THE
UNION
WAR

THE
UNION
WAR

GARY W. GALLAGHER

HARVARD UNIVERSITY PRESS
Cambridge, Massachusetts
London, England
2011

For my graduate students
at Penn State University and the University of Virginia,
with admiration for their contributions to our field

Publication of this book has been supported through the generous
provisions of the Maurice and Lula Bradley Smith Memorial Fund.

Frontispiece image Library of Congress, Prints and Photographs Division,
reproduction number LC-DIG-cwpb-04104

Library of Congress Cataloging-in-Publication Data
Gallagher, Gary W. (Gary William)
The union war / Gary W. Gallagher.
p.   cm.
Includes bibliographical references and index.
ISBN 978-0-674-04562-0 (alk. paper)
1. United States—History—Civil War, 1861–1865.
2. United States—Politics and government—1861–1865.
3. Political culture—United States—History—19th century.
I. Title.
E468.G349 2011

973.7—dc22   2010051977

Contents

INTRODUCTION

The loyal American citizenry fought a war for Union that also killed slavery. In a conflict that stretched across four years and claimed more than 800,000 U.S. casualties, the nation experienced huge swings of civilian and military morale before crushing Confederate resistance. Union always remained the paramount goal, a fact clearly expressed by Abraham Lincoln in speeches and other statements designed to garner the widest popular support for the war effort. What Walt Whitman said of Lincoln and Union in the wake of the president's assassination applied equally to most loyal Americans. "UNIONISM, in its truest and amplest sense, form'd the hard-pan of his character," wrote the poet, who defined it as "a new virtue, unknown to other lands, and hardly yet really known here, but the foundation and tie of all, as the future will grandly develop." That hardpan of unionism held millions of Americans to the task of suppressing the slaveholders' rebellion, even as the human and material cost mushroomed. "By many has *this Union* been conserv'd and help'd," continued Whitman's tribute to Lincoln and Union, "but if one name, one man, must be pick'd out, he, most of all, is the Conservator of it, to the future. He was assassinated—but the Union is not assassinated—*ça ira!* One falls, and another falls. The soldier drops, sinks like a wave—but the ranks of the ocean eternally press on. Death does its work, obliterates a hundred, a thousand—President, general, captain, private—but the Nation is immortal."[1]

Whitman celebrated a Union that carried great meaning for the mass of loyal citizens who joined him in equating it with "the Nation." It represented the cherished legacy of the founding generation, a democratic republic with a constitution that guaranteed political liberty and afforded individuals a chance to better themselves economically. From the perspective of loyal Americans, their republic stood as the only hope for democracy in a western world that had fallen more deeply into the stifling embrace of oligarchy since the failed European revolutions of the 1840s. Slaveholding aristocrats who established the Confederacy, believed untold unionists, posed a direct threat not only to the long-term success of the American republic but also to the broader future of democracy. Should armies of citizen-soldiers fail to restore the Union, forces of privilege on both sides of the Atlantic could pronounce ordinary people incapable of self-government and render irrelevant the military sacrifices and political genius of the Revolutionary fathers. Secretary of State William Henry Seward encapsulated much of this thinking in one sentence pertaining to the Republicans' agenda: "Their great work is the preservation of the Union and in that, the saving of popular government for the world."[2]

Issues related to the institution of slavery precipitated secession and the outbreak of fighting, but the loyal citizenry initially gave little thought to emancipation in their quest to save the Union. By the early summer of 1862, long before black men donned blue uniforms in large numbers, victorious Union armies stood poised to win the war with slavery largely intact. Setbacks on battlefields in Virginia dictated that the bloodletting would continue, however, and as months went by, casualties mounted, and a shortage of manpower loomed, emancipation and African American military service assumed increasing importance. Eventually, most loyal citizens, though profoundly prejudiced by twenty-first-century standards and largely indifferent toward enslaved black people, embraced emancipation as a tool to punish slaveholders, weaken the Confederacy, and protect the Union from future internal strife. A minority of the white populace invoked moral grounds to attack slavery, though their arguments carried less weight than those presenting emancipation as a military measure necessary to defeat the Rebels and restore the Union. African American freedom still seemed problematic in the bloody summer of 1864, when Union armies bogged down in Georgia and Virginia and antiemancipation Democrats looked hopefully toward the November elections. Only striking victories at Atlanta and in the Shenandoah Valley in September and October retrieved the situation, setting up Lincoln's reelection and guaranteeing that slavery's extinction would be a nonnegotiable condition for peace.

Union armies composed of citizen-soldiers occupied a central position in the grand drama. Their hard and costly service salvaged the Union and, more than any other factor, made possible emancipation. They functioned as the most powerful national symbol and unifying institution, bringing together men from all over the country regardless of political affiliation. In a conflict marked by deep divisions within the loyal states, they represented self-sacrifice reminiscent of the Continental soldiers who had followed George Washington. They confirmed notions of American exceptionalism based on a long-standing antipathy toward professional soldiers and large standing armies. Observers who watched 150,000 veterans parade down Pennsylvania Avenue in the Grand Review at the end of the war gloried in the fact that the men soon would be on their way home—citizens who had performed their civic duty with the expectation of returning to civilian pursuits as soon as the Rebels capitulated. The wartime generation viewed surviving veterans and the Union dead—300,000 of the latter reinterred in national cemeteries established soon after Appomattox—as honored reminders of a free society's reliance on citizen-soldiers.

This book seeks to recover what Union meant to the generation that fought the war. That meaning has been almost completely effaced from popular understanding of the conflict; indeed, "Union" as defined in a political sense in the nineteenth century has disappeared from our vocabulary. Students and adults interested in the Civil War are reluctant to believe that anyone would risk life or fortune for something as abstract as "the Union." A war to end slavery seems more compelling, something powerfully reinforced by films such as *Glory*—easily the best of Hollywood's treatments of the conflict—and *Gettysburg*. Although Lincoln remains a towering figure in the popular imagination, few Americans associate him with the widely held idea of the Union, as he put it in his second annual message to Congress in December 1862, as "the last best, hope of earth." Even within the specialized world of Civil War enthusiasts who purchase prints and other contemporary artworks, the Union and its military idols take a decidedly secondary position behind such Lost Cause icons as Robert E. Lee and "Stonewall" Jackson. Apart from Col. Joshua Lawrence Chamberlain and his 20th Maine Infantry, the Army of the Potomac's famous Irish Brigade, and various commanders and episodes at the battle of Gettysburg, the Union cause scarcely exists in that art. Were it not for Michael Shaara's Pulitzer Prize–winning novel *The Killer Angels,* Ken Burns's documentary *The Civil War,* and the director Ron Maxwell's film version of Shaara's book, even Chamberlain would be largely unknown.[3]

Much Civil War scholarship over the past four decades has diminished the centrality of Union. Slavery, emancipation, and the actions of black people, unfairly marginalized for decades in writings about the conflict, have inspired a huge and rewarding literature since the mid-1960s. No longer can any serious reader fail to appreciate the degree to which African Americans figured in the political, social, and military history of the war. This has been one of the most heartening developments in the field since the great successes of the civil rights movement in the 1950s and 1960s. But the focus on emancipation and race sometimes suggests the war had scant meaning apart from these issues—and especially that the Union victory had little or no value without emancipation.

Historical context is crucial on this point. Anyone remotely conversant with nineteenth-century U.S. history knows that democracy as practiced in 1860 denied women, free and enslaved African Americans, and other groups basic liberties and freedoms most white northerners routinely attributed to their republic. Almost 99 percent of the residents in the free states were white (96.5 percent in the loyal states, which included slaveholding Missouri, Kentucky, Maryland, and Delaware), and their racial views offend our modern sensibilities.[4] Yet a portrait of the nation that is dominated by racism, exclusion, and oppression obscures more than it reveals. Within the context of the mid-nineteenth-century western world, the United States offered the broadest political franchise and the most economic opportunity. Vast numbers of immigrants believed that however difficult the circumstances they might find, relocation in the United States promised a potentially brighter future. As one Irish-born Union soldier put it in early 1863, "this is my country as much as the man that was born on the soil and so it is with every man who comes to this country and becomes a citezen." If the Union lost the war, he added, "then the hopes of millions fall and. . . . the old cry will be sent forth from the aristocrats of europe that such is the common end of all republics." Without an appreciation of why the loyal citizenry went to great lengths to restore the Union, no accurate understanding of the era is possible.[5]

The Union War focuses on one part of the population in the United States—citizens in the free states and four loyal slaveholding states who opposed secession and supported a war to restore the Union. This group encompassed Republicans as well as the portion of the Democratic Party that stridently opposed emancipation and other policies of the Lincoln administration but remained committed to a war against the rebellion. African American refugees who made their way to Union lines, soldiers in the United States Colored Troops (USCT), and antiwar Democrats or Copperheads receive some attention but remain peripheral to my main line of inquiry. White unionists in the Confederacy fall outside my purview. Many U.S. soldiers, it is important to keep in mind, acted from motives unrelated to unionist or any other ideology, including an indeterminate number of poor men who enlisted primarily for financial reasons. Similarly, some of their fellow citizens on the home front exhibited minimal interest in the war's large issues, hoping for the least possible disruption in the usual rhythms of their daily lives.[6]

By exploiting evidence relating to the substantial majority of the U.S. population that supported a war for Union, this book examines three fundamental questions. What did the war for Union mean in mid-nineteenth-century America? How and why did emancipation come to be part of the war for Union? How did armies of citizen-soldiers figure in conceptions of the war, the process of emancipation, and the shaping of national sentiment? Consideration of these questions proceeds from knowledge that pro-Union support could be grudging, especially as emancipation became more prominent and the central government took unprecedented steps to raise money and find manpower. The Lincoln administration dealt with political fissures, war weariness, apathy, and fluctuating levels of outright hostility to the war. Yet loyal citizens remained steadfast enough to push through to victory, despite far more casualties than in any previous American war and the absence of a direct physical threat from Rebel armies to their homes, farms, businesses, towns, and cities. They did so because they believed to do otherwise would betray the generation who established the Union as well as future Americans who would reap its political and economic benefits.

Although concerned with ideas about nation, this is not a study of the formation of American nationalism. I do not believe a new nation was born amid military upheaval in 1861–1865—though the service of more than 2 million men surely strengthened bonds of nationhood across the free states and to a lesser degree in the Border States except for Kentucky, which so loathed emancipation that it aligned with the defeated Confederacy after Appomattox. Nation building had been in progress for a long time, and an expansionist, democratic republic built on the blueprint of the Constitution and convinced of American exceptionalism had used diplomacy and violence to overspread the continent by mid-century.[7]

Continuity marked loyal citizens' opinions and attitudes between 1860 and the early postwar decades. They routinely deployed "United States," "the Union," "the country," and "the nation" as synonyms. A Republican broadside from the 1864 presidential election perfectly captured this phenomenon, referring to Union, nation, and country in just a few sentences: "CITIZENS OF MICHIGAN! To-day is to be decided whether this Nation *lives, or dies* at the *hands of traitors!* . . . Be sure and vote for the Union, GOVERNMENT, AND COUNTRY. If the Union and government is not maintained, the nation is disgraced before the CIVILIZED WORLD."[8] The citizens who labored to save the Union subscribed to a vision of their nation built on free labor, economic opportunity, and a broad political franchise they considered unique in the world. They believed victory over the slaveholders confirmed the nation, made it stronger in the absence of slavery's pernicious influence, set the stage for the country's continuing growth and vitality, and kept a democratic beacon shining in a world dominated by aristocrats and monarchs. It is this belief that led them into battle and ultimately to victory over the Confederacy.

1

....

The Grand Review

*T*he Grand Review of United States forces in Washington, D.C., on May 23–24, 1865, represented a celebration of military victory after four grueling years of war. Soldiers who marched in the two-day event and spectators who crowded along Pennsylvania Avenue to watch and cheer believed that hard-won military success had preserved the Union, ensured the viability of democracy, and vanquished the forces of southern oligarchy inimical to the intent of the founding generation. Everyone present that day knew United States armies had shouldered the burden of suppressing the Confederate rebellion, and those on parade in Washington could claim more achievements on famous battlefields than any others. Their seemingly endless ranks bespoke the impressive military power of a mobilized citizenry, while their state and national flags, many of them little more than tattered remnants, summoned emotional images of both the nation's constituent parts and its triumphant whole. The soldiers who marched under the colorful banners had risked all in a brutal war and stood as exemplars of disinterested patriotic sacrifice.

Americans who regarded the Grand Review in such terms could not have anticipated that future generations would take a far different view. Much recent commentary finds in the events of May 23–24 a template for what was wrong with the war's winning cause. Too militaristic, too avowedly nationalist, and, most troubling, too white, the review laid bare the flawed nature of Union triumph. Strip away the waving flags and celebratory chest-thumping, and what remained was a soon-to-be-reunited nation that looked much like the racist, exclusionary, oppressive United States of the prewar era. How should we reconcile these conflicting interpretations of the Grand Review? The answer to that question opens inquiry into broader topics such as the meaning of Union, the role of African Americans and emancipation in the effort to destroy the Confederacy, and the relationship between the loyal citizenry and the men who campaigned in their armies.

Anyone hoping to understand the origins and composition of the Grand Review must keep in mind that the war had not officially ended by the third week of May 1865. Rebel forces remained active in the Trans-Mississippi Theater, a French puppet regime in Mexico posed a potential threat, and United States soldiers were needed east of the great river to maintain order and oversee details of the transition from war to peace. The major bodies of troops encamped near Washington were Maj. Gen. George G. Meade's Army of the Potomac (less its Sixth Corps), Maj. Gen. William Tecumseh Sherman's Armies of the Tennessee and Georgia, and Maj. Gen. Philip H. Sheridan's cavalry. Conflicting rumors had been circulating through the city. "From what I gather," General Meade wrote his wife on May 12, "I infer the armies are to be disbanded at once. The review or parade has been talked about, but there appears to be nothing settled, and I rather think it will fall through." As late as May 16, General in Chief Ulysses S. Grant did not know whether a review would take place. Sherman heard nothing definitive until May 19, when, after reading about the final plans for May 23–24 in newspapers, he chided Chief of Staff John A. Rawlins, "I am old fashioned and prefer to see orders through some other channel, but if that be the new fashion, so be it."[1]

Although difficult to imagine in light of the scale and impact of the review, there was an *ad hoc* dimension that dictated which troops would

be present.[2] Most of the slightly more than 1 million United States soldiers active in the field were too far from Washington. Typical was the
Fourth Corps of Maj. Gen. George H. Thomas's Army of the Cumberland. A much-bloodied organization that had fought in the Tennessee
and Georgia campaigns of 1863–1864, it deferred to no other unit in its
battle honors or service to the republic. Yet because it was stationed at
Nashville in May 1865, it had no chance of participating in the Grand
Review. Its 19,000 men had enjoyed "a spectacular review" in the Tennessee capital on May 9. The Army of the Potomac's Sixth Corps, left
in Southside Virginia after Appomattox, did not reach Washington in
time for the Grand Review—settling for a separate parade in the city on
June 8. Even General Sheridan missed the chance to lead his troopers
down Pennsylvania Avenue. Behind only Grant and Sherman as a popular Union war hero, "Little Phil" received word from the general in chief
on May 17 to hurry westward "to restore Texas, and that part of Louisiana held by the enemy, to the Union in the shortest practicable time."
Because of the French military presence in Mexico, Grant also alerted
Sheridan that "a heavy force should be put on the Rio Grande . . . The
25th Corps is now available and to it should be added a force of White
Troops say those now under Maj. Gn. Steele." Sheridan asked Grant for
permission to put off his departure until after the review, explaining later,
"I had a strong desire to head my command on that great occasion." Although fond of his young lieutenant, Grant refused with the comment
that "it was absolutely necessary to go at once."[3]

All the men in the three armies near Washington in mid–May 1865
were white—as were the large majority of those in units posted elsewhere. In early December 1864, United States Colored Troops (USCT)
units in the Department of Virginia and North Carolina had been con-
solidated in the Twenty-Fifth Corps and assigned to the Army of the
James. The corps, commanded by Maj. Gen. Godfrey Weitzel, had served
alongside the Army of the Potomac during the Appomattox campaign
and then been sent to City Point, at the confluence of the James and
Appomattox rivers. On April 29, Maj. Gen. Henry W. Halleck, in charge
of the Military Division of the James with headquarters in Richmond,
sent Grant a harsh evaluation of Weitzel's corps. "General [E. O. C.] Ord

[commanding the Department of Virginia] represents that want of discipline and good officers in the twenty-fifth Corps," reported Halleck, "renders it a very improper force for the preservation of order in this department." Soldiers from the corps had been charged with a number of rapes, and their "influence on the colored population is also reported to be bad." Halleck recommended removal of the corps "to garrison forts or for service on the Southern coast" and requested that the Sixth Corps temporarily replace the Twenty-Fifth.[4]

Grant must have taken Ord's and Halleck's opinions of the black troops seriously. He replied to Halleck on April 30, making the Sixth Corps available and ordering that the Twenty-fifth be placed "in a Camp of instruction" near Petersburg "until some disposition is made of them for defense on the seacoast." In early May, before anyone was thinking seriously about a grand review, all "detached companies and regiments" of African American soldiers in the Department of Virginia were ordered to report to Weitzel. On May 17, the chief of staff ordered the quartermaster general to provide seagoing vessels "with as little delay as practicable, for the Twenty-Fifth Army Corps." The next day, Grant issued instructions for Weitzel "to get his Corps in readiness for embarkation at City Point immediately upon the arrival of ocean transportation." The corps would rendezvous with Maj. Gen. Frederick Steele in Mobile, after which it would continue on to the Rio Grande frontier. Grant deemed that duty, as his instructions to Sheridan on May 17 made clear, a high national priority because thousands of French regulars in Mexico posed a potential threat. Although Halleck's and Ord's comments raise the possibility that prejudice influenced their assessments, Grant's final decision, which sent the black units and many thousands of white soldiers to an important theater, suggests the general in chief considered the Twenty-Fifth Corps trustworthy. On May 23, during the Army of the Potomac's part of the Grand Review, Weitzel informed Grant that "steamers to transport my Corps" had arrived at City Point.[5]

The fact that neither Meade's nor Sherman's forces contained any USCT units largely explains the absence of black soldiers on May 23–24. Noah Andre Trudeau states matter-of-factly in *Like Men of War: Black Troops in the Civil War, 1862–1865:* "Since there were no black units then

serving in either of those commands, the only African Americans participating in the Grand Review were contraband laborers whose squads
had toiled to build roads for Sherman's legions."[6] Could planners have
scheduled the event to make certain black troops were present? The answer must be yes. They also could have waited to summon from other
theaters representative white units that had as much claim to a place in
the parade as USCT regiments, or, perhaps most obviously, arranged for
some of the navy's 50,000 sailors to participate. Instead, working on a
short timetable amid considerable uncertainty, they opted to stage the
event with the republic's greatest and most famous armies—which collectively had won decisive victories in Georgia and Virginia in 1864,
captured Atlanta and Richmond, assured Abraham Lincoln's re-election,
and forced Robert E. Lee and the most important Rebel army to capitulate at Appomattox Court House.

It is worth noting that black units had been given public credit in
ways that undercut any notion of a conspiracy to render their service
invisible by banning them from the Grand Review. Although accounts
vary regarding which Federal troops first marched into Richmond after
its fall, many newspapers awarded the palm to black soldiers. Thomas
Morris Chester, an African American correspondent for the *Philadelphia
Press,* reported on April 4 that "Brevet Brigadier General [Alonzo G.]
Draper's brigade of colored troops . . . were the first infantry to enter Richmond. The gallant 36th U.S. Colored Troops, under Lieutenant
Colonel B. F. Pratt, has the honor of being the first regiment." George
Templeton Strong, the famous diarist who followed the war from his
home in New York City, commented, with some rough language, on
April 3: "Thus ends a day *sui generis* in my life. We shall long remember
that the first troops to enter Richmond were niggers of Weitzel's corps.
It is a most suggestive fact." On April 29, *Frank Leslie's Illustrated Newspaper* featured a full-page wood engraving, titled "The Union Army
Entering Richmond, Va. April 3—Reception of the Federal Troops in
Main Street," showing USCT soldiers of General Weitzel's command being welcomed by black residents of the city. *Harper's Weekly* had given its
readers a two-page illustration of the same scene a week earlier, observing in accompanying text that "Most of Weitzel's men were negroes, and

their advent excited the greatest enthusiasm among the swarthy denizens of the rebel capital."[7]

Notable examples of black soldiers included in important events had come with Lincoln's second inauguration and in the wake of his death. The inaugural parade took place on a soggy March 4, 1865, but nonetheless attracted a crowd estimated at 30,000. "The military escort," reported one newspaper, "consisted of two regiments of the Invalid Corps, a squadron of cavalry, a battery of artillery, four companies of colored troops, and several bands of music." Despite muddy conditions occasioned by the weather, spectators "manifested the utmost enthusiasm" as the mile-long procession moved along Pennsylvania Avenue. Six weeks later Lincoln lay dead, and military officers in Washington worked feverishly on April 16 to prepare for the funeral procession. Assistant Adjutant General T. S. Bowers instructed Maj. Gen. E. O. C. Ord, who at that time headed the Army of the James, to send "one of the best regiments of colored troops you have, to attend the funeral ceremonies of President Lincoln." The order passed to Weitzel, who selected the 22nd U.S. Colored Infantry. On April 20, reported a correspondent, the 22nd awaited the funeral cortege in front of the Metropolitan Hotel on Pennsylvania Avenue. The regimental band "struck up a dirge" as the head of the column approached, and the 22nd "immediately moved forward, thereby becoming the head of the procession."[8]

The approximately 150,000 white veterans who marched in Washington on May 23–24 probably devoted little attention to absent units.[9] Perfect weather greeted them, warming from a low of 68 degrees at 7:00 A.M. to a high of 75 degrees at 2:00 P.M. on both days. The District of Columbia's fire department swept and watered down Pennsylvania Avenue, which effectively suppressed dust. Units formed early each morning near the Capitol, recently draped in mourning black for President Lincoln but on the 23rd festooned with red, white, and blue bunting. A huge banner on the newly domed building that symbolized American democracy proclaimed: "The Only National Debt We Never Can Pay, Is The Debt We Owe To The Victorious Soldiers." Leading units stepped off about 9:00 A.M. and proceeded down Pennsylvania Avenue, passing the Treasury Department, the Executive Mansion, and the War Department. President Andrew Johnson, members of the cabinet, General Grant, and other dignitaries took in the pageant, which consumed between six and seven hours each day, from a reviewing stand erected near the Executive Mansion. Packed several people deep along most of the route, the crowd included men and women, black and white, young and old—many dressed up as for a formal occasion. Newspapers and other observers estimated that 50,000 to 100,000 visitors flooded into the city, augmenting the ranks of residents who sought to honor their heroes.[10]

The Army of the Potomac took center stage the first day, followed by Sherman's western commands on the second. Officers and soldiers in the ranks left vivid accounts of the stirring experience. William Ray, an enlisted man whose 7th Wisconsin Infantry formed part of the Army of the Potomac's celebrated Iron Brigade, recorded in his journal that the "streets & evry available place to see was crowded with Spectators & prominent among them was the President & cabinet & the heads of all the different departments & Bureaus & all the Foreign Ministers . . . There were boxes fixed so as all the Officials could have seats where they could [see] all with ease." No blunders marred the procession, added Ray, who concluded, "Today was a grand affair." A member of the 120th New York Infantry admitted to being "very tired & foot sore" after marching four miles in the review. He marveled at how "the streets are crowded with spectators," among them "[m]any of our wounded boys in Hospital" who managed to "come out to see us."[11]

A member of the 10th Illinois Infantry provided more detail in diary entries that betrayed an uncertain mastery of spelling conventions. "The streets or rather side walks were crowded with people of all ages and sex with buckets filled with ice water or cold spring water, inviting the soldiers to drink," observed John Hill Ferguson, a Scottish immigrant and veteran of Sherman's campaigns in the Deep South. Young girls "gaily dressed scipped along with their hands full of roses, presenting the soldiers with bowquets" and remarking that the "private soldiers are the ones that dun the hard fighting, and they are the ones that needs the prais." Loud cheering from either side of the avenue washed over the men, "a duzin heads" peered from windows in "every house and apartment," and "many white handkerchiefs fluttered over our heads and in many cases flowers were thrown down amongst us from the windows and the house tops at every place." Ferguson noted the "jijantic" banner on the Capitol, though substituting "our Union Defenors" for "The Victorious Soldiers"—a telling change that suggests the centrality of Union to soldiers' conception of what had been at stake in the conflict. Taking pride in the appearance of the western soldiery, Ferguson wrote on May 26: "The paper speaks very highly of our review and acknoladges . . . that Sherman's Army went far a head of the Army of the Potomac."[12]

Maj. Gen. Oliver Otis Howard, just appointed head of the new Freedmen's Bureau, enjoyed a perspective on the parade's atmosphere quite different from that of infantrymen such as Ray and Ferguson. Howard had commanded the Army of the Tennessee during most of the Georgia and South Carolina campaigns of 1864–65, but Sherman asked him to allow Maj. Gen. John A. Logan to ride at the head of the command on May 24. Although disappointed, Howard generously agreed, requesting permission to accompany Sherman's staff during the parade. "No, Howard, you shall ride with me," Sherman answered, and the two went side by side down Pennsylvania Avenue. "Our Western armies, competing in a friendly way with the Eastern, behaved magnificently at that Review," recalled Howard, who was impressed by the "vast multitude of people lining the streets, occupying every elevated stand, even covering the roofs of buildings from the Capitol to the War Department." Appreciative cheering and shouting reached such a level that "none of the soldiers who participated could ever forget that day or that magnificent recognition of their work."[13]

For his part, Sherman later described how, "attended by General Howard and all my staff," he slowly proceeded down Pennsylvania Avenue past "crowds of men, women, and children, densely lining the sidewalks, and almost obstructing the way." Mary Ann Bickerdyke, whose tireless labors to provide medical care for western soldiers won her the sobriquet "Mother Bickerdyke," had earned Sherman's admiration; riding sidesaddle in a plain calico dress, she accompanied officers of the Fifteenth Corps, the general's command during the middle phase of the war. Turning to look back up the avenue from near the Treasury building, the officer second only to Grant in the nation's estimation marveled at a "simply magnificent" sight: "The column was compact, and the glittering muskets looked like a solid mass of steel, moving with the regularity of a pendulum." When the last soldier had completed the march, continued Sherman, "thousands of spectators still lingered to express their sense of the confidence in the strength of a Government which could claim such an army."[14]

Colonel Charles S. Wainwright similarly alluded to the powerful connection between the nation and its armed citizenry. He wrote a long entry in his journal just after the review, expressing relief that the spectacle had unfolded "without a single accident or drawback." A native of upstate New York and able artillerist who had fought throughout the war in the Eastern Theater, Wainwright acknowledged a widespread belief that Sherman's men "marched somewhat better than the Army of the Potomac." He attributed this to "the fact that the Western armies have lost far less men than we in Virginia, and consequently four-fifths of Sherman's men are old soldiers while full a half of the Army of the Potomac have not been in service over a year." The eastern officers and artillerists excelled their western counterparts, insisted Wainwright, and overall Meade's army exhibited more military discipline. Wainwright took special pride in what he considered the *American* character of the review. Europeans would have made "much more of a show of it than we do," he commented. In Washington, "[a]ll the ornamenting of the streets and buildings was very crude," and the armies lacked "the variety, style, and showiness of uniforms" typical in European military forces. "Still, it was a grand sight" perfectly appropriate for a democratic republic, "citizen soldiers, with everything for service and not a particle for appearance. Had it been a European review, it would have been less American."[15]

General Grant devoted a brief passage in his *Personal Memoirs* to the scene on May 23–24. Pleased with the orderly appearance of the massed soldiers, he noted that the "National flag was flying from almost every house and store." Spectators who filled windows in all the buildings along Pennsylvania Avenue enjoyed an elevated view. Below them, at street level, "door-steps and side-walks were crowded with colored people and poor whites who did not succeed in securing better quarters from which to get a view of the grand armies." Grant concluded that the people who had poured into the capital for the two days approximated the number who typically visited on "inauguration day when a new President takes his seat."[16]

Commissioner of Public Buildings Benjamin Brown French offered impressions from the sidelines. A longtime resident of Washington, he fastened a gilded eagle over his front door, hung a large American flag across the front of his residence, and placed a quotation from Isaiah in a window: "Speak ye comfortably to Jerusalem, and cry unto her that her warfare is accomplished, that her iniquity is pardoned." Soldiers trod past in a constant stream, Brown recorded in his journal on May 24, some of whom cheered when they noticed the biblical passage. At one point, Brown climbed up in the Capitol Dome, whence he "could see troops by the thousands in every direction—I presume there were more than 50,000 in sight at one time . . . It was a grand and a brave sight." Brown closed with a paean to volunteers who had salvaged the work of the founding generation. "God Bless them all," he wrote: "I saw them depart for the war, and my eyes moistened with grief, as I thought how many of them would never return! I have seen many of them come back—brave veterans who have fought and bled to preserve the liberties for which their fathers fought so well, and my eyes moistened with joy to think that they were on their way *home*."[17]

Mary Logan, wife of Gen. John A. Logan, spoke to Brown's theme of soldierly sacrifice for Union in her retrospective account of the review. "Our republic had been saved by our invincible army," she affirmed, "and in order to confirm the faith of the nation in them, it was a wise suggestion to have the review." All those who witnessed the massed armies knew "what the final triumph had cost," and Logan doubtless reflected a common attitude in pronouncing awareness of how many members of the marching units had given their lives to be "the one cloud over the matchless pageant that can never be repeated on American soil." Overall, thought Logan, the review "aroused the patriotism of every American heart." The soldiers, she added perceptively, combined longing for a quick return to home and family, sadness at leaving an army that had accomplished so much through patriotic service, and knowledge that neither time nor distance could "break the bonds cemented by the experience of soldiers who have marched, suffered, and bivouacked together."[18]

Newspaper coverage of the Grand Review dealt with the meanings of victory, attitudes toward African American military service, and conceptions of the nation and soldiers' place in it. Overwhelmingly celebratory and exceptionalist in tone, the reporting lauded citizens in uniform from across the loyal states who had waged sanguinary battles to save the Union—and by extension to confirm the rule of constitutional law and to preserve the example of democratic self-government for people around the world. The *Philadelphia Press,* edited by Republican John W. Forney, affirmed that the nation owed soldiers "benefits and tokens of its gratitude during all their future lives" because they had won what would be considered an immortal "struggle for the salvation of the republic." Restoration of the Union, explained the *Baltimore American,* stood as "a success filled with assurances of reunion and peace, of law vindicated and order restored, of returning industry and prosperity, of freedom and national strength, of invigorated manufacture and renewed commerce, of domestic and foreign tranquility." The Republican *Chicago Tribune* offered a lesson on the difference between winning and losing a war with a terse comparison of Washington and Richmond: "The Union Capital enthusiastic with the cheers of our heroes, the rebel Capital silent and deserted."[19]

James Gordon Bennett's *New York Herald,* a Democratic sheet with a robust domestic circulation and the largest European readership among all American newspapers, captured the triumphal character of most public and private reactions to the Grand Review. It took a decidedly international stance regarding the meaning of Union, applauding the accomplishments of United States soldiers in salvaging democracy in a world dominated by monarchs, oligarchs, and aristocrats. All democracy-loving people of the world owed a great debt to blue-clad soldiers who "have secured the perpetuity of that Union upon which the hopes of the oppressed of all climes and countries depend. They are the champions of free governments throughout the world. The applause which greets them comes not from the Washington crowds alone, nor from the millions of their fellow-citizens in all the States, but we can hear it ringing across the Atlantic, echoed alike from the Alps and the Andes, and swelled by the majestic chorus of republican voices from Mexico to Denmark." From one end of the earth to the other, concluded the *Herald* with a hyberbolic flourish, the souls of the men would march on long after their deaths, "On—till the soldiers of Grant, Sherman, and Sheridan have saved the world as they have saved the Union."[20]

The two leading American illustrated newspapers offered prose as well as stirring wood engravings of the review. *Harper's Weekly* devoted many pages to the subject, reminding readers of the direct connection between citizen-soldiers on storied battlefields and salvation of the republic. It led with a large engraving of General Meade and his staff passing the president's reviewing stand, shown draped with banners bearing names such as "Petersburg" and "Richmond" (at the center of the stand) and "Donelson" and "Shiloh" (to either side). Other illustrations depicted Sheridan's cavalry and Sherman's men. "It was no ordinary pageant that turned all the people's eyes and so many of their steps toward Washington," observed the text. No "mere idle curiosity" had animated the spectators, but rather "pride mingled with infinite pathos—pride in the youthful strength of a republic tried and found steadfast—pathos from the remembrance of countless heroes . . . who died many of them while the strife seemed uncertain." Emphasis on the Union's survival as a republic, together with the absence of any mention of emancipation, surely aligned with how most readers would have assessed the meaning of victory.

Frank Leslie's Illustrated Newspaper chose language similar to that of its competitor. A wood engraving of Sherman passing the reviewing stand graced the front page, and the following text declared that United States soldiers "returned from the field covered with the glory which appertains to those who fight for the rights of man and the estimable privileges belonging to freedom. The war through which they have fought, and in which they have so signally triumphed, was not a contest for supremacy and territory, but a conflict for the maintenance of national integrity and the destruction of a rebellion against law, order, and the dictates of humanity." Like *Harper's Weekly, Leslie's* nowhere mentioned emancipation or the destruction of slavery directly, though some readers could have interpreted the language regarding freedom and the dictates of humanity to include African Americans. Most white northerners, within a mid-nineteenth-century context, probably would not have done so.[21]

Neither publication commented on the absence of United States Colored Troops in the parade, though both described African American noncombatants who accompanied Sherman's armies. *Harper's Weekly* termed them the "transportation brigade of the 'Bummers' Corps'" and noted that they "caused much amusement" among spectators. *Frank Leslie's* included an illustration, explaining that "our Artist has chosen to represent the passage of some of Sherman's 'bummers' and the indigenous fruits of the sacred Southern soil collected by their industry." The "indigenous fruits" included horses, donkeys, mules, cattle, chickens, ducks, corn, flour, and other things that had "supplied the fighting legions of Sherman" in Georgia and the Carolinas. "The ludicrous grand division of foragers and bummers," stated *Leslie's* in language with a cruel edge, "furnished a life-like picture of an army of invasion carrying the terrors of the law into the vitals of rebellious States." Both newspapers conflated two groups of black people in the parade—African American pioneers, who performed various types of labor in support of Sherman's operations, and contrabands, including women and children, who followed the Union armies as they swept through the Confederate hinterland. Sherman described the former as marching "abreast in double ranks, keeping perfect dress and step" in advance of each division of infantry; the latter, added to the parade by some of the division commanders, included "families of freed slaves . . . with the women leading their children." The papers also misused the term "bummers," which properly referred to white soldiers who foraged without close supervision during the March to the Sea and in the Carolinas.[22]

Other newspapers did refer to the absence of African American soldiers, as well as to the presence of contrabands and black pioneers with Sherman's armies. A few, such as the *Daily Illinois State Journal,* raised accusative questions. The *Journal* did not know if any black soldiers had been stationed near Washington, but if so they "had a right to be repre-

sented here as they were on the field of battle." Most coverage, however, manifested a clear understanding of why no black soldiers marched
on May 23–24. Lois Bryan Adams, a Republican who covered the parade for the *Detroit Advertiser and Tribune,* informed readers that no black
troops "were on review either day, except the few with Sherman's army
who were attached to the Pioneer corps and armed with picks and shov-
els." USCT regiments, she explained, remained in the field with "the
army of the James, or at the West and Southwest." Writing for the *Sacra-
mento Daily Union,* correspondent Noah Brooks recorded that many onlookers in the crowd wondered why they saw no black units. "That was
explained by the fact that all the colored troops are massed at City Point,
preparatory to being sent to Texas," wrote Brooks: "They would have
had a welcoming cheer from the brilliant assembly today, no doubt, for
they have deserved and have earned the plaudits of a generous people."
The *Daily National Intelligencer,* a fixture in Washington for more than a
half-century, noted without embellishment that with some of Sherman's
corps "we noticed colored men carrying spades and axes, and moving as
pioneers."[23]

Important newspapers challenged the notion of deliberate exclusion.
Henry J. Raymond's *New York Times,* a solidly Republican voice widely
admired for its dispassionate analysis of leading issues, pronounced "very
silly, and scarcely worthy of notice" the idea circulated among some
"over-zealous friends of the colored race" that black units had been
barred from the review. The government had no thought of "casting a
slight on the gallant soldiers who, on so many battle-fields, have dis-
played such signal courage and devotion. They were not excluded from
the review any more than the white troops who were not present on
that occasion." African American units were stationed at various places in
the South, and "certainly no higher compliment could have been paid to
their bravery, their good discipline, and their devotion to their country,
than their selection for this service." Their deployment represented an
"emphatic endorsement of their soldierly qualities" by General Grant,
concluded the *Times,* an honor for which they could forego the "mo-
mentary triumphs of the grand review."[24]

William Lloyd Garrison's *The Liberator* examined the issue carefully.

A story carried in some papers about "brave colored troops . . . debarred from participation in the late military review, much of course, to their disappointment, and to the indignation of those who have watched their brilliant career of soldierly exploits," raised questions at *The Liberator*. Subsequent investigation revealed the report to be groundless, "as the colored division of the Ninth Corps, which marched through Washington under Burnside last spring, was transferred to the Army of the James soon after the Petersburg mine disaster, and there have been no negro troops in the Army of the Potomac for nearly a year." Unlike the illustrated newspapers, *The Liberator* accurately described Sherman's black pioneers who "marched shoulder to shoulder, in the review, with their white comrades, under the same flag." Garrison echoed Raymond in asserting that "Our Generals are more just than to refuse due honor to any soldier, white or black, who has battled nobly for the cause of the Union."[25]

One last factor should put to rest notions of exclusion from the review based on race. Most of the USCT men, unlike the mass of soldiers in Meade's and Sherman's armies, had enlisted in 1864 and thus had a good deal of time left in uniform. Because no one knew how long the Texas campaign might last, it made sense not to deploy short-time units. Many black soldiers undoubtedly joined white comrades in hoping for a quick return to civilian life. But Thomas Morris Chester described others who took a different stance. Chester had covered the Army of the James since August 1864 and knew its men very well. He described pride in the ranks about what the soldiers considered important duty. "That the negro corps, under General Weitzel, has received marching orders is well known throughout their camps," he observed on May 22, "and they are beginning to put on the war-paint with the impression that they are going to Texas. They look forward to the period of embarkation with a great deal of satisfaction." Chester gave no hint here or elsewhere that members of the Twenty-Fifth Corps felt aggrieved in any way about missing the review. Many of the black men, who by law had been treated as little better than cattle just a few years before, probably considered it an honor to be selected to guard the national border.[26]

Numerous accounts alluded to other groups and prominent individuals left out of the review. Although disappointing, these absences surprised few people because it was widely understood that the war dragged on in many parts of the Confederacy. Some observers framed their comments broadly, as when *Harper's Weekly* reported that many commands "equally worthy of notice were not permitted to take part in the spectacle, because of their distance or from the pressure of active duty in the field or in garrison." Another paper informed readers that most of Sherman's cavalry "remains in Georgia and the Carolinas, and will probably do so until affairs there are more settled." A correspondent for the *New York Tribune* singled out the Army of the Potomac's Sixth Corps, a much-honored unit "necessarily detained at Danville and vicinity until last week." Many in the crowd, wrote Noah Brooks, "were disappointed at not seeing Sheridan, who is on his way to Texas." A hero of the 1864 Shenandoah Valley campaign and the pursuit of Lee's army to Appomattox, the fiery Sheridan undoubtedly would have proved a favorite among the spectators. The night before the review, Sheridan's troopers and musicians from several military bands had serenaded him, attracting a large crowd of civilians who responded to lusty cheering. Walt Whitman stood among those who saw the general "on a balcony, under a big tree, coolly smoking a cigar. His looks and manner impress'd me favorably."[27]

The most obvious missing figure at the Grand Review generated considerable comment. Secretary of the Navy Gideon Welles delayed a trip to attend both days of the review and marveled at the number of people "who wished to see and welcome the victorious soldiers of the Union." He sat where "the President, Cabinet, generals, and high naval officers" shared space with their wives and others. His voluminous diary includes nothing regarding the decision to limit the parade to soldiers, though surely he believed men who had served aboard United States naval vessels to be equally deserving of acknowledgment. "But Abraham Lincoln was not there," Welles wrote sadly of the man above all others who should have been present. "All felt this." The correspondent for the *Philadelphia Press* "did not hear a coarse word, nor notice an unseemly act" during the entire first day's procession, because, he ventured, "the thought of our great loss of our murdered Lincoln came in to temper the feeling and to suppress any vulgar or violent exultation." A Baltimore paper spoke to the bond that had grown between Lincoln and the soldiers. The martyred president "who called the men composing the splendid pageant now passing home from their peaceful firesides to protect the Government he had sworn to support would have been most glad and happy to have bidden them kindly greeting on their return." Adopting a bitter tone unusual in coverage of the review, the paper blamed Rebels for Lincoln's death: "What has Secession and Slavery to answer for?"[28]

Those present rather than those missing on May 23–24 preoccupied most observers, for whom the marching men personified a diverse citizenry brought together in a mighty and successful enterprise. The diversity most obvious and remarked upon was geographical. Geography was surely the leading frame of reference within a mid-nineteenth-century American context. Sectionalism nearly sundered the Union, but the Grand Review showed how sprawling parts had been fused into an irresistible whole. The soldiers had come forth in "tribute to free government, and to the democratic institutions under which they were reared," affirmed one newspaper, "representatives of every loyal State, to struggle, shoulder to shoulder, for their common country. They were our friends and brothers and sons, our fellow-citizens, our *people*." *Frank Leslie's,* among numerous other publications, highlighted the mingling of western and eastern men. Amid ringing applause from a largely eastern audience along Pennsylvania Avenue, most of Sherman's veterans strode behind banners of western states. They would "carry to their far western homes, in Indiana, Illinois, Iowa, Wisconsin, Missouri, Michigan, and Ohio, grateful remembrance of the day when they marched through the capitol of the nation." Another paper remarked that Sherman's forces also contained easterners (thirty regiments hailed from the East, compared to 156 from western states), uniting men from "all the States of the Great West, and also regiments from Pennsylvania, New York, New Jersey and Connecticut." In Pennsylvania, the *Franklin Repository* listed all the regiments from the Keystone State that participated in the review with Meade's army (forty-two infantry, five cavalry, and one artillery battery) and with Sherman's (seven infantry and one artillery battery).[29]

As Ferguson and Wainwright suggest, a leitmotif of sectional rivalry ran through soldiers' accounts of the review. Civilian testimony followed suit, creating an image of Meade's army as more spit-and-polish and of Sherman's as looser in marching style, physically more impressive, and less attentive to dress. These descriptions reflected common regional stereotypes—rugged westerners who sometimes bridled at convention versus easterners reared in more urban and regulated settings—as well as the fact that Sherman's troops wore uniforms grown shabby from long campaigning. Eliza Woolsey Howland, an educated and perceptive New Yorker married to an officer in the Army of the Potomac, described Sherman's soldiers alliteratively as "great big, brave, brawny men with faces brown as Indians" who moved with "an easy swinging gait" and "seemed half a head taller" than their eastern counterparts. Walt Whitman described the westerners as "larger in size" but "more slow in their movements, and in their intellectual quality also." A Philadelphia newspaper stressed that Meade's soldiers exhibited "very fine" marching and presented a "handsome appearance" in "clean, bright uniforms." *Frank Leslie's* accorded a full measure of praise to western forces but insisted the Army of the Potomac, because it confronted Robert E. Lee, had shouldered the greatest military burden: "Against them the power of the rebellion was mainly concentrated and consumed. Whether attacking or defending, it was the Army of the Potomac, with its mighty sledge, that battered the traitor fabric into the dust." Most accounts agreed that the second day's review attracted a larger crowd, owing in part, some speculated, to greater curiosity about armies that had fought far from Washington.[30]

A few individual units stood out as especially colorful. Zouaves from the Army of the Potomac, with their distinctive uniforms based on French North African infantry, "brought out a rapturous volley of applause," and Maj. Gen. George A. Custer's Third Division of cavalry donned long red neckties that added a swaggering edge to their already formidable presence near the van of the first day's parade. Custer's troopers, recalled Elizabeth Bacon Custer proudly, were "distinguishable far down the street by the scarlet neckties." Yet no body of troops cut a more impressive figure than the famous Irish Brigade, its ranks cruelly thinned by appalling casualties on battlefields such as Antietam, Fredericksburg, and Gettysburg. Part of the Army of the Potomac's Second Corps, the brigade "gave out their cheers with such stentorian vim as roused the multitude to tumultuous excitement." Lois Bryan Adams told her Midwestern readers of its "fine appearance, every soldier in it having a sprig of green box in his cap . . . The green flag of Erin was carried beside the national colors, and the tattered battle flags give token of the hard service they have seen."[31]

Few other regimental flags were as recognizable as the green Irish banners, but they all joined the national colors to touch a deep chord among the audience. Describing Sherman's armies as especially warlike, one young woman thought "their flags looked as if they had *met* the enemy and conquered, some of them nothing left but the fringe and tassels, some with the staff broken & spliced." A member of the 105th Ohio Infantry informed his mother on May 27, "We had many praises, cheers, and hurrahs heaped on us, on seeing our tattered flag." The proximity of state and American flags provided another reminder of how constituent parts had coalesced into a national military whole. Charles A. Page of the *New York Tribune* dwelled on this phenomenon. "One thing, both yesterday and to-day," he wrote on May 24, "never failed to call forth cheers, and that was the old flags, the tattered, torn, stained flags, frayed to shreds, staffs with a few sprays of lint-like silk,—these were loudly cheered time after time." A Massachusetts regiment, its state colors reduced to "a few shreds," had attached "a score of bright new streamers, each having the name of one of the battles of the regiment—and wasn't *that* cheered!" Gazing up Pennsylvania Avenue on May 23, the *New York Times*'s correspondent described "a continuous moving line, as far as the eye could reach, of national, state, division, brigade, regiment, and other flags. Some of them were new, the stars of gold leaf glittering in the sun, and these contrasted strongly with flags borne in the procession, tattered in battle, or mere shreds. Other flags were thickly covered with names and dates of battle-fields where victories were won by these proud veterans." A third newspaper pronounced some of the ragged flags "so funereal that they seemed to have been playthings in the grave rather than fashioned by the soft fingers of woman."[32]

The emphasis on flags carried in combat and streamers inscribed with the names of individual battles underscores the profound tie between military events and a continuation of the Founders' republic. The many national flags in evidence on May 23–24—hanging from buildings along the route, in the hands of bystanders along Pennsylvania Avenue, and adorning President Johnson's reviewing stand—would have served a shallow and merely symbolic purpose but for the soldiers' hard and costly work. Absent northern victory, a United States flag with eleven fewer stars that stood for a shrunken republic would, for many people in the loyal states, mock the political and military achievements of previous generations and serve as a constant reminder of their own failure to suppress the rebellion.

Obviously wounded officers stood out among a cavalcade of leaders, inspiring emotions similar to those aroused by scarred regimental standards. A heartfelt reception greeted maimed commanders such as General Howard, who had lost his right arm in the battle of Fair Oaks on June 1, 1862. "Every officer who wore an empty sleeve, or showed that he had been wounded," observed the *Baltimore Sun,* "was heartily cheered by the crowds along the sidewalk. The gallant Major General Howard was thus distinguished throughout the day." The press and onlookers also lavished attention on other generals, most notably Sherman and the various corps commanders. One newspaper reported that "great applause" greeted Sherman everywhere, "and he was the recipient of many fine bouquets and wreaths. Indeed, so lavish were the ladies with bouquets, that the General was obliged to call members of his staff to his assistance to take care of them." General Custer, inveterately focused on himself and always seeking the limelight, attracted attention on May 23 when his horse bolted near the president's reviewing stand. A superb horseman, Custer lost his flamboyant hat but garnered appreciative applause when he regained control of the animal.[33]

Above all, the throngs who attended the Grand Review celebrated the fact that Meade's and Sherman's soldiers would soon revert to their prewar status of American citizens. This reversion represented continuity in its most important meaning—from the revolutionary example of George Washington and the Continental Army, to Andrew Jackson and his Tennessee and Kentucky volunteers at New Orleans in 1815, to the soldiers who brought Rebels to heel all across the Confederacy. Americans cherished few things so much as the idea that their national history, unlike those of all the European powers, rested on the republican virtue of citizens willing to sacrifice in times of military crisis. What other nation could boast of anyone like George Washington, an American Cincinnatus who gave up supreme military power to resume his civilian pursuits at Mount Vernon after the Revolutionary War? The veterans in the Grand Review, in their more modest way, followed directly in Washington's republican footsteps.[34]

General Logan's farewell address to soldiers in the Army of the Tennessee, thousands of whom had marched on May 24, dwelled on the theme of virtuous citizenship. "You pledged your brave hearts and brawny arms to the Government of your fathers," stated Logan, yoking the efforts of 1861–1865 to those of 1776 and 1787, "rallying as the guardian of man's proudest heritage, forgetting the thread unwoven in the loom, quitting the anvil, abandoning the workshops, to vindicate the supremacy of the laws and the authority of the Constitution." The men's reward lay in the gratitude of the citizenry, in the "consciousness that, in saving the Republic, you have won for your country renewed respect and power at home and abroad," and, most of all, in the pride and glory central to "that loved boast, 'I am an American citizen.'" The citizen-soldiers had earned their accolades by humbling the "haughtiness" of oligarchs in the slaveholding states and thus positioned themselves to be objects of veneration by all lovers of republican liberty.[35]

Newspaper articles about the Grand Review anticipated Logan's sentiments by a few weeks. The *Daily National Intelligencer* asked, "Has the world ever seen a spectacle more truly sublime than this?" Success in combat paled before the prospect of a rapid demobilization following victory: "These are only dutiful American *citizens,* coming home to disband after a long successful work in behalf of their country!" Neither boastful nor threatening, the "armies of the North feel no other exultation than that which springs from the assured hope of a united and fraternal country." A Baltimore paper placed the veterans' work "alongside the events of the Revolutionary generation," attributing "moral sublimity" and overriding importance to one dimension of their work: "It is the significance of the transition from the soldier to the citizen. The soldier of yesterday is the citizen of to-day." Lois Bryan Adams quoted an Englishman in the crowd who affirmed he had never seen a more impressive military parade and thought "the grandeur of it all is that these men are citizens." Adams agreed in a brief tribute to the soldiers as "citizens who know the value of their country and their Government; they saw the danger menacing both, they made heroes of themselves, they have averted the danger, have given a progressive interpretation to the old Constitution, and are now quietly disbanding to go home and be citizens again."[36]

Adams left her readers with one last thought about the first day's review. After discussing at some length how individuals and groups used music, flowers, wreaths, and cheers to express thanks and admiration, she confessed disappointment at how little the crowd could do. "[O]h, how poor, how empty does all this pageantry and cheering seem," she lamented, "compared with what we owe to these bronzed and war-torn veterans. Shouts and songs and fading flowers seem almost like mockery when offered to such men who have accomplished a work so grand, and yet what else had these gratified crowds to offer?"[37]

Many loyal citizens lamented missing the Grand Review. From Boston, John Codman Ropes, a lawyer who had lost a brother killed at Gettysburg, conveyed his disappointment to Maj. John C. Gray, Jr., a friend serving with the judge advocate's office in Hilton Head, South Carolina. "I missed, partly through stupidity, and partly through business, going on to Washington to attend the Reviews," he wrote on May 29: "I shall never cease to regret it." Ropes urged Gray to attend commencement week at Harvard, during which the college would commemorate the military service of its graduates. The ceremony would be "a great occasion," predicted Ropes, who obviously saw it as a chance to make up for his decision to forego a trip to Washington.[38]

Much of the contemporary excitement and enthusiasm accompanying the Grand Review and its celebration of the restored Union is missing from some recent studies. Cecilia Elizabeth O'Leary's *To Die For: The Paradox of American Patriotism* asserts that the review marked a crucial first step in "the ritualization of male warrior heroism on a national scale . . .

Nationalists used the parade to commemorate the war's achievement and to make mythic heroes out of the Boys in Blue rather than dwell on the horrors of war." United States flags joined the soldiers who fought under them as "the most important symbols of the enduring power of the nation-state." This celebration of military success against Rebel armies, she claims, "provided a ritualized occasion for emphasizing the gender divide" between the marching men and thousands of women along Pennsylvania Avenue who were "spatially and symbolically removed to the sidelines." United States Colored Troops were also missing from the parade, with newspaper accounts only mentioning "two tall black sol- diers riding small pack mules who provided what the *New York Times* called a 'comic scene' for the white spectators." Among soldiers who did participate, "the Irish Brigade appeared wearing the green, but will- ingness to fight for the United States was not guaranteed to halt nativ- ist attacks." An emphasis on famous military engagements also bothers O'Leary: "Directly in front of the White House, flags and bunting omi- nously inscribed with names of battlefields covered the principal review- ing stand." Lest anyone underestimate how gender, race, ethnicity, and militarism compromised the Grand Review, O'Leary closes with this: "Patriotic culture emerged from war deeply fractured and ambivalent."[39]

The absence of United States Colored Troops on May 23–24 has re- ceived the most attention in recent years. As a "symbol of the new na- tion," observes Melinda Lawson in her study of mid-nineteenth-century American nationalism, the Grand Review demonstrated the power of Federal arms that had sustained the Union. But perhaps "most signifi- cantly, there were no black regiments represented in either Meade's or Sherman's Armies . . . Though viewed as an emblem of a nation re- born, the review's racial exclusion was disturbingly reminiscent of the old Union." Stuart McConnell voices comparable concern in his study of United States veterans. The "awesome size and scope" of the march- ing columns, which conveyed to observers a sense of national order and power, could not conceal the "exclusion from the parade of the black Union regiments"—a feature that in turn sent "a clear message about the sort of Union the white veterans felt they had preserved." McCon- nell anticipates O'Leary in mentioning that people who "watched from the sidewalks—women, children, men who had never enlisted—were obvious enough exclusions under the circumstances." Looking toward the future, McConnell wonders whether the veteran would remain a "privileged savior of the nation . . . If so, then the privileged were a peculiarly narrow group: white, male, largely rural in origin, and mostly (considering the make-up of the armies) of British, Irish, or German extraction."[40]

Still others have detected malicious purpose among the review's organizers or referred without explication to the lack of black soldiers on May 23–24. "One characteristic of the Grand Review that is seldom mentioned is the total absence of black troops, who made up nearly 10 percent of the Union Army at war's end," states William B. Holberton in his book on Union demobilization. "Their absence from the festivities celebrating the victorious conclusion of the war," he adds, "appears to have been deliberately planned." A recent survey of common soldiers blames "the army's official view of the war as a white man's crusade," adding incorrectly that "both armies represented in the Review had included African-American troops." Terry L. Jones's overview of the conflict avers that "few people probably noticed [that] . . . African American combat soldiers were nowhere to be seen." No evidence suggests veterans from units such as the 54th Massachusetts Infantry or the Louisiana Native Guards had been invited, Jones continues: "The guns had not yet fallen silent, yet the contribution black soldiers had made to final victory was already being forgotten." Even more troubled by the review is Harry S. Stout in his "moral history" of the war: "In a dark omen of what was to become of race relations in the reunited nation, no black military units were included in the parades as they had been at Lincoln's funeral." Other contemporary assessments note the absence without much speculation in such passages as "the Grand Army of the Republic (minus the black troops) passed in review"; "Unrepresented . . . were the thousands of African-American volunteer soldiers who had also paid in blood for the victory signified by the grand review"; and "After the Grand Review of Grant's army on May 24 and Sherman's the following day (parades that almost entirely excluded black troops) down Pennsylvania Avenue in Washington, the vast majority of the men soon entrained for home."[41]

A pair of studies devoted to African American troops after the Civil War echoes these other works. Donald R. Shaffer finds the seeds of postwar discrimination against USCT veterans in the events of May 23–24. "From the earliest days after the war," he comments in a passage that levels two charges against organizers of the review, "black veterans were slighted. They were excluded from the Grand Review of the Union Army. . . , although some black military laborers were allowed to march for the amusement of the spectators." In her book on black soldiers in the postwar decades, Elizabeth D. Leonard, who deals with only part of the newspaper's coverage, states that the *New York Times* "failed to acknowledge the USCT's absence—or, for that matter, its existence." Leonard implies deliberate purpose in this "not-so-easily explained lack of representation," linking it to callousness regarding the question of political rights for black veterans. "One could certainly argue that the effacing of black soldiers' sacrifices for and contributions to the nation's survival began here," she concludes, "as did many white Americans'—even white Northerners'—dismissal of the notion that blacks' military service during the war should be rewarded with their swift and uncompromising elevation to full citizenship." As with other accounts that proclaim an exclusionary purpose among planners, neither Shaffer's nor Leonard's cites any military documents barring USCT units from the Grand Review.[42]

The most expansive treatment of the review in the past twenty-five years closes Charles Royster's *The Destructive War: William Tecumseh Sherman, Stonewall Jackson, and the Americans.* Understandably focused on Sherman, it captures the sights and sounds on May 23–24 and accords considerable attention to the western soldiers' desire to outshine their eastern counterparts. "Many of these westerners believed that they had done far more than the Army of the Potomac to defeat the rebellion," states Royster, and the "review would give them a chance to show that they were veterans who surpassed the paper-collar soldiers of the east in every way." Captivating as a piece of descriptive prose, Royster's coda neither remarks on the absence of USCT units nor marshals contemporary testimony regarding how the soldiers and their military success had saved the Union and kept alive America's democratic promise. Instead, it presents the review as a public sanctioning of Sherman's style of brutal warfare, a festive tribute to militarism and violence in which the destructive capacity of the soldiers invigorated throngs of adoring observers.[43]

Understanding the Grand Review can prove elusive without sufficient attention to historical time, place, and documents. Too often the Grand Review has been reduced to little more than an exercise in reprehensible racial exclusion, with its marching soldiers defined most obviously as armed agents of a racist republic. Using race as the dominant analytical lens assumes bureaucratic ill will and ignores critical factors that shaped Grant's decision to deploy the Twenty-Fifth Corps to the Rio Grande. The use of "American" in nineteenth-century descriptions such as those by Colonel Wainwright, Mary Logan, and others, who clearly equated "Union," "nation," and "America" in a moment of victory over power-hungry southern oligarchs, loses all analytical value. By far most important, the meaning and promise of Union and the value of citizen-soldiers have no place in these exclusionary narratives. The importance of such things among onlookers at the Review, whether in uniform or not, loses all relevance to modern readers. Thus the Grand Review and how it has been portrayed over the past fifty years compels a renewed exploration of the meanings of Union, emancipation, black military service, and citizen-soldiers in the Civil War era and their legacy for Americans today.[44]

A view up Pennsylvania Avenue from near the Treasury building. Spectators fill all available spaces to watch mounted officers followed by batteries of artillery and infantry units stretching back toward the Capitol. (Library of Congress, Prints and Photographs Division, reproduction number LC B811–3310)

The presidential reviewing stand, featuring a huge flag, stars made of evergreen cuttings, and the names of battles such as Petersburg and Richmond sewn on bunting. Among the identifiable people in the front row (from the viewer's left to right) are General Grant (with a child on his left knee), Secretary of War Stanton, President Johnson, Secretary of the Navy Welles (with white beard), and General Sherman (looking to his right). (Francis Trevelyan Miller, ed., *The Photographic History of the Civil War,* 10 vols. New York: Review of Reviews, 1911, 9:259)

Frank Leslie's Illustrated Newspaper sought to convey the scale of the review and the size of the crowds in this illustration, which showed part of the Army of the Potomac on May 23. (Paul F. Mottelay and T. Campbell-Copeland, eds., *The Soldier in Our Civil War: Columbian Memorial Edition. A Pictorial History of the Conflict, 1861–1865,* 2 vols. New York: Stanley Bradley Publishing Company, 1893, 2:377–378)

This engraving graced the front page of *Frank Leslie's Illustrated Newspaper* on June 10, 1865. General Sherman raises his sword to the presidential party on May 24, with General Howard, his empty right sleeve pinned to his jacket, immediately behind him and General Logan on the rearing horse. (Paul F. Mottelay and T. Campbell-Copeland, eds., *The Soldier in Our Civil War: Columbian Memorial Edition. A Pictorial History of the Conflict, 1861–1865*, 2 vols. New York: Stanley Bradley Publishing Company, 1893, 2:377–378)

Harper's Weekly devoted a front cover to General Meade and his staff passing the main reviewing stand on May 23. (*Harper's Weekly*, June 10, 1865)

United States Colored Troops received considerable attention in the illustrated weeklies prior to the Grand Review. *Frank Leslie's* published this large engraving of USCT men entering Richmond to the applause of African American residents shortly after the Rebel capital fell. The caption read: "The Union Army Entering Richmond, Va. April 3—Reception of the Federal Troops in Main Street." (*Frank Leslie's Illustrated Newspaper,* April 29, 1865)

Participation by USCT units in various important events suggests there was no official effort to exclude them from the Grand Review. This photograph shows African American soldiers in Washington on the day of Lincoln's second inaugural (lower center and right, with muskets on their shoulders). (Library of Congress, Prints and Photographs Division, reproduction number LC B811–1284)

2

UNION

In his fourth annual message to Congress, dated December 6, 1864, Abraham Lincoln got to the heart of northern motivation in a war that had taken the lives of more than a third of a million United States soldiers. He mentioned the proposed Thirteenth Amendment to abolish slavery, which had passed the Senate eight months earlier but failed to garner the requisite two-thirds majority in the House of Representatives. The issue should be revisited, he argued, in light of Republican success in the recent national elections. Those returns represented "the voice of the people now, for the first time, heard upon the question." Lincoln framed his call for another vote in the House with reference to what he knew to be the bedrock of sentiment among loyal Americans. "In a great national crisis, like ours, unanimity of action among those seeking a common end is very desirable—almost indispensable," he observed: "In this case the common end is the maintenance of the Union," and the amendment stood "among the means to secure that end." Five and a half months later, in the wake of United States victory, William Tecumseh Sherman echoed Lincoln's words in a congratulatory order to veterans he had led in Georgia and the Carolinas. "Three armies had come together from distant fields, with separate histories," he said, "yet bound by one common cause—the union of our country, and the perpetuation of the Government of our inheritance."[1]

Maintenance of the Union, as Lincoln and Sherman made clear, always ranked first among war aims for most citizens in the United States. Anyone interested in why the mass of northern people supported crushing the rebellion, even at hideous cost, must come to grips with this crucial fact. Union was the key, and for many in the loyal states it had a meaning that extended far beyond the United States. Victory meant keeping aloft the banner of democracy to inspire anyone outside the United States who suffered at the hands of oligarchs. It meant affirming the rule of law under the Constitution and punishing slaveholding aristocrats whose selfish actions had compromised the work of the founding generation. And it meant establishing beyond question a northern version of the nation—of America, of the United States—that left control in the hands of ordinary voting citizens who were free to pursue economic success without fear of another disruptive sectional crisis.

Most Republicans and many Democrats eventually accepted emancipation as a useful tool to help defeat the Rebels and punish the slaveholding class most northerners blamed for secession and the outbreak of war. Most also came to believe that only a Union without slavery would be safe from internal threats in the future. Except among abolitionists and some Radical Republicans, however, liberation of enslaved people took a back seat to saving the Union. This fact does not drain all value from a war for constitutional law and a democratic republic on the northern model. For the wartime generation, Union promised liberty, freedom, and opportunity that, while restricted in many ways even with emancipation, would expand as the republic moved through the nineteenth century and into the twentieth. That expansion often proceeded at a depressingly slow pace—even stopped altogether at various points—but likely would have been far more problematical if the Confederacy had succeeded, slavery had survived in some of the loyal states, and the specter of additional groups of states separating themselves from a diminished Union had lingered on the political landscape.

American democracy as practiced in 1860 exhibited glaring weaknesses. Women, free and enslaved black people, and others did not partake fully of what most northerners would have defined as liberties and freedoms at the center of their popular republic. But it is important to remember the global context within which the Civil War generation lived and fought—within which, over the preceding decades, political and economic opportunity had been on the rise in the United States while privilege, with the failure of the European revolutions of the late 1840s, had seemed to gain a greater stranglehold on other nations in the western world. Falling far short of perfection (as all governments and political systems everywhere and always do), the American republic nonetheless followed a trajectory toward expansion of opportunity for its citizenry and functioned as a great magnet for immigrants seeking to improve their economic and political circumstances. Across the Atlantic, the United States stood for possibilities and change. The International Workingmen's Association congratulated Abraham Lincoln on his reelection in 1864, presenting him with an address drafted in late November. Europe's laboring men "felt instinctively that the star-spangled banner carried the destiny of their class" and believed "their hopes for the future, even their past conquests were at stake in that tremendous conflict on the other side of the Atlantic."[2]

Much recent Civil War scholarship obscures the importance of Union for the wartime generation. Two interpretive threads run through such literature. The first and more prominent suggests the Union of 1860–1861 scarcely deserved to be defended at the cost of any bloodshed. The second argues that a major shift in war aims occurred when northerners realized that only emancipation made their level of sacrifice worthwhile. In both instances, modern sensibilities distort our view of how participants of a distant era understood the war.

The sense of promise bequeathed by the republic's founders that motivated northern unionists often lies hidden beneath recent elaborations of American shortcomings. In *The Age of Lincoln,* Orville Vernon Burton states that the republic threatened by southern secession in 1860–1861 was "grounded in ruthless ideas of inequality of race, class, and gender." The cherished right of property so important to unionists concerned with their own freedom and liberty "had been rooted directly and indirectly in slavery." David Williams's *A People's History of the Civil War* unsurprisingly champions the "common people" (a group never clearly identified) against venal capitalists and their political lackeys such as Abraham Lincoln. Yet even Williams's common folk could not always resist the corrupting influences of the time, "giving in to a culture and politics of fear, bigotry, sexism, and racism" that prompted them "to resist expansions of freedom." One passage, sketching a bleak landscape featuring mass false consciousness among the befuddled plain folk, counters the idea of worthwhile purpose in the war: "In the name of patriotism, patriarchy, religion, and white supremacy, common people worked against each other, even slaughtered each other by the hundreds of thousands, and felt themselves righteous in doing so."[3]

Pulitzer Prize–winning historian Walter A. McDougall's *Throes of Democracy: The American Civil War Era, 1829–1877* concedes little of value to a fight for Union. "If preserving the Union was the war's deepest meaning," McDougall asserts in a text alternately acerbic and humorously entertaining, "then it merely restored the *status quo ante bellum*." Even emancipation did no more than enable the United States to catch up with the rest of "Christendom," scarcely a triumph "within the context of world history." (Brazil and Spanish Cuba must have occupied some other realm in this formulation.) Although Lincoln loved the Union because "its liberty under law permitted people to enjoy the fruits of their labor and apply their genius to the service of human progress," his "constituents, not to say his opponents, rarely or barely grasped that." Yankee victors, convinced of the "moral and material superiority of northern civilization," celebrated a war that rendered "millions of Caucasian, African, and Native American men and women . . . losers in terms of pursuing their happiness." The North unfortunately embraced more than ever "the myth of America as a 'New Israel' destined to regenerate the whole human race." Unmoved by what advocates of Union thought they had accomplished, McDougall implores his readers: "Let no one persuade you that the American Civil War was anything but a catastrophe."[4]

McDougall's allusion to a "New Israel" reflects a pervasive discomfort with expressions of American exceptionalism that often surfaced when unionists explained why they must defeat the Confederacy. Harry S.

Stout, a leading scholar of religion in America, manifests obvious unease with the fact that many northerners "supported the rightness of the war because at some profound level they believed in Lincoln's characterization of America as the world's last best hope." He adds, somewhat cryptically, "I can only conclude that for reasons Americans don't deserve or understand, we are." In a similar vein, Adam I. P. Smith warns of the dangers implicit in the idea "that progress is inevitable in American history, that wars have progressive purposes." Far too many people since Appomattox, he observes, "have found it as hard as the Americans who actually lived through the war to resist imposing a sort of providential meaning on the events of 1861–1865."[5]

Much recent work on the Civil War describes a troubling nationalism—often tied to exceptionalist attitudes and military might in the form of a powerful Yankee nation-state. Mark R. Wilson's *The Business of Civil War: Military Mobilization and the State, 1861–1865* illuminates the Quartermaster Department's influence on the Union war effort and describes the conflict as a great turning point. "Prefiguring developments that would emerge most explosively in the world wars of the twentieth century," Wilson argues, "the Civil War stood for half a century as the best illustration of the fearsomely destructive potential of military mobilizations conducted by industrialized nation-states." What Wilson labels "exceptionalist history," he believes, has overlooked how "modern America, as a child of the Civil War, had nonetheless been shaped by a partial militarization of business and government. Although this process did not necessarily promote a militarist national culture, it surely enhanced American war-fighting capacities during the era of the world wars and beyond, when the military foundations of the modern United States would shape the triumphs and horrors of the 'American century' and its aftermath."[6]

Harry Stout yokes the Union government and its military forces to a modern projection of United States power. His bridge from the nineteenth to the early twenty-first century was the decision, reached by U. S. Grant and Abraham Lincoln in 1864, to strike at the logistical capacity of the Confederacy in the Shenandoah Valley and the interior of Georgia. This represented "a moral touchstone of the war" because civilians and their property would become targets. Apparently unaware that noncombatants and their possessions had suffered terrible damage long before Grant planned his grand offensive in 1864, Stout claims that the one available moral justification lay in projecting the enemy as "not only a nation of Confederates but a nation of guerrillas as well." Although sufficient "as a moral lever for escalating the military destruction of armies in the field," emancipation could not justify harming civilians, most of them nonslaveholders, in the Shenandoah Valley. "There needed to be a terrorist threat to justify the destruction of nonmilitary targets," concludes Stout with what most readers in 2006 would have taken as an unmistakable reference to United States actions in the Middle East, and "that is precisely what the Union generals, and Lincoln, and, to be sure, pesky rebel bushwhackers, provided." Stout's anachronistic insertion of a "terrorist threat" into Grant's strategic formulations betrays an uncertain grasp of Civil War military affairs but abets his search for immorality in high counsels.[7]

Michael Fellman trumps Stout's analysis with a sweeping claim of state-sponsored terrorism. *In the Name of God and Country: Reconsidering Terrorism in American History,* a present-minded treatment featuring a long section on the Civil War, claims: "From the beginning of the American state (and before), terrorism has pervaded American war making, social transformation, and political development" and been "ultimately related to wider patterns of social inequality and domination—especially, though not exclusively, to divisions of race and class." A biographer of William Tecumseh Sherman and chronicler of Missouri's guerrilla war, Fellman revisits those topics to paint a picture of brutality that engulfed civilians—even as both the United States and the Confederacy invoked "contradictory versions of Christian civilization and the maintenance of liberty." Troubled by a "Civil War historical mainstream" that "tends toward unionist triumphalism," Fellman remarks in an interview published shortly before publication of his book that "where others stress the advance of freedom I see some of that and a lot more continuity of domination and oppression."[8]

From a modern American perspective, few things more effectively diminish the Union cause than to underscore the northern tendency to think in terms of a white democratic republic. Melinda Lawson's *Patriot Fires: Forging a New American Nationalism in the Civil War North,* for example, observes that "From the Revolution to the eve of the Civil War, American citizens—with the exception of a small abolitionist minority—imagined themselves as a uniquely democratic and exclusively white community." Similarly, Peter Parish draws on the work of George Fredrickson and others to remark that "between the Revolution and the Civil War, the United States became more conspicuously and self-consciously a white man's country." The antislavery crusade notwithstanding, "there was, until war and then emancipation came, virtually no conception and no serious discussion of a future American republic that might include several million free and equal black citizens."[9]

Other authors carry this theme into a postwar era dominated by rampant racism, nationalism, and imperialism. Christopher Waldrep finds no evidence that the war, won by soldiers who wrote "letters home on stationery that proclaimed 'THE UNION, THE CONSTITUTION—AND THE ENFORCEMENT OF THE LAWS,'" had made any long-term difference. In a study of Vicksburg in the national memory, Waldrep charges that postwar "American nationalism—more than white southern sectionalism—revived racial memories of the Civil War, putting reconciliation ahead of racial justice. For every major war or national crisis between the Civil War and World War II, northerners and the national government mobilized memories of Confederate heroism. Civil War gallantry consistently served American militarism, imperialism, and nationalism." Edward J. Blum develops a strong religious theme in *Reforging the White Republic: Race, Religion, and American Capitalism, 1865–1898,* which centered on "how the post–Civil War reunification of whites, the decline in American race relations, and the rise of a militarized, imperialistic nation were permitted, even encouraged, by northern whites" who had turned their backs on African Americans.[10]

Barbara J. Fields renders a succinct verdict regarding the value of a war for Union in the illustrated volume that accompanies Ken Burns's PBS documentary *The Civil War.* That kind of war arrayed different groups of "free, white citizens" against one another over such issues as whether states could withdraw from the federal compact or whether free-soilers would have their way in the territories. "Those appointed or self-appointed as spokesmen for 'respectable' opinion in the loyal states agreed on that premise even when they disagreed heatedly on the conclusion to be drawn from it," which meant that the war "should be decided on the basis of what would best promote such citizens' desires and interests." Restoration of the Union within such a framework, states Fields, distilling much of the literature into a single sentence, represents "a goal too shallow to be worth the sacrifice of a single life."[11]

In a time when the word "Union" as deployed in the mid-nineteenth century has passed out of our political vocabulary, it is difficult to recapture why it once resonated so powerfully. Readers in search of discussions of the concept of Union as a motivating force for the loyal populace will find almost no help in indexes of Civil War–era surveys. They will discover entries for, among other things, "Union" as a synonym for "United States," "Union Army," "Union Leagues," "Union Party," "Unionists" (meaning loyalist dissenters in the Confederacy), and "Unions" (labor organizations)—but just one for "Union: concept of," in the fourth edition of James M. McPherson's *Ordeal by Fire: The Civil War and Reconstruction*, the first three editions of which had no such an entry. Publishers rather than authors, it is important to note, are often responsible for the length and even the content of indexes.[12]

Careful readers will find some discussion of Union as a concept in almost all surveys, but often in very brief form or compared unfavorably to emancipation as a worthy goal of the war. For example, Scott Nelson's and Carol Sheriff's *A People at War* devotes about two pages to "Northern Causes," noting that some soldiers "wrote about protecting 'the best government on earth' or maintaining their nation's republican heritage" as an example to the rest of the world. Only over time "the idea of ending slavery—not necessarily because it was the right thing to do but often because it would deal secessionists a blow—would become increasingly popular among Northern soldiers and civilians." Another textbook lists a number of "motivations to enlist," among them for some early volunteers "a strong love of Union" and a belief that a southern slaveocracy "threatened their free-labor economy." These men "were none too keen on the notion of emancipation," add the authors, who leave unaddressed why many in the United States resisted what they saw as a direct assault on republican government from an oligarchic slaveholding class. In the postwar decades, white northerners, "anxious to downplay the role of slavery in the conflict and to appreciate the notion of a hierarchical white society," remembered the conflict "as a contest to save the Union."[13]

If saving the Union meant no more than fulfilling the self-interested objectives of white people in an exclusionary republic, or setting the stage for a militaristic nation-state to assert its will at home and abroad, such dismissive language would suffice as an explanation. But harsh critiques of the loyal citizenry and their embattled republic suggest a number of questions. More than 1.2 million men enlisted before conscription went into effect, while preservation of the Union remained the only official goal of the northern war effort. Did they all act from motivations unworthy of respect? Virtually all of the volunteers fit at least part of Stuart McConnell's demographic profile of "privileged saviors." They almost exactly mirrored the pool of military-age males in the wartime United States, so why label them "peculiarly narrow?"[14] Can we criticize the North's Civil War generation for not envisioning what the nation has become? Finally, would a failed war for Union have hindered progress in many admirable dimensions of American society?

There are many different ways to approach the era of the Civil War. One explores what it meant to Americans who lived through it. This avenue of inquiry requires seeking letters, diaries, newspapers, books, broadsides, illustrative materials, and other evidence produced at the time. It involves trying to discern how people used language and what key words and phrases and expressions meant to a past generation. No words require more careful attention than "liberty" and "freedom," both of which figured prominently in discussions of the war's origins and purposes by those who struggled over Union, secession, and emancipation. Such inquiry seeks not to decide whether we like or dislike the Civil War generation but to *understand* them and their actions.

A second approach seeks insight into topics of interest—or problems—in modern American culture. Edmund S. Morgan's *American Slavery, American Freedom* (1975) and C. Vann Woodward's *The Strange Career of Jim Crow* (1955), to name two influential examples, were emotionally satisfying because they identified the historical origins of contemporary problems. The Civil War era bristles with meanings of current relevance. For example, mid-nineteenth-century debates about the proper relationship between central and local authority, between advocates and opponents of unfettered capitalism, and about the degree to which civil liberties should be compromised in the midst of war often sound very current. Most obviously, black and white Americans of the time struggled with the problem of ordering a biracial society in a way that afforded fair treatment to all. Wrangling over the Thirteenth, Fourteenth, and Fifteenth Amendments (which ended slavery, guaranteed the equal protection of the law to all citizens, and conveyed the franchise to black men) anticipated modern discussions about race in the United States.[15]

A third approach, often closely linked to the second, assesses the motivations and behaviors of the Civil War generation through the analytical prism of current social and cultural norms. A largely ahistorical exercise, it almost always creates an impression of a benighted, unworthy North. Although it is important to know how northern society dealt with race and gender and how it conceived of freedom, liberty, and opportunity, simply describing the many ways in which wartime northerners fell short of later standards of acceptable thought and behavior yields little understanding.[16]

Inquiring more critically, it is clearer why, until well into the war, few white northerners gave serious consideration to a biracial society with anything approaching equal rights for all. Most thought in terms of a white republic because, in almost every way that mattered in their quotidian lives, they inhabited one. Demographic data illuminate a dominant antebellum society and culture conducive to forming a white-centered worldview.[17] In 1860, the free states and territories contained 19,048,849 people, of whom 18,822,654 (98.8 percent) were white and 226,195 (1.2 percent) black. Seven states met or surpassed the overall average of 1.2 percent, five of which shared access to the Atlantic Ocean along a coastline stretching from Rhode Island Sound on the northeast to Delaware Sound on the southwest. New Jersey had the largest percentage of African Americans with 25,336 out of 672,053 residents (3.8 percent), followed in descending order by Rhode Island (3,952 out of

174,601—2.3 percent), Pennsylvania (56,949 out of 2,906,208—2 percent), and Connecticut (8,627 out of 460,131—1.9 percent). Only three other states surpassed 1 percent in black population: Ohio (36,673 out of 2,339,481—1.6 percent), New York (49,005 out of 3,880,595—1.3 percent), and California (4,086 out of 327,253—1.2 percent). African American populations in the Midwestern states beyond Ohio composed less than 1 percent of population: Michigan (6,799 out of 742,941—.92 percent), Indiana (11,428 out of 1,350,138—.85 percent), Illinois (7,628 out of 1,711,919—.45 percent), Iowa (1,069 out of 674,848—.16 percent), Minnesota (259 out of 169,654—.15 percent), and Wisconsin (1,171 out of 774,864—.15 percent).

Even these sparse numbers do not reveal the degree to which white people could go about their lives without encountering many, if any, African Americans. Large cities contained a significant percentage of all black residents, leaving the smaller towns and rural areas even more blindingly white. For example, New York City and Brooklyn counted 17,471 African Americans among their populations in 1860, which represented 36 percent of all black people in the state. Similarly, 39 percent of black Pennsylvanians, a total of 22,185, lived in Philadelphia in 1860. In the Midwest, Chicago boasted 6.3 percent of the Illinois population but 12.5 percent of its black people, and in Ohio both Cincinnati and Cleveland possessed a higher percentage of African Americans than the rest of the state.[18]

Scholars in the mid-1960s cast into unsparing relief the unlovely relationship between white racial attitudes and demographics in the Midwest and West. In *The Frontier Against Slavery,* Eugene H. Berwanger explores exclusionary laws in Illinois, Indiana, Kansas, and Oregon (173,816 of 218,520 of votes cast in the four states supported them) and other antiblack legislation, demonstrating that much opposition to abolition stemmed from the specter of liberated slaves migrating northward and westward. V. Jacque Voegeli's *Free But Not Equal: The Midwest and the Negro during the Civil War,* which appeared the same year as Berwanger's study, gets right to the point in the opening sentence: "On the eve of the Civil War, the great majority of Americans believed in the innate superiority of the Caucasian race and were determined to maintain white supremacy." Outside the South, continues Voegeli, the Middle West "was the region most firmly committed to white supremacy. To most Midwesterners, negroes were biologically inferior persons to be shunned by all respectable whites." Even the Midwestern states witnessed vociferous debates about abolition that revealed some support for extending basic rights—such as control over property—to free black people. The overwhelming weight of sentiment, however, fell on the side of unequivocal white dominance.[19]

But while almost all white northerners would have responded in prejudiced terms if asked about African Americans, they were not as consumed with race as much of the recent literature would suggest. Most people did not begin each day by thinking immediately about the need to protect a privileged status conveyed by their "whiteness."[20] It is crucial to assess what people did discuss, what concerns most engaged their attention. Farmers worried about weather or pests or the market for their crops. Merchants thought about goods and consumers, bankers about loans and specie and paper notes, and parents about the well being of their children and extended families. Most were alert to the threat of ill health. Then as now economic concerns—whether in the form of dealing with hardship during crises such as the panic of 1857 or seeking to make good on a promising venture—often predominated.

The journals of two midwesterners afford revealing glimpses into the daily concerns of antebellum citizens. Writing on December 31, 1859, an Illinois farmer named John Edward Young reviewed a year that he termed "in some respects . . . a remarkable one." His detailed entry discussed the weather (some of it violent in northern Illinois); his "fair average crop of all kinds of farm products"; generally good health; prices for pork, beef, wheat, hay, and corn; and, in one of the longer passages, "the brightest most beautiful and extensive Auroraborelis" ever seen. "Financial matters," he recorded, "has not materially improved money is scarce and stock and articles of trade has ruled low." Although Young's diary as a whole reflected an interest in politics (he was a Republican), the summary of 1859 included no reference to John Brown's raid on Harpers Ferry, debates about the extension of slavery, or any other political issue—never mind anything suggesting that maintenance of white supremacy was on his mind that last day of December.[21]

In Indiana, banker and farm owner Calvin Fletcher kept an extraordinarily detailed diary. Crops, financial affairs, family issues, and the weather contended for much of his attention, and political events and issues often appeared in entries as well. The diary betrays scant concern about Fletcher's whiteness, but it does express considerable uneasiness about the state of the Union as the secession winter of 1860–1861 unfolded. "I fear that the South are determined on violence," he wrote in his final entry for 1860: "No one can now know what dire calamities await [us] as a nation or as individuals." Fletcher blamed slaveholders for the threats to Union, selecting language that juxtaposed a republican North against southern oligarchs who, together with their northern allies such as "the poor old imbecial President Buchanan," had undermined the intent of the Constitution. By late February, as Abraham Lincoln's inauguration drew near, Fletcher cheered that the "reign of a democratic dynasty is approaching its end . . . The power of the South must decline." He hoped the free states, armed with "the physical & moral power," would "exercise their power to the glory of God & the good of their country." Alluding to Baltimore, through which Lincoln passed on his way to Washington and where the 6th Massachusetts Volunteer Militia would be attacked by pro-secessionists on April 19, Fletcher dismissed the possibility of free and orderly government wherever a powerful slaveholding class held sway: "Tyranny is the rule or mob—A republic can not exist in a slave state."[22]

Americans of the late antebellum years who shared Calvin Fletcher's concern for the Union—almost all of whom were infused with a sense of national exceptionalism—often quoted the stirring rhetoric of Daniel Webster. "I speak to-day for the preservation of the Union," Webster famously proclaimed on March 7, 1850, "Hear me for my cause." The Massachusetts senator went on to explain why the American model of government, once again tested by sectional tensions related to slavery, excelled that of the European nations: "We have a great, popular, constitutional government guarded by law and by judicature, and defended by the affections of the whole people. No monarchical throne presses these States together, no iron chain of military power encircles them; they live and stand under a government popular in its form, representative in its character, founded upon principles of equality, and so constructed, we hope, as to last forever." Twenty years earlier, in the midst of a crisis prompted by South Carolina's posturing about nullification, Webster had uttered his most famous words from the floor of the Senate, "Liberty *and* Union, now and forever, one and inseparable." Published as a pamphlet, that speech sold nearly 150,000 copies and influenced generations of American schoolchildren. Although abolitionists denounced Webster's Seventh of March speech, the white majority applauded it. They followed Webster in yoking liberty to Union in explaining why they fought in United States armies during the Civil War. Like Webster, they championed their Union as a place where citizens ruled, a bulwark against the forces of oligarchy personified in the American context by proud aristocrats from the slaveholding states.[23]

Recapturing how the concept of Union resonated and reverberated throughout the loyal states in the Civil War era is critical to grasping northern motivation. No single word in our contemporary political vocabulary shoulders so much historical, political, and ideological meaning; none can stir deep emotional currents so easily. Devotion to the Union functioned as a bonding agent among Americans who believed, as a citizenry and a nation under the Constitution, they were destined for greatness on the world stage. For devout unionists, the Constitution had been framed by the people rather than created as a compact among states. It formed a government, as President Andrew Jackson insisted during the nullification crisis of the early 1830s, "in which all the people are represented, which operates directly on the people individually, not upon the States." Secession, added Jackson in language that anticipated unionist arguments in 1860–1861, "does not break a league, but destroys the unity of a nation." Kenneth M. Stampp's influential essay on the concept of perpetual Union used the writings and speeches of Jackson, Webster, John Quincy Adams, and other figures from the early republic to make a salient point: "By 1833, to the nationalists the Union had become an absolute, an end in itself; and, in retrospect, it seems clear that by then the time had passed when the people of a state might resort to the remedy of secession without confronting the coercive authority of the federal government."[24]

Historians W. R. Brock and Elizabeth R. Varon, across a period of thirty-five years, present two thoughtful analyses of the concept of Union. Citizens in the northern states believed "the idea of American nationalism was bound up with the ideals of human betterment," writes Brock in a survey of the mid-nineteenth-century United States: "This explains the intensity of emotion that focused upon the word 'Union': it was not a mere political arrangement but the only way in which an American could summarize his romantic concept of national existence." In her exploration of the coming of the Civil War, Varon concludes that "the word 'Union' connoted 'nation' and 'country,' and called to mind the geographic, linguistic, cultural, and historical bonds that held America's citizenry together." Moreover, it "was synonymous with the republic—America's unique experiment in self-rule 'by the people'" and had "a transcendent, mystical quality as the object of their patriotic devotion and civic religion." The word "disunion," while not precisely an antonym, evoked a chilling scenario within which the Founders' carefully constructed representative government failed, triggering "a nightmare, a tragic cataclysm" that would subject Americans to "the kind of fear and misery that seemed to pervade the rest of the world."[25]

In a revealing interdisciplinary study that ranges from the American Revolution to the Civil War and across the Atlantic world, Nicholas and Peter Onuf similarly explore the relationship between Union and nation. "The union Lincoln would fight to preserve was not the bundle of compromises that secured the vital interests of both slave states and free," they argue, "but was, rather, the *nation*—the single, united, free people— Jefferson and his fellow Revolutionaries supposedly had conceived and whose fundamental principles must never be compromised." A critical moment in America's history, the Civil War proved the Union—the nation—could survive a potentially lethal internal threat, achieving redemption and presenting itself to the world as more than an experiment in self-government by a free citizenry. Lincoln "invoked Jefferson in order to establish legitimating genealogy for the American nation and to define its world historical destiny," but he also accepted the need for wartime concentrations of central power many of the founders had linked to despotic rule. "The character of the American union," observe the Onufs, "was transformed between Jefferson's time and Lincoln's." Its unique strengths, Lincoln almost certainly would have been quick to add, were not.[26]

That many in the slaveholding South saw menace rather than protection in the Union following Lincoln's election highlighted a fundamental division foreshadowed by John C. Calhoun almost exactly thirty years earlier. At a dinner on April 13, 1830, in honor of Thomas Jefferson's birthday, President Jackson had toasted, "Our Union. It must be preserved." Vice President Calhoun, his hands shaking slightly as he struggled to master his emotions, answered in what unionists at the time and thereafter would construe as inflammatory language: "The Union, next to our liberty most dear. May we all remember that it can only be preserved by respecting the rights of the states and by distributing equally the benefits and the burdens of the Union."[27] Many northerners might wonder how the Union threatened slaveholders and their liberty. Its Constitution, with a three-fifths clause that counted nonvoting slaves for purposes of national representation, made every ballot cast in a slave state worth more than one cast north of the Ohio River and Mason's and Dixon's Line. Slaveholders and their allies also had dominated the presidency since the nation's founding. For these and other reasons, Calhoun's toast, and innumerable similar statements from slaveholding politicians over the succeeding decades, struck northern unionists as self-serving defensiveness.

Abraham Lincoln spoke eloquently for all those who loved the Union and believed it guaranteed rather than threatened liberty. His statements designed for public consumption reflect a remarkable consistency regarding the centrality of Union to the war effort. As a group, the messages, letters, and speeches reveal how the president, whose political skills matched those of anyone who has held the presidency, sought to galvanize support for a massively destructive war. Throughout the conflict, Lincoln evoked the multiple meanings of Union—as a priceless inheritance from the founding generation, a guarantor of liberty and freedom and opportunity, and a gonfalon of democracy in a world sadly dominated by oligarchs and monarchs. He also dealt with Union in ways that aligned very closely with his definition of a nation, which, he observed in December 1862, "may be said to consist of its territory, its people, and its laws." Shaped by Lincoln's reading of public opinion, these statements regarding Union reach across a century and a half to help clarify what motivated most white northerners.[28]

The president's first inaugural address, delivered on March 4, 1861, gave a history lesson regarding the Union. Older than the Constitution and "perpetual," it stemmed from the Articles of Association in 1774, the Declaration of Independence in 1776, the Articles of Confederation in 1778, and, finally, the Constitution in 1787—whose framers during a stifling summer of debate in Philadelphia had built on the documents from 1774–1778 *to form a more perfect union.* Summoning images of a shared democratic destiny, Lincoln closed on a lyrical note that tied Americans in 1861 to all previous generations: "The mystic chords of memory, stretching from every battle-field, and patriot grave, to every heart and hearthstone, all over this broad land, will yet swell the chorus of the Union, when again touched, as surely they will be, by the better angels of our nature."[29]

Four months later, in a message to Congress called into special session to deal with the war, Lincoln developed important themes related to Union—which together anticipated his later definition of nation. He labeled the conflict "essentially a people's contest," phrasing tied to the opening words of the Constitution's preamble and certain to touch all who considered themselves part of "We the people." Ballots had "fairly, and constitutionally" decided the election of 1860, and it remained for "our people . . . to demonstrate to the world, that those who can fairly carry an election, can also suppress a rebellion." Lincoln also moved beyond the boundaries of the United States, staking out lofty ideological ground in arguing that secession "presents the whole family of man, the question, whether a constitutional republic, or a democracy—a government of the people, by the people—can, or cannot, maintain its territorial integrity, against its own domestic foes." (Had Lincoln *spoken* the words "of the people, by the people," as he would later in his address at Gettysburg, his emphasis surely would have been on "people" rather than on the prepositions.) Finally, he explained precisely what Union promised those who lived under the protection of its government. The "lead-ing object, is to elevate the condition of men—to lift artificial weights from all shoulders—to clear the paths of laudable pursuit for all—to af-ford all, an unfettered start, and a fair chance, in the race of life." This last section aligned perfectly with the Republican Party's devotion to free labor ideology, which promised an opportunity, through the careful ap-plication of one's own labor, to move from the laboring to the proper-tied class.[30]

The summer of 1862 found the Union beset by a shortage of man-power, military defeats in Virginia at the Seven Days and Second Bull Run, and political wrangling over emancipation. Lincoln's administra-tion flirted with the idea of conscription before finding other ways to meet immediate goals for enlistments. Winning battles lay beyond the president's immediate control, but he wrote an unequivocal reply to an editorial by Horace Greeley, published in the *New York Tribune* in mid-August and titled "The Prayer of Twenty Millions." Greeley had urged a more rigorous effort to free slaves owned by Rebels, as authorized by the Second Confiscation Act. Such action would hurt the Confederacy and "fight Slavery with Liberty." Lincoln answered on August 22 (his response appeared in Washington's *Daily National Intelligencer* the next day), reiterating his "oft-expressed *personal* wish that all men every where could be free" but leaving no doubt about his overriding goal. "My para-mount object in this struggle," stated Lincoln, "*is* to save the Union, and is *not* either to save or to destroy slavery. If I could save the Union with-out freeing *any* slave I would do it, and if I could save it by freeing *all* the slaves I would do it; and if I could save it by freeing some and leav-ing others alone I would also do that. What I do about slavery and the colored race, I do because I believe it helps to save the Union; and what I forbear, I forbear because I do *not* believe it would help to save the Union." These three sentences summarized Lincoln's "purpose accord-ing to my view of *official* duty."[31]

The reply to Greeley has inspired numerous attacks on Lincoln as a racist who cared little about enslaved people, as well as elaborate defenses of his reasoning. In fact, the letter stands as a straightforward expression of his consistent commitment to and invocation of Union to rally the largest segment of the loyal states' white population—which at the same time signaled the president's willingness to consider emancipation as one tool to suppress the Rebels.

The next few months brought three examples of Lincoln tying emancipation to Union. In each instance, he sought to dampen widescale and vociferous hostility among Democrats who would support a war for Union but not one for the liberation of slaves. The United States could prevail against the Confederacy only if it maintained at least a degree of bipartisan support for the military effort, which prompted Lincoln to justify emancipation as a war measure necessary to deny vital labor to the Rebels. In the preliminary Emancipation Proclamation, issued on September 22, 1862, he announced "that hereafter, as heretofore, the war will be prosecuted for the object of practically restoring the constitutional relation between the United States, and each of the states, and the people thereof, in which states that relation is, or may be, suspended." The final proclamation of January 1, 1863, rested on the power vested in Lincoln as "Commander-in-Chief, of the Army and Navy of the United States in time of actual armed rebellion against authority and government of the United States, and as a fit and necessary war measure for suppressing said rebellion." Later in the document, Lincoln characterized it as "an act of justice, warranted by the Constitution, upon military necessity." Neither version alluded in any way to the morality of ending slavery, though Lincoln invoked the "gracious favor of Almighty God."[32]

In between the proclamations, Lincoln took up emancipation in his annual message to Congress of December 1, 1862. Well aware of opposition in the Border States and within the ranks of the Democratic Party, he outlined a case for gradual, compensated emancipation accompanied by voluntary colonization of freedpeople. His plan, which included three proposed amendments to the Constitution, would not harm free white labor, he assured those fearful of competition with black workers, but would discomfit the Rebels and safeguard the freedom and liberties of all loyal citizens. Admonishing members of Congress that they, and he, would be called to account by subsequent generations for their actions during the "fiery trial through which we pass," Lincoln remarked: "We know how to save the Union. The world knows we do know how to save it. We—even *we here*—hold the power, and bear the responsibility. In *giving* freedom to the *slave,* we *assure* freedom to the *free*—honorable alike in what we give, and what we preserve." Looking beyond the borders of the United States, as he had in his message to Congress on July 4, 1861, he spoke of American democracy as a great beacon of promise. "We shall nobly save, or meanly lose, the last best, hope of earth," he said in raising the stakes for emancipation as a tool to help vanquish the Rebel threat to Union. "Other means may succeed; this could not fail," he concluded, "The way is plain, peaceful, generous, just—a way which, if followed, the world will forever applaud, and God must forever bless."[33]

In 1864, Lincoln and his supporters dropped the name "Republican" and ran on a Union Party ticket with Democrat Andrew Johnson of Tennessee as the vice presidential candidate. Secretary of State William Henry Seward had supported a Union Party movement in the first spring of the war, observing in a memorandum to Lincoln that "we must *Change the question before the Public from one upon Slavery, or about Slavery* for a question upon *Union* or *Disunion*." Throughout the conflict, a number of Republicans had run on the state level as Union candidates. A grim military situation in the summer of 1864 spread despair across the loyal states and weakened Republican prospects, prompting Lincoln's famous blind memorandum of August 23, which he asked his Cabinet to endorse on the verso. "This morning, as for some days past," read the text, "it seems exceedingly probable that this Administration will not be re-elected. Then it will be my duty to co-operate with the President elect, as to save the Union between the election and the inauguration; as he will have secured his election on such ground that he can not possibly save it afterwards." The Union ticket might attract Democratic votes in November 1864, as well as help lay the groundwork for a national party when Confederate states returned to the fold. In the end, William Tecumseh Sherman's capture of Atlanta and Philip H. Sheridan's decisive victories in the Shenandoah Valley transformed civilian morale and re-elected Lincoln. But jettisoning the party label "Republican" speaks to the power of Union as a rallying cry—or at least to a pervasive belief in such power.[34]

Some Democrats responded as those who supported a Union ticket expected. At the Baltimore convention that nominated Lincoln, the temporary chairman, Robert J. Breckinridge of Kentucky, said to the delegates: "I see before me not only primitive Republicans and primitive Abolitionists, but I see also primitive Democrats and primitive Whigs . . . As a Union party I will follow you to the ends of the earth." If Lincoln were running as candidate of the Republican Party, added Breckinridge, a prominent Border State Presbyterian who held moderately antislavery views, "I will not follow you one foot."[35]

Lincoln's last annual message to Congress reiterated the main points of the platform on which he and his party had mounted their successful campaign. The platform's first resolution defined as the "highest duty of every American citizen" a willingness to maintain the integrity of the Union, its Constitution, and its laws against rebels and traitors. The second expressed determination to prosecute the war until Confederates surrendered unconditionally. The third pronounced slavery "the cause and now . . . the strength of this rebellion," condemned it as "hostile to the principles of republican government," and proposed an amendment to the Constitution forever prohibiting it in all parts of the United States. Buoyed by the results of the election, Lincoln celebrated its unequivocal message that most loyal citizens stood ready to finish the work of saving the Union. The wavering sentiment of July and August 1864 seemed far distant. More votes were cast in 1864 than in 1860 (including many thousands by United States soldiers in the field), which demonstrated, said the president, "the important fact . . . that we have *more* men *now* than we had when the war *began;* that we are not exhausted, nor in process of exhaustion; that we are *gaining* strength, and may, if need be, maintain the contest indefinitely." Union would be protected, the people's "common end" achieved.[36]

A mass of evidence from all four years of the conflict confirms Lincoln's astute reading of the loyal citizenry. Herman Melville put the case very directly in the dedication for his collection of war poetry: "The Battle-Pieces In This Volume Are Dedicated To The Memory Of The THREE HUNDRED THOUSAND Who In The War For The Maintenance Of The Union Fell Devotedly Under The Flag Of Their Fathers."[37] Attachment to Union, more than any other factor by far, motivated loyal citizens bent on defeating the rebellion. Because such factors are impossible to quantify, scholars can argue about their relative importance and whether they waxed and waned under the stress of an expanding war.

But the preeminence of Union cannot be denied by anyone immersed in the written, illustrative, and other materials from the war years. A look at several categories of evidence will indicate the tenor of the overall body.

A good place to begin is with George F. Root's *The Battle-Cry of Freedom,* probably the most popular song among loyal soldiers and civilians.[38] Its lyrics not only shed light on what mattered to those who sang and listened to it, but they also demonstrate the importance of ascribing contemporary meanings to words deployed by the Civil War generation. "Freedom" is the key word, and in the twenty-first century it most often conjures thoughts about African Americans and emancipation. A reasonable conclusion might be that when Root composed the song, in the summer of 1862, he believed the North should embrace a war for black liberation. Congress already had outlawed slavery in the District of Columbia and the federal territories (on April 16 and June 19, 1862, respectively), and discussion of more general emancipation grew increasingly heated inside and outside Congress. Here was a compelling plea for men to enlist and end the practice of human bondage by force of arms.

However plausible, such an interpretation fails to account for the origins of the song and its great appeal in the United States. "I heard of President Lincoln's second call for troops one afternoon while reclining on a lounge in my brother's house," Root recalled in his memoirs. "Immediately I started a song in my mind," he continued, "words and music together:

'Yes, we'll rally round the flag, boys, we'll rally once again,
Shouting the battle-cry of freedom!'

I thought it out that afternoon, and wrote it the next morning . . . From there the song went into the army, and the testimony in regard to its use in the camp and on the march, and even on the field of battle, from soldiers and officers, up to generals, and even to the good President himself, made me thankful that if I could not shoulder a musket in defense of my country I could serve her in this way."[39] Lincoln's call for the governors of loyal states to supply 300,000 three-year volunteers, dated July 1, 1862,

and released to the press the next day, made no mention of possible black
enlistment. Emancipation almost certainly did not preoccupy Root as he
composed what he termed a "rallying song"; rather, he sought to boost
volunteering among white men across the United States. National conscription lay many months in the future, as did enlistment of African
Americans, so anything that might encourage white men to enlist would
assist the Lincoln administration.[40]

For the song's targeted audience, Union provided the hook, with preservation of existing American freedom as one of the obvious benefits of
vanquishing the Rebels. The chorus conveyed the principal message:

> The Union forever, Hurrah, boys, Hurrah!
> Down with the traitor, Up with the star; while we rally round the flag
>   boys,
> Rally once again, Shouting the battle-cry of Freedom.

Echoing Daniel Webster's "Liberty and Union, now and forever," the
chorus supported the idea of a perpetual Union so dear to Lincoln and
countless others. It also featured the stars and stripes, easily the most vis-
ible representation of the Union. The second verse tied prospective volunteers to those who had enlisted during the first great rush to the colors, casualties among whom left units shorthanded:

> We are springing to the call
> Of our brothers gone before,
> Shouting the battle cry of Freedom,
> And we'll fill the vacant ranks
> With a million Free men more,
> Shouting the battle cry of Freedom.

The third verse invited all classes of men to step forward with a promise
of rights within the Union:

> We will welcome to our numbers
> The loyal, true, and brave,

Shouting the battle cry of Freedom,
And although he may be poor
He shall never be a slave,
Shouting the battle cry of Freedom.

The last verse spoke to a national effort uniting geographical sections:

So we're springing to the call
From the East and from the West,
Shouting the battle cry of Freedom,
And we'll hurl the rebel crew
From the land we love the best,
Shouting the battle cry of freedom.

Root's lyrics brilliantly engaged all segments of the loyal states' pool of military-age white men—"free men" who, by taking up arms, would guarantee continued "freedom" and prevent their becoming slaves to southern slaveholders. These words appealed on the basis of a free-labor vision of the American nation—a northern version of Union with a Constitution and representative form of government, to quote Lincoln once again, designed "to clear the paths of laudable pursuit for all—to afford all, an unfettered start, and a fair chance, in the race of life." Many in the North believed that slaveholding oligarchs denied such a path, and thus real freedom, to nonslaveholding white people in the South, and that the Slave Power's inordinate influence in the antebellum federal government had presented a continuing obstacle to greater expansion of political and economic opportunity. Whether consciously or not, Root translated Webster's soaring rhetoric into a paean to Union, with an in-fectious melody and well-crafted lyrics that "proved amazingly successful at patriotic gatherings." An alternate set of lyrics, described as a "battle song" by Root, included lines more directly beholden to Webster:

Yes, for Liberty and Union we're springing to the fight,
And the vict'ry shall be ours,
for we're rising in our might.

This version "formed an ideal marching air," noted a pair of historians of Civil War music, and "it literally belonged to the soldiers."[41]

Civilians and soldiers who embraced *The Battle-Cry of Freedom* had long since begun using patriotic envelopes that also reflected a devotion to Union.[42] The envelopes featured a number of predictable motifs, most prominently the figure of Columbia, American flags, eagles, the Union shield, soldiers and sailors, and famous military and political leaders. Jefferson Davis—most often being hanged, mocked, or otherwise reviled—turned up frequently as the prime traitor seeking to undo the Union. In one typical example, he dangled from a gallows with text above and below: "Jeff. Davis, 'President' of Traitors, Robbers, and Pirates; the Nero of the 19th century" (above); and "On the Last 'Platform' of the Southern Confeder-ass-y 'Rope, Beam & Co.,' Executors" (below). African Americans and emancipation, neither a major subject of the envelopes, often appeared as unflattering caricatures. Some examples reflected Democratic unhappiness with emancipation, as with one showing a man with large red lips and the caption, "The Cause of All Our Troubles." Others dealt with contrabands—a man shining a shoe and saying, "By golly Massa Butler, I like dis better dan / workin' in de field for old Secesh massa"; a black couple in grotesque caricature with the caption, "Bress de Lor, we am Contraban." Still others relied on stereotypes associated with minstrelsy—a grinning, dancing character singing, "I'm glad I'm not in Dixie! / Hooray! Hooray!"

Envelopes most often combined images and text to remind citizens about the value of a war for Union. The massive amount of correspondence passing between the armies and the home front assured wide dissemination of the envelopes—though what percentage of letters traveled in them cannot be established. Richard Eddy, chaplain of the 60th New York Infantry in the Army of the Potomac's Twelfth Corps, served as postmaster for his unit, noting in April 1863, "I mailed for the regiment 3855 letters during the month." The volume of letters surely varied by season, with more sent during winter encampments than amid active campaigning between late April and early autumn. A conservative annual estimate might be 15,000 for the 60th, which mustered 273 men on the battlefield at Gettysburg in July after suffering nine killed, forty-four

wounded, and thirteen captured at Chancellorsville in early May. The
Army of the Potomac comprised 238 infantry regiments, 29 cavalry regiments, and 65 artillery batteries during the Gettysburg campaign, some
two months after Chaplain Eddy made his count. If men in all units
wrote home at approximately the same rate as the New Yorkers, more
than a million letters could have left the army in a single month. United
States armies altogether counted 698,802 men in their ranks on January
1, 1863 (another 219,389 were absent for various reasons), a total roughly
six times that in the Army of the Potomac. The staggering volume of
mail that emanated from the armies—and incoming letters greatly expanded the total correspondence—underscores the ubiquitous presence
of patriotic envelopes.[43]

Americans who sent and received mail were reminded of their democratic republic and its Constitution, Daniel Webster's unionist pro-
nouncements, and links between the war against secession and the
founding generation. Columbia, the feminine personification of the
United States in the nineteenth century, often conveyed messages of
Union. One envelope placed her opposite a Websterian text, "Liberty &
Union Now & For Ever," below which the designer turned to the final
stanza of Francis Scott Key's poem "Defence of Fort McHenry," adapted
as lyrics for *The Star-Spangled Banner:* "Then conquer we must, our cause
it is just,/And this is our motto, 'In God is our trust.'" Another limited
its text only to Webster: "Liberty & Union Now & For Ever." A third
placed Columbia in a world setting, looking forward with a message that
America's perpetual Union would continue to serve all who believed in
self-rule:

> Columbia, Columbia, to glory arise
> The queen of the world and the child of the skies;
> The genius commands thee, with rapture behold;
> While ages on ages thy splendors unfold.

The extra-legal nature of secession dominated a fourth envelope, "Our
Union and Our Laws we must maintain / And drive foul treason from

our land again," while a fifth offered a Columbia given to plodding le-
galistic wording rather than phrasing likely to cause hearts to soar: "Proclaim liberty throughout all the / land unto all the Inhabitants thereof."

The Founders appeared on envelopes in various ways, most often in
the person of George Washington. One mailed from Worcester, Massachusetts, included a bust of the first president and this quotation:

Every portion of our country
finds the most commanding
motives for carefully guarding and
preserving the union of the whole.

Another combined a bust and part of Washington's Farewell Address:

To the efficacy and permanency of our
UNION, a government for the whole
is indispensable.

A third situated Washington astride a rearing horse to the left of "THE
WAR FOR THE UNION" rendered in block letters adorned by stars and
stripes. Among other founders, Patrick Henry made an appearance with
the call for "Liberty or Death" attributed by Civil War–era Americans to
his famous speech before Virginia's House of Burgesses in March 1775.[44]

Allusions to Union also accompanied various other symbols. Representative envelopes offered "Union Forever" on an embossed flag,
"Union" surrounded by the names of the loyal states, and "Union" in the
middle of a large star. On an especially effective envelope, a locomotive
with "Union For Ever" emblazoned on its smokestack smashed through
Rebels along a railroad. Should the letter's recipient miss the obvious
message, a caption explained: "The Union locomotive clearing the Secession track." Soldiers and flags graced many envelopes alongside such
slogans as "The Constitution and the Laws" and "Maintain the Government." General in Chief Winfield Scott, a septuagenarian Virginian
whose decision to remain in United States service personified unionism,

proved a prime early-war subject for those who produced envelopes. The designers most often located his massive head, topped by unruly hair and often surrounded by flags, above quotations about Union:

> Gen. Winfield Scott.
> Brave in the Field,
> Wise in Council,
> A true Patriot,
> Loyal to the Constitution and the Union;

or, "The Union Must and Shall Be Preserved."[45]

George B. McClellan was a frequent subject. General in chief of United States armies and commander of the Army of the Potomac for parts of 1861 and 1862, he also ran for president on the Democratic ticket in 1864. McClellan adamantly opposed forced emancipation and was most popular among those who wanted a war for Union unadulterated by attention to black freedom as a secondary goal. Examples of patriotic envelopes acknowledged both his time as a general and his political candidacy, often with a message of Union. One of the former juxtaposed his portrait above draped flags opposite "The War for the Union"; another, simpler design placed a plain three-quarters bust just to the left of "Liberty and Union." Among the political envelopes, a striking example surrounded McClellan with flags and a shield and quoted him at some length: "'Love and reverence for the Union, the Constitution, the Laws and the Flag.' 'The Union at All Hazards.' 'Re-establishment of the Union in all its integrity.' 'The Union the one condition of peace— we ask no more.' McClellan."[46]

Surviving evidence does not reveal whether patriotic envelopes maintained a steady popularity throughout the conflict. Some political and military figures prominent early in the war appear more frequently than those whose fame came later. For example, the Union's first real martyr, Col. Elmer Ellsworth, was a subject more often than Ulysses S. Grant or William Tecumseh Sherman. This raises the possibility that the impact of symbols and texts on envelopes diminished as the conflict dragged on. On the other hand, it could be that generic symbols such as flags and Columbia simply proved more durable. One thing seems beyond debate: for countless Americans who came into contact with these envelopes, the dominant patriotic message concerned the need to preserve the Union.[47]

The importance of the concept of Union to loyal officers and soldiers similarly cannot be gainsaid, though how it related to other factors in promoting enlistment and keeping men in the ranks defies precise quantification. Since Bell I. Wiley's pioneering work on common soldiers in the 1940s and 1950s, historians have consulted solders' letters and diaries to examine motivation, behavior in combat, political attitudes, racial assumptions, the degree to which ideology influenced the men, and other questions. The most diligent scholars visited repositories across the United States to survey collections of letters, as well as a smaller number of diaries, en route to generalizing about soldiers' experiences. They strove for representativeness, looking at soldiers of different classes (perhaps inevitably, wealthier and better-educated men often predominated), from different regions, and with varying types of service (those in mainline armies who participated in famous campaigns appeared more often than those relegated to rear-echelon service). No one employing this methodology has claimed a truly "representative" sample—and rightly so, because such would be impossible no matter how many letters were read.[48]

Chaplain Eddy and his nearly 4,000 letters from one regiment in a single month come to mind. More than 2 million men served in United States military units, and they wrote many millions of letters. Serendipity initially shaped which letters were saved by families and intervened again to determine how many found their way to accessible repositories. Time, funding for research, and pressure from publishers in turn affected how many letters and diaries a single scholar could consult. As a result, all studies of common soldiers are to a significant degree impressionistic. Indeed, this literature has reached a point of diminishing returns in regard to gauging the importance of such things as ideology, attitudes toward slavery and emancipation, and level of national sentiment. The plethora of firsthand testimony from soldiers allows historians to marshal support for virtually any argument. Those willing to overlook substantial bodies of contrary evidence can present what might seem to be especially strong cases.[49]

Letters, diaries, and other testimony from soldiers must be placed in conversation with additional types of evidence to assess the importance of Union. The conclusions here rest in part on writings from more than 350 United States soldiers during the period 1861–1866, an admittedly small sample that includes officers and enlisted men from every major theater whose experiences ran the gamut from significant combat to backwater duty in supportive roles. Collectively, these men articulated Union-centered sentiments that often linked the struggle of 1861–1865 to that of 1776–1783. They fit comfortably in the tradition exemplified by Daniel Webster, and eloquently carried forward by Lincoln, that accepted as an article of faith the importance of preserving the Union. American exceptionalism, the value of a democratic republic, the threat posed by slaveholding oligarchs, and the worldwide implications of Union victory appear frequently enough to be denominated themes. Many of the soldiers also addressed emancipation—mostly as an ancillary dimension of the war but sometimes as a necessity if the Union were to remain safe or as the just course to take regarding African Americans. This triumphal interpretation of Union must be taken seriously as representative of very widely held attitudes.

Many earlier books have quoted passages from innumerable wartime letters and diaries relating to the concept and meaning of Union.[50] A few examples will establish patterns. Wilbur Fisk's letters to *The Green Mountain Freeman* of Montpelier, Vermont, afford a readily accessible starting point. A private in Company E of the 2nd Vermont Infantry, Fisk observed on April 7, 1864, that "Slavery has fostered an aristocracy of the rankest kind, and this aristocracy is the bitterest foe that a really free government can have." Most rebellions saw the mass of people rise against a tyranny of the few to demand liberty, but in "this war it has been different. The people have not rebelled against the few, but the few have rebelled against the people. Our government is the people's, and against this government the proud slaveholder has rebelled." Was the republican experiment of the founders, "which has been our pride and boast so long, to be a failure after all? If the North will do her duty, we answer, Never!" Six months later, Fisk quoted an orderly sergeant from the 139th Pennsylvania Infantry who supported pursuing the war to final victory. "The North and South must find out who is master," the sergeant proclaimed, "The South had rebelled against our common Government, and the Government must compel them to cry Enough, or it would be no Government at all." An Illinois officer echoed Fisk's comments about aristocracy. "I have faith in an overruling Providence," affirmed D. S. Parker of the 113th Illinois Infantry, "that He will not permit the triumph of so wicked and justice-destroying an Oligarchy as the Southern confederacy."[51]

A sergeant in the 75th Indiana Infantry similarly spoke of the "Glorious Republic." A self-described Douglas Democrat, William Bluffton Miller noted in his diary on December 26, 1862, that his comrades missed home during the holidays but knew they must persevere. "There are thousands no[w] sleeping in unknown Graves," he wrote sadly, "and many more yet will have to die martyrs to perpetuate the best Government in the world." Almost a year later, while recuperating from a wound at his father's home in Indiana, Miller inveighed against local Democrats who opposed the war. "My Democracy does not consist of being a 'Rebel' against the Laws and Government," he fumed: "I had several warm discussions and talked in a way that some of [them] here dont like but that makes no difference. I tell them there is no political parties. It is a disolution of the Union and tryumph of Secession or their Surrender and the tryumph of Law and order." Miller classified anyone who opposed the Union army "as Rebels and I can give them no other name." Indeed, some of his old friends seemed little different from "the Johnies" when it came to the war—they rejoiced over Union defeats yet "call themselves Democrats."[52]

Andrew Joseph Duff, a Catholic in the 78th Pennsylvania Infantry, put Confederates and northern peace Democrats in one traitorous category. In a letter to his aunt in October 1863, he looked back on two years' service in Tennessee. Men who enlisted to support "Our Country's cause" had endured cruel separation from loved ones caused by "haughty tyrants" from the slaveholding South. Some old friends in western Pennsylvania had turned their backs on the soldiers, which made those "whose sympathy was for the defender of our Beloved Country" all the more cherished. Duff wrote again on March 18, 1864, upset that Copperheads had enticed a fellow soldier to desert. Peace Democrats "grossly insult the Soldiers who now are willing to lay down their lives to save our bleeding Country," remarked Duff, "The innocent blood of thousands mingled with the undying revenge of every Union loving Soldier is against them, hoping & believing that their effort will be fruitless, that their treason will fail in its object."[53]

Higher up the chain of command, Col. Robert McAllister addressed Union at two crucial moments during the final months of the conflict. In a letter to his wife on November 2, 1864, the commander of a brigade in the Army of the Potomac's Second Corps explained why he would vote for Lincoln and the Union ticket. "Tell them that we in the army send our bullets and ballots in the same way—against our enemies and in favor of law, order, Constitution, and Union," he admonished Ellen McAllister, closing with a wish to "hear a good report from New Jersey next Tuesday." (New Jersey cast its electoral votes for George B. McClellan—the only free state to do so.) Six months of additional campaigning took McAllister to Appomattox Court House, where on the day of Lee's surrender he celebrated the "glorious results." Citizen-soldiers could return to their homes having accomplished something that transcended reestablishment of the old national boundaries. They had "the proud satisfaction that it has been our privilege to live and take part in the struggle that has decided for all time to come that Republics are not a failure."[54]

Three last quotations illustrate how Daniel Webster's words, the concept of citizen-soldiers performing a republican duty, and visceral reactions to a perceived threat to American liberty as exemplified in Union pervaded soldiers' correspondence. A captain in the 2nd Ohio Cavalry, part of George A. Custer's Third Cavalry Division in the Shenandoah Valley, recorded thoughts about the national election in his diary on November 8, 1864: "The decisive day of the nation. If the cause of the Union prevails today, liberty and union will be ours forever." A sergeant in the 14th New Jersey Infantry alerted his parents on May 21, 1865, that men who had completed their service looked forward to resuming their prewar pursuits as citizens. Those who "survived this Grand struggle for the maintenance of the old Union," observed Sgt. Albert C. Harrison, "will be glad to live in quietude the remaining days of their lives." Just more than four years before Harrison wrote, an enlisted man in Battery B of the Chicago Light Artillery struggled to articulate why he thought it necessary to fight. "Our two American principles of freedom and liberty must be preserved," William T. Shephard told his mother. Beset by powerful emotions, he confided, "Often when thinking of the great question of the day my heart jumps—sending a chill through my veins, inspiring my soul with courage to do anything in the cause of my country & liberty. I *never had such feelings* before[.] It seems as though I must do something to rescue my Native land from destruction and ruin, though my efforts be ever so weak."[55]

A rich vein of testimony regarding the centrality of Union lies largely untouched in sixty-eight regimental histories published between 1863 and 1866.[56] The larger genre to which these books belong, produced between the last years of the conflict and the early twentieth century, often has been dismissed by military historians as too romantic or antiquarian and by nonmilitary historians as too focused on drums-and-bugle topics.[57] Yet early regimentals, written while the war was fresh in soldiers' minds, contain extensive material relating to the conflict's meaning. Usually compiled without thought of profit and produced by local printers rather than publishing houses, the regimentals sought to commemorate the war for members of the units and their families. The intended audience had experienced the same things as the authors, which increased the likelihood that narratives would accurately reflect collective attitudes. Timing also was crucial. The regimentals provide extensive firsthand testimony from a period when soldiers thought about what their service had meant but, because they had returned to civilian life, no longer wrote letters home.[58]

Although not a perfect representation of all kinds of units, the early Union regimentals boast a remarkably diverse body of evidence. The sixty-four here embraced seventeen loyal states and Colorado Territory, with New York (13), Pennsylvania (7), Ohio (7), Illinois (9), and Indiana (4), the five most populous in 1860, leading the way. Dominated by infantry units, as was the Union army as a whole, the roster includes five regiments of cavalry and three batteries of artillery. Twenty-five of the units served only in the Eastern Theater, eighteen only in the Western Theater, and six only in the Trans-Mississippi. Three saw duty in South Carolina and Florida, three in Louisiana and Virginia, four in the Army of the Potomac and Sherman's armies, four in South Carolina and Virginia, and one in the Trans-Mississippi and Western Theaters. Thirty-two entered service in 1861, twenty-seven in 1862, one in 1863, and four in 1864. Most enlisted for three years—though a number were two-year, nine-month, or three-month regiments. In terms of types of activity, eighteen witnessed enough combat to make William F. Fox's roster of "Three Hundred Fighting Regiments," others participated in extensive campaigning and some combat, and several performed largely noncombat roles. Historians sometimes worry that famous fighting units get undue attention from those who study common soldiers, a bias certainly not present in the early regimentals.[59]

Authorship also covered a wide spectrum of personnel in the units. Noncommissioned officers and privates wrote slightly fewer than a third of the texts, with chaplains accounting for nearly a quarter. Field-grade officers—colonels, lieutenant colonels, and majors—penned just 10 percent of the total, with the remainder distributed among company-grade officers (captains and lieutenants), surgeons, and staff officers. Members of the regiments often contributed diaries, letters, and other materials to assist the authors, who seem not to have been selected on the basis of their political views. They self-consciously strove for accuracy within the bounds of available evidence.[60]

Early regimentals yield abundant evidence of Union as a powerful symbol and its preservation as the conflict's overriding objective. Congressman Roscoe Conkling addressed the 117th New York Infantry upon its return to Oneida County after nearly three years in the field. In what the regimental historian termed an "appropriate and eloquent manner," the future Republican senator echoed Lincoln's reference to "unanimity of action among those seeking a common end" in his December 1864 message to Congress. "In all this career of glory, of duty, and of daring exploit," affirmed Conkling, "a common purpose has inspired you, a common hope has led you on. What was it? Peace. Peace

with the Government and the constitution of our fathers established, has
been the object of the war, and the prayer of every patriot and of every
soldier." In other homecomings, civilians thanked the soldiers for saving
the Union, as when the 114th New York Infantry was greeted with "a
tasteful evergreen arch, bearing this motto: 'Welcome the Brave Defenders of our Union.'" The chronicler of the 86th Illinois Infantry noted
warm welcomes at various points along the regiment's route home: "Every one seemed rejoiced that the soldier boys were coming home from
the bloody wars, in every way showing their grateful feeling of warmest
sympathy for the services they had rendered to Union and liberty."[61]

Many accounts mentioned success in protecting the Constitution, a
government of laws, and republican liberty, each widely considered a
fundamental benefit of life under a perpetual Union. The historian of
the 14th New Jersey Infantry asserted that the regiment "will ever be
remembered by the people of the State as the defenders of our Union
and Constitution." Confederates had "learned a terrible lesson, that this
Union can never be broken, and as a united nation will live forever."
Ephraim J. Hart, a sergeant in the 40th Illinois Infantry writing in 1864,
described a "public heart swelling with a pure devotion to the principles of *national Union,* resolved to do or die for the perpetuation of the
Government which they had been taught to love and respect from infancy." Hart doubtless had some quotation by Webster in mind among
the things he had been taught, as did many others such as Surg. Harris H.
Beecher of the 114th New York Infantry. "Think, oh! think of what they
have done," wrote Beecher of soldiers in the regiment who had campaigned in Louisiana and Virginia: "Think of the ark of constitutional
liberty they have aided to rescue from assault. Think of the Union they
have helped to preserve, with all its blessings, all its memories, and all its
hopes."[62]

Hatred of slaveholding oligarchs who tyrannized poorer white southerners and would undo the Union and its free-labor promise emerged
from the pages of many regimentals. Evan M. Woodward, adjutant of
the 2nd Pennsylvania Reserves, excoriated slaveholders who preferred
"a system of labor that gave wealth and luxuriant ease to the few, at the
expense of the prosperity and elevation of the masses, and the degrada-

tion of labor." A daily journal kept in the 192nd Pennsylvania, a 100-day regiment, reveled in how the arrival of Union forces in Charleston, West Virginia, had improved the lives of both poor white residents and former slaves. "Free press, free speech, and freedom generally, not heretofore enjoyed in this part of the world," read the entry, "are no longer under the heel of the slaveholders. His power over the minds and souls of this people has departed from him, never to return . . . and instead of being all slaves, (white and black,) they are all free,—they and their posterity henceforward forever." Fletcher W. Hewes of the 10th Michigan Infantry painted an unsparing portrait of how slaveholders' rule had blighted the Sequatchie Valley of Tennessee. He found no schools, great ignorance, and lack of ambition among the people. "Thrift and enterprise were entirely absent," he noted disapprovingly of a population and social system that wasted agricultural resources: "Here was a rich tract of land, a good fruit country, and yet scarcely a fruit tree of any kind."[63]

Hewes typified many Union soldiers who criticized slaveholders' misuse of land. They raised the specter of how an expanded empire of slavery could frustrate the free-soil vision of western lands peopled by independent, productive yeomen farmers. Chaplain M. D. Gage of the 12th Indiana Infantry used the area surrounding McPhersonville, South Carolina, to censure slaveholders for their neglect of good farming techniques. Thousands of acres once devoted to cotton production had been "abandoned on account of sterility . . . This is the Southern mode of cultivation, under the influence of slavery, the very ground being cursed in consequence of the sin of the people." Rather than use fertilizers to replenish the soil, planters left exhausted fields to be claimed by pine forests while they moved on to break new ground elsewhere. This process had left McPhersonville, once situated "among fields of snowy cotton," marooned amid "a vast pine forest, a curious spectacle to eyes accustomed to scenes of beauty and fertility in the vicinity of rural villages of the North."[64]

James Mowris of the 117th New York Infantry usefully summarized why so many loyal soldiers believed it necessary to vanquish slaveholding oligarchs. "A practical Democracy," he affirmed, "engenders no distinct class of 'poor white trash' groveling in hopeless ignorance over beyond

the impassable gulf of social class." In the nondemocratic South, however, the planter class exploited its poorer white neighbors: "The illiter-
ate condition of the 'poor whites,' their necessary lack of grace and af-
fluence, made them mentally and externally distinct from the aristocracy.
They were thus *excluded from the sympathies* of the rich. In the presence of
bonded black laborers they were regarded a superfluous class, and therefore a *cheap war material.*" Confederate leaders headed a rebellion that
represented "the consummation of a social disorder," and, to ensure safety
from another sectional rupture, Union victory would have to be followed by "removal of the social conditions which induced secession."[65]

In contrast to their negative view of lower-class Confederates manip-
ulated by slaveholders, the regimentals applauded loyal citizen-soldiers
who defended a democratic republic that valued their patriotic service.
"The preservation of the government was paramount to all other objects," averred H. M. Davidson of Battery B, 1st Ohio Light Artillery,
and forty-two of the battery's men had died to achieve it. The war had
"been no man's triumph, but a people's will and a nation's fame." Having
performed honorably, the artillerists deserved lasting admiration because
"the citizen soldier of the army of the Republic is the grandest embodi-
ment of intelligence, patriotism and bravery the world has yet developed.
By them the great experiment of self government has been settled for all
people, in all countries beneath the sun." Less verbose than Davidson,
Edwin B. Houghton of the 17th Maine Infantry agreed entirely with his
sentiments. Once the Stars and Stripes floated over a reunited nation,
nothing remained for the men of the 17th "but to return to home and
friends, and, resuming the pursuits from which they had been called at
the voice of duty, enjoy the blessings of the government they had sustained, and rescued from the hands of traitors." In a passage on the
38th Massachusetts Infantry's homecoming, the historian of the regiment quoted the *Cambridge (Mass.) Chronicle*. The newspaper took a republican approach that muted any class difference, reporting that "the
whole people, the young and the old, the rich and the poor, united together to do honor to the citizen soldiers who went forth to secure the
blessings of Liberty, Union, and Peace to a distracted country."[66]

Union victory also safeguarded the possibility of liberty beyond

American shores. Regimental historians reserved some of their most dramatic rhetorical flourishes, and most spread-eagled exceptionalist claims, for this topic. Chaplain M. D. Gage of the 12th Indiana Infantry thought the world should learn from the American war. "The important lesson inculcated by a careful review of the conflict is the permanency of republican institutions and the self-preserving power of a free people," he stated, something suitable for "instruction of the nations of the earth." European monarchs could no longer hope to dismiss republican government as impracticable: "The capacity of a representative democracy to resist and suppress insurrection and rebellion against the constituted authority of the people has been fully tested and triumphantly established." Another chaplain, Thomas G. Murphey of the 1st Delaware Infantry, easily excelled Gage in purple-tinged verbosity. "Our temple of liberty and the republican constitutional government would have been undermined and its fall inevitable," he insisted, "if we had not struggled to establish our nationality. Remove one block from the arch of liberty, and is it not insecure? Will it not yield to the rude storm, and be thrown to the ground?" Had secession gone unchallenged, the "political storms which so often sweep over our people must unavoidably dash it to the ground, and bury beneath it for ever the hopes of the world for a free republican form of government." A civilian speaker who addressed the 33rd New York Infantry when it returned from the front credited the men with furthering a great project. Every foot of American soil soon would rest comfortably under the "Bird of Liberty," who "shall again expand her pinions, with one wing touch[ing] the sun-rise, and the other the sunset, and cast her shadow over the whole world."[67]

Lieutenant Osceola Lewis connected the promise of democracy and economic opportunity inherent in Union victory with immigration. When his regiment, Pennsylvania's 138th Infantry, received new flags from civilians in Norristown and Bridgeport in late 1864, several officers prepared a letter of thanks on behalf of the regiment. It touted the Union as a free land where downtrodden people from around the world could escape oppression from monarchs or oligarchs—a place guarded by the "noblest Government ever bequeathed to man." Like the officers, Lincoln's last annual address to Congress strongly supported immigration, offering the practical argument that immigrants filled "one of the principal replenishment streams which are appointed by Providence to repair the ravages of internal war, and its waste of national strength and health." The president opposed conscripting immigrants and urged affording them "effective national protection."[68]

Rampant ethnic prejudice should not obscure the widespread belief, typified by Lewis's and Lincoln's comments, that the promise of Union extended to foreigners who might emigrate to the United States.[69] Acutely aware of the failed European revolutions of the late 1840s (though often concerned about the radical turn many of them took regarding labor), unionists thought it natural that anyone devoted to republican government should look to America. Karl Marx agreed in November 1861, crediting the American nation with "the highest form of popular self-government till now realized" and predicting that defeat of "the oligarchy of three hundred thousand slaveholders" would open the expansive American West to settlement by European workers who might obtain their own small parcels of land.[70] In practice, even German and Irish Catholics could acquire the franchise, participate in local politics, pursue careers in the law, and otherwise make their way in an American society that alternately beckoned and scorned them. Thus could Charles O'Conor, the Catholic son of an immigrant from County Roscommon, Ireland, ascend to the front rank of New York City's lawyers, and immigrants such as Michael Corcoran, Thomas Francis Meagher, Carl Schurz, and Franz Sigel reach positions of military and political prominence.

Berlin-born Francis Lieber, who headed New York's Loyal Publication Society, laid out in detail the Union's appeal for German immigrants. In a pamphlet written to boost support for Lincoln during the presidential canvass of 1864, Lieber emphasized economic opportunity and democratic refuge from aristocratic rule. Working men had left Germany "because you had heard that in the United States you would find a country wherein you and your children would enjoy all the rights of the free citizen; where skill and industry would surely find their reward, and where your children would never find themselves debarred from any merited attainment by the privileges of others." Democratic victory at the polls might substitute, "in place of this Union, a land where the working man should be delivered over to a grinding tyranny far worse than any endured in the oppressed countries of Europe, . . . to the dominion of the Southern landholders." Confederate success would confirm "the prerogative of the owners of the soil, the privilege of using the working man, whether white or black, as the instrument of their power, their pleasure, and their arrogance."[71]

Two years after Appomattox, the first historian of the Irish Brigade wrote about motivation among the thousands of Irish men who had fought for the Union. "The Irish people in New York, and throughout the Northern States, were not slow in declaring for the Union and volunteering for its defence," stated David Power Conyngham, an Irish nationalist and wartime correspondent for the *New York Herald*. Long the victims of oligarchic rule in Ireland, they "felt that not only was the safety of the great Republic, the home of their exiled race, at stake, but also, that the great principles of democracy were at issue with the aristocratic doctrines of monarchism. Should the latter prevail, there was no longer any hope for the struggling nationalities of the Old World." Utterly unconcerned with the condition or fate of African Americans, Irish soldiers rejected emancipation as a rallying cry. "The safety and welfare of his adopted country and its glorious Constitution were imperiled," so the Irish soldier enlisted "to sustain the flag that sheltered him when persecuted and exiled from his own country, the laws that protected him, and the country that, like a loving mother, poured forth the richness of her bosom to sustain him." Although Conyngham's prose neglected widespread opposition to the war among Irish Americans after 1863, many of whom took to New York's streets to oppose conscription in July of that year, it captured how the promise and reality of Union had affected many others.[72]

Harper's Weekly devoted its lead editorial on May 23, 1863, to a remarkable phenomenon—increasing immigration amid a massive American war. The editors identified a general consciousness throughout Europe "that the contest in which we are engaged . . . is really the final decisive contest between free popular government on the one side, and government by an oligarchy or a monarch on the other." Landed aristocrats ruled Great Britain; "despotic emperors" controlled France, Austria,

Russia, Turkey, China, and Brazil; and a combination of aristocracy and the middle class held sway in Spain and Italy. Free citizens stood supreme only in the United States and tiny Switzerland, but Union victory would silence "the haters of liberty" and prove conclusively the "human capacity for self-government." Confederate triumph would mean that "the cause of the working-man and of human rights will be thrust back perhaps for several generations . . . the oligarchs of Europe will well say that republics are impracticable, and human self-government a delusive dream." In the absence of Union success, rulers around the world would restrict suffrage, strengthen privileged classes, reduce popular rights, and increase burdens on poor men whose economic opportunities would shrivel. Pulling out all the stops in a period of virulent controversy regarding emancipation and conscription and despair over a shattering Union defeat at Chancellorsville, the editors projected calamity if friends of the Union failed to rally: "We shall have brought self-government and humanity itself into merited contempt. It is, in part, to avert this dire calamity that the working-men of Europe are coming here in vast numbers."[73]

This unequivocally exceptionalist reading of America's role in the world aligned perfectly with how loyal citizens explained the importance of Union. It also aligned with reality. Europeans did continue to pour into the United States, where they found a society, however unfair and oppressive by twenty-first-century standards, more conducive to economic and political freedom than those they had left behind. The Union's republican form of government featured a franchise broader than any in the major European nations, granting most voting-age men in loyal states a direct voice in politics. Upward movement between economic classes fell short of claims by ardent advocates of the free labor ideology but far exceeded that typical elsewhere. Unionists need look no further than to their president, or Pennsylvania's powerful radical congressman Thaddeus Stevens, or a host of other leaders for unimpeachable evidence of opportunity to rise on the basis of hard work and intelligence. Any reading of the mid-nineteenth-century United States that overlooks or minimizes such visions cannot yield anything approaching a true understanding of the era.

Just before voters went to the polls in the presidential election of 1864, editor Henry Raymond the *New York Times* reminded readers of what Union offered in a piece titled "The Only Issue and the Only Solution." A respected political voice who influenced and echoed Lincoln, Raymond said the North fought not to kill slavery, destroy the doctrine of state rights, or "subdue or degrade the Southern people." It waged the war "purely and simply to save the unity of the nation." Declaring such unity "indispensable to the continuance of free and good Government on this continent," the newspaper predicted that without restoration of the Union "ceaseless conflict" would exhaust the physical and human resources of both regions until chaos engulfed the whole. A plea for support of the Union Party, this piece targeted potential voters who were devoted to the Union but cared little about emancipation. Without stating so directly, it also framed the conflict as a struggle to define the postwar nation. A northern victory would validate one of the two competing antebellum sectional visions—the one trumpeting free soil, free labor, and democratic rule by free citizens unencumbered by the narrow class interests of a slaveholding oligarchy. Although the *Times* insisted that in "no form or degree is the adherence of the South to slavery a part of our *casus belli*," most unionists by 1864 had come to embrace emancipation as necessary for the long-term success of the American project.[74]

In his second reply to Sen. Robert Y. Hayne of South Carolina on January 27, 1830, Daniel Webster famously called for "Liberty *and* Union, now and forever, one and inseparable." His phrasing quickly became a touchstone for advocates of Union, and the dramatic moment on the floor of the Senate inspired artist G. P. A. Healy to paint the scene. This engraving, titled "Webster Replying to Hayne," is based on the painting. (Henry Cabot Lodge, *Daniel Webster.* Boston: Houghton Mifflin, 1899, opposite p. 178)

This Republican lithograph from the 1860 presidential campaign captures the political and economic promise loyal Americans would have pronounced central to understanding why "The Union Must and Shall be Preserved." Its support for the rights to free speech and settlement in free federal territories invites censure of the slaveholding South, while the figures of a blacksmith and woodcutter celebrate free laborers. (Library of Congress, Prints and Photographs Division, reproduction number LC USZ62–5884)

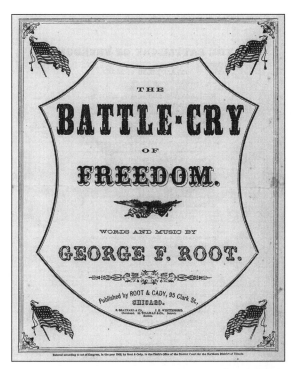

Cover of the sheet music for George F. Root's *The Battle-Cry of Freedom,* the chorus of which included the tune's powerful message: "The Union forever, Hurrah, boys, Hurrah!" The publisher sold several hundred thousand copies of the music, and President Lincoln was quoted, perhaps apocryphally, as saying Root helped the Union cause more "than a hundred generals and a thousand orators." Members of the 45th Pennsylvania Infantry defiantly sang the chorus during the battle of the Wilderness in May 1864. (Historic American Sheet Music, Music B-988, Duke University Rare Book, Manuscript, and Special Collections Library)

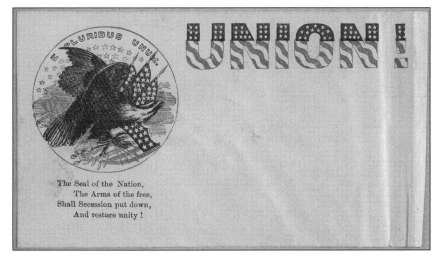

This patriotic envelope includes popular symbols including the United States flag and a bald eagle but relies mainly on the bold deployment of "UNION!" The four lines of verse include a reference to "Nation," which most loyal citizens would have considered a synonym for Union. (Courtesy of the Henry E. Huntington Library, San Marino, California)

THE UNION VOLUNTEER.

Devotion to the Union helped spur a rush to the national colors of more than 750,000 men in 1861. This Currier & Ives lithograph, titled *The Union Volunteer* and probably issued during the first months of the war, employs themes of Union, love of flag, constitutional law, and treason:

> O'er Sumter's walls OUR FLAG again will wave,
> And give to traitors all a bloody grave.
> OUR UNION and OUR LAWS maintain we must;
> And treason's banner trample in the dust."

(Library of Congress, Prints and Photographs Division, reproduction number LC USZ62–91516)

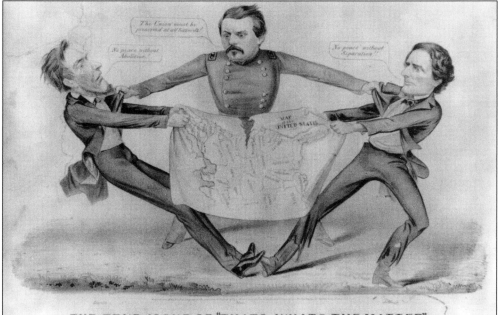

THE TRUE ISSUE OR "THATS WHATS THE MATTER".

"THE TRUE ISSUE OR 'THATS WHATS THE MATTER.'" Both major political parties in 1864 knew that support for the Union was crucial to getting votes. This Democratic cartoon presents McClellan as the genuine pro-Union candidate. "The Union must be preserved," states McClellan, who tries to hold the nation together while Lincoln insists on "No peace without Abolition!" and Jefferson Davis calls for "No peace without Separation." (Library of Congress, Prints and Photographs Division, reproduction number LC USZ62–13957)

The Mower, an anti-Copperhead print by A. Troschsler published in 1863, juxtaposes a free farmer in the foreground and a slaveholder (presumably Confederate) and enslaved African Americans in the background. The farmer's scythe cuts a poisonous snake, while hounds chase a fleeing slave. The caption seeks to rally loyal friends of the Union:

> We have battles to fight, we have foes to subdue,
> Time waits not for us, and we wait not for you!
> The mower mows on, though the adder may writhe
> And the copperhead coil round the blade of his scythe.

(Library of Congress, Prints and Photographs Division, reproduction number LC USZ62–55538)

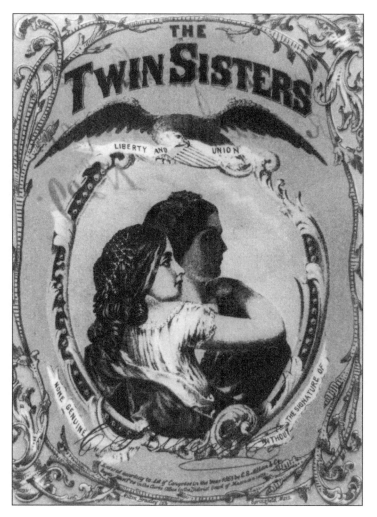

This tobacco label from 1863 attests to the ubiquity of Daniel Webster's pro-Union rhetoric, offering "The Twin Sisters" of "Liberty and Union" with an eagle. Although the sisters appear to be of different generations rather than twins, the patriotic message would have been clear to purchasers. (Library of Congress, Prints and Photographs Division, reproduction number LC USZ62–90679)

Southern Ass-stock-crazy.

"Southern Ass-stock-crazy (Southern Aristocracy)" This cartoon from 1861 expresses the widespread antipathy among friends of the Union toward what they considered slaveholding oligarchs who had engineered secession. (Library of Congress, Prints and Photographs Division, reproduction number LC USZ62–91445)

3

EMANCIPATION

*I*n the third week of August 1864, Abraham Lincoln discussed emancipation with two Republicans from Wisconsin. One of the pair, Judge Joseph T. Mills, recorded the president's comments in his diary. The upcoming election occupied Lincoln's attention, and he spoke in animated fashion about the relationship between ending slavery and the war for Union. The Democratic Party's call to jettison emancipation presaged disaster, he observed, because returning "the mastery & control of millions of blacks" to the Rebels would render the Confederacy "sure of ultimate success." African American soldiers and laborers in Union service were essential. "Abandon all the posts now possessed by black men," Lincoln said, "& we would be compelled to abandon the war in 3 weeks. We have to hold territory." The president also spoke admiringly of black combat veterans—the "warriors of Port Hudson and Olustee." To Democrats who accused him of "carrying on this war for the sole purpose of abolition," Lincoln answered plainly: "It is & will be carried on so long as I am President for the sole purpose of restoring the Union. But no human power can subdue this rebellion without using the Emancipation lever as I have done." Two hundred thousand black

men born on southern soil had come under loyal control with more to
follow, which denied a vast amount of labor to the Confederacy. "My
enemies condemn my emancipation policy," Lincoln noted: "Let them
prove by the history of this war, that we can restore the Union without
it." Judge Mills, who went into the interview expecting the president to
be a "pleasant joker," left with an impression of "a man of deep convic-
tions & an unutterable yearning for the success of the Union cause."[1]

Lincoln's comments regarding emancipation and the use of black soldiers mirrored opinions widely held in the United States by early 1864.
Newspapers, letters, diaries, early regimentals, and other sources reveal
key themes. Most important, white soldiers and civilians overwhelmingly supported emancipation as a tool to help restore the Union and
protect it against future slavery-related threats rather than as a grand
moral imperative. Only a sweeping assault on the Confederacy's slave-
based social and economic systems—which between them undergirded
Rebel efforts on the battlefield—seemed likely to yield victory. Loyal
citizens also consistently voiced a desire to punish treasonous oligarchs
by freeing their slaves and agreed that USCT units played a useful and
praiseworthy, though not decisive, role in Union military affairs. A small
number thought black veterans had earned the right to vote. Among
Union soldiers, exposure to slavery in the Confederacy yielded varying
results—many expressed greater compassion for the enslaved people
while others hardened existing negative stereotypes (the exact propor-
tions of these two responses defy precise calculation). For most loyal
Americans, it had become impossible to think of a postwar Union still
fettered by slavery.

Almost all Democrats and some Republicans initially expressed strong
opposition to freeing slaves and arming black men, but military events
changed attitudes. The war for Union came close to success in the first
half of 1862 without resort to emancipation. Only Robert E. Lee's defeat
of George B. McClellan in the Seven Days battles reversed a seemingly
irresistible tide of Union success, reinspiriting the Confederate people
and setting the stage for a much longer war. In the face of continuing
slaughter, the loyal populace endorsed measures that would have been
unthinkable for most people when the conflict began. They accepted, in

other words, what Lincoln had hoped to avoid in 1861—"a violent and remorseless revolutionary struggle" that precluded restoration of the antebellum Union comprising slaveholding and nonslaveholding states. Emancipation became, as Mark Grimsley observes in his study of a turn toward "hard war" by the United States, "a symbol of Northern resolve, a touchstone of its intention to smash the slaveholding aristocracy that had spawned secession."[2]

It was not a question of whether restoring the Union justified fighting a massive war—most loyal Americans never doubted that as a transcendent goal—but whether the nation could be restored and made safe in the future without killing slavery and enlisting African American soldiers. A struggle for a different kind of Union emerged, support for which sprang from related impulses to win the war, punish oligarchic slaveholders, and remove the irritant that had vexed the nation from 1787 to 1860. Without slavery and the various issues related to its expansion, most white northerners could envision no serious internal threat to their beloved Union. Genuine concern for African Americans seldom preoccupied a population that remained profoundly prejudiced—though a minority in the North consistently argued that any Union true to the founding documents would extend basic human rights to all black people. The idea of black military service met with varying degrees of enthusiasm. White northerners typically thought of African American soldiers in garrisons—deployed "to hold territory" as Lincoln said in his interview with the Republicans in Wisconsin—or assigned to fatigue duty, more than as participants in battles.[3]

Assessing the number of Democratic voters who consistently approved of a war for Union and those who favored peace above victory poses a special challenge to anyone attempting to parse loyal sentiment. In the presidential election of 1864, for example, Democratic candidate George B. McClellan polled 45 percent of the popular vote and exceeded that rate in populous states such as New York (49.4 percent), Pennsylvania (48.2 percent), Illinois (45.6 percent), and Indiana (46.4 percent). Because he called for Union before any peace negotiations while the party's platform demanded an end to fighting and then discussions with the Confederates, Democratic ballots could indicate very different attitudes toward the war. A substantial majority almost certainly favored victory and reestablishment of the Union—an even larger proportion would have accepted reunion with slavery still intact in at least part of the nation. Soldiers cast a far higher percentage of their votes for Lincoln than did the general electorate, and it is safe to assume that considerably fewer than 45 percent of Democrats in uniform opted for McClellan. Had the primary issue in 1864 been emancipation rather than continuance of a war to save the Union, McClellan's part of the soldier vote likely would have increased significantly.[4]

Beginning in the 1970s, historians embarked on a massive reevaluation of emancipation and black military participation as elements of the Union war effort. This development reversed a longstanding and pernicious tendency to treat African Americans as powerless pawns in a great sectional bloodletting waged by white people. More broadly, it served as part of a cultural imperative to frame a more expansive view of race in the United States around black people as agents of their own improvement and participants in the long national effort to forge a more just democracy. Within the field of Civil War history, it aligned perfectly with the concomitant tendency to dismiss or lament devotion to Union as the most powerful animating factor among the loyal white population. This literature took up fundamental questions such as what drove the process of ending slavery, whether emancipation joined Union as a major goal for the United States, and the degree to which white racial attitudes in the North evolved. The scholarship did not speak with one voice, but an overarching consensus stood largely unchallenged: anyone hoping to understand the trajectory and meaning of the conflict must look primarily to slavery, emancipation, and race. The effect has been to illuminate many hitherto hidden dimensions of the war while at the same time creating a new set of distortions.

Any attempt to comprehend the roles of slavery and emancipation must differentiate between the war's causes and the goals for which most loyal citizens fought. Abraham Lincoln spoke the truth about causation in his Second Inaugural Address, observing that in 1860 4 million slaves "constituted a peculiar and powerful interest. All knew that this interest was, somehow, the cause of the war." He meant *all Americans*—not just those who remained loyal—had known slavery was the key, a fact borne out by ample testimony from leading Confederates. On April 29, 1861, for example, Jefferson Davis informed the Confederate Congress that efforts to bar slavery from the federal territories had the effect of "rendering the property in slaves so insecure as to be comparatively worthless, and thereby annihilating in effect property worth thousands of millions of dollars." Slaveholding states embraced secession, Davis continued, "to avert the danger with which they were openly menaced" by Republican success in 1860. Neo-Confederates intent on distancing the Confederacy from slavery and writers who find dark economic conspiracies at play with Lincoln and other Republicans might pretend otherwise, but it is beyond dispute that controversies relating to slavery precipitated secession and by extension the outbreak of fighting in 1861.[5]

Recent interpretations addressing how the loyal population dealt with emancipation and black military service leave far more room for debate. The principal distortion, sometimes implied and sometimes stated outright, posits the emergence of emancipation as an overriding northern goal. What can be called the Appomattox syndrome comes into play here. The surrender of Lee's army effectively ended a war that both restored the Union and destroyed slavery; therefore, it seems logical that a war begun to save the Union had been transformed into a war for Union and emancipation as equally worthy outcomes. The interesting question for many has become when and how emancipation emerged as the second grand goal. Discussions of timing, in turn, open up subtopics such as whether emancipation was a prerequisite to Union success, the importance of black soldiers in crafting victory, and the degree to which white racial prejudice weakened as the war ground along.

The editors of the Freedmen and Southern Society Project, whose labors have yielded five massive volumes of rich testimony on slavery and emancipation during the Civil War era, emphasize the shift toward a war against slavery. As the conflict unfolded, the actions of slaves profoundly affected white soldiers and civilians: "On both sides of the line of battle, Americans came to know that a war for Union must be a war for freedom." Lincoln's Emancipation Proclamation also contributed to the revolution in war aims. Although not applicable to slave states in the

Union or areas controlled by United States military forces, it nonetheless "fundamentally transformed the character of the war. The war for the Union became a war against slavery." Barbara J. Fields couches it in terms of the need for African Americans to educate the white North. "The burden of teaching that lesson fell upon the slaves," she avers in the companion volume to Ken Burns's documentary: "Their stubborn actions in pursuit of their faith gradually turned faith into reality. It was they who taught the nation that it must place the abolition of slavery at the head of its agenda."[6]

Chandra Manning's book on Civil War soldiers departs from almost all other such studies in locating substantial, and early, antislavery sentiment within the Union ranks. After observing that "Union soldiers cared about the United States government . . . because its survival mattered for the survival of ideals like liberty, equality, and self-government for all humanity," Manning moves her spotlight to slavery. "This book rescues slavery from the periphery of soldiers' mental worlds, where subsequent generations have tried to relegate it," she explains, "and returns slavery to its rightful place at the center of soldiers' views of the struggle." Contact with African Americans as Union armies moved southward influenced attitudes about slavery and race, building support for emancipation. In the end, soldiers gave three reasons why the peculiar institution had to end: it bolstered the Confederate war effort; it mocked the ideals for which the men fought; and "no lesser outcome could make the trauma of the war worthwhile . . . The senseless destruction had to be converted to purposeful sacrifice offered for a goal that was large enough to make the carnage worthwhile." Manning situates loyal soldiers ahead of Lincoln in realizing the nation "must reform rather than merely preserve itself." They concluded that "preservation of the Union, though important, was not enough, unless accompanied by the end of slavery." In this reading, emancipation joined—or even superseded—Union as a widely held, intrinsically worthy goal.[7]

Manning's discussion of her methodology in determining soldiers' responses to the Emancipation Proclamation underscores the difficulties inherent in generalizing from a limited body of testimony. She notes a "wide range of outlooks" but settles on a "predominant view . . . best summed up by a soldier who explained, 'slavery is the primary cause, or the root of the matter'; therefore, the Emancipation Proclamation made good sense, because 'to distroy the tree root & branch is the surest way to brake this rebellion.'" How did Manning decide that more than three-quarters of Union soldiers endorsed Lincoln's proclamation? "I categorized the statements of the first approximately one hundred . . . Union soldiers I encountered who explicitly mentioned the Emancipation Proclamation and clearly expressed an unequivocal opinion about it between September 1862 . . . and June 1863," seventy-nine of whom voiced active support. "Subsequent soldiers did not change the proportion established by this set," she continues, "so I saw no further need to inflate the numbers." The sample included men from all theaters and "ordinary enlisted men and junior officers"—in other words, "they were average soldiers, not men preselected on the basis of likely views." Manning concedes that "a perfect statistical ratio is impossible" but believes her handling of the evidence established "a convincing pattern of support."[8]

A pattern did emerge from her small sample, but several questions come immediately to mind. How many soldiers did not mention the proclamation? Can anything be inferred from their silence? How many did not use the key words for which Manning searched? She counted those "who specifically named the Emancipation Proclamation (or an obvious synonym, such as 'the President's Proclamation') in their writings in this specific time frame and took a stance on it." How did she determine that these were "ordinary enlisted men and junior officers"— and what, precisely, did she mean by that term? How many were officers (some studies have found higher rates of support for emancipation among them than among men in the ranks)? Could she determine political affiliation for many—or any—of the soldiers? These questions are especially pertinent because Manning's portrayal of widespread support for the proclamation at this stage of the war—a stage that ended just before ugly antiemancipation sentiment erupted in the New York City riots of July 1863—challenges much of the previous literature.

A pair of books on veterans from the 123rd New York Infantry and the Army of the Cumberland similarly showcase emancipation as a powerful goal. Ross D. Reid traces an arc of ascending enthusiasm within the

123rd, a regiment that fought in the Eleventh Corps in the Eastern Theater and in the Twentieth Corps with Sherman's forces in the West. Exposure to slavery on Confederate ground revealed the "arrogance and
cruelty of slaveholders" and helped create "an army of liberation." In
Reid's telling, the transformation extended to a stunning reversal of
long-standing racial attitudes. "By war's end," after campaigns through
the Deep South, "the vast majority of soldiers in Sherman's army either
believed in social and political equality for blacks or at worst held only a
slight degree of prejudice against them." Reid relegates Union to a decidedly secondary position, with support "most clearly demonstrated by
the border states, where slavery was permitted." Robert Hunt's study of
how the Cumberland army's veterans remembered the war detects a radical alteration of war aims. "The Lincoln administration replaced the goal
of restoring the Union," states Hunt unequivocally, "with the idea that
the Slave Power was a corruption of the American mission and that this
social system had to be destroyed completely."[9]

Garry Wills interprets Lincoln's most famous speech as the signal moment that converted the war into a struggle to destroy slavery and make
true equality possible in the reunited nation. Easily the most influential
book on the Gettysburg Address, *Lincoln at Gettysburg: The Words that Remade America* credits the president with "one of the most daring acts of
open-air sleight-of-hand ever witnessed by the unsuspecting. Everyone
in that vast throng of thousands was having his or her intellectual pocket
picked." On a late autumn day in Gettysburg, Lincoln transformed the
war—and more than that, reshaped all the inherited baggage from the
founding generation. The spectators streamed away from Evergreen
Cemetery "into a different America. Lincoln had revolutionized the
Revolution, giving people a new past to live with that would change
their future indefinitely." Without using the word *slavery,* Lincoln had
promised "a new birth of freedom" guaranteed by a "government of the
people, by the people, for the people." He had cleansed the Constitution
"by appeal from its letter to the spirit, subtly changing the recalcitrant
stuff of that legal compromise, bringing it to its own indictment." Far
more important than the Emancipation Proclamation, which had been
"only a military measure, an exigency of war," the remarks at Gettysburg

set a goal for "a nation trying to live up to the vision in which it was conceived."[10]

Wills's soaring claims for the Gettysburg Address can seduce the unwary into connecting the speech to wartime conceptions of what was at stake. In fact, Wills allocates almost no attention to contemporary reaction. He focuses most on a single article in the *Chicago Times,* a Democratic sheet that interpreted "a new birth of freedom" in emancipationist terms and chided the president for straying from his constitutional duty. "It was to uphold this constitution, and the Union created by it," stated the piece, "that our officers and soldiers gave their lives at Gettysburg. How dare he, then, standing on their graves, misstate the cause for which they died, and libel the statesmen who founded the government?" Did proemancipation citizens, soldiers, and newspapers discern Lincoln's deft reconfiguration of national goals? More to the point, did those who supported a war for Union decide they must embrace emancipation as the preeminent goal rather than as one of many tools to help defeat the Rebels?[11]

The conception of the address as a pivotal moment of reorientation has migrated from Wills to a number of other studies. Russell F. Weigley's military and political history of the war accepts Wills's reading, observing that "the war gave birth to a new and different American Republic, whose nature is to be discerned less in the Declaration of Independence than in the Address Delivered at the Dedication of the Cemetery at Gettysburg." James Oakes's exploration of the relationship between Lincoln and Frederick Douglass takes a similar tack. "The founders, Lincoln said, had set out to establish a nation 'conceived in Liberty and dedicated to the proposition that all men are created equal,'" affirms Oakes, "A nation without slavery: That, Lincoln said, is what this civil war is all about. For that the soldiers buried beneath them at Gettysburg had given their lives. It was 'the cause for which they gave their last full measure of devotion.'" Lincoln scholar Douglas L. Wilson terms *Lincoln at Gettysburg* "a book that has shed more light on its subject than any other" and concurs that the speech closed with a strong statement against slavery. Although he does not mention Wills, Eric Foner concurs that "no one could mistake the meaning of the 'new birth of freedom' to which [Lincoln] alludes."

The Gettysburg Address "offered a powerful definition of the reborn nation."[12]

Yet none of these authors established any direct connection between Lincoln's remarks at Gettysburg and the loyal citizenry's ideas about the war's overarching purpose. Indeed, most evidence from the time points to only tepid interest in Lincoln's remarks. Within the cabinet, treasury secretary Salmon P. Chase mentioned Lincoln's departure for Gettysburg on November 18 but in letters dated November 19, 23, and 25 ignored the content of the address. Chase told his daughter Kate that he remained in Washington rather than accompany the president because too much work crowded his desk. Secretary of the Navy Gideon Welles mentioned that he was "strongly urged by the President to attend the ceremonials at Gettysburg, but was compelled to decline, for I could not spare the time." He offered no comment on the substance of the speech. Both Chase and Welles expressed far more interest in the president's upcoming message to Congress (in which Lincoln would reference both emancipation and black military service). John Hay, Lincoln's young secretary, also focused on the annual message, jotting down a perfunctory description of the day in Gettysburg: "Mr Everett spoke as he always does perfectly—and the President in a firm free way, with more grace than is his wont said his half dozen lines of consecration and the music wailed and we went home through crowded and cheering streets." Another attendee in Gettysburg, the perceptive Benjamin Brown French, also lavished praise on Edward Everett, who brought "his audience to tears many times during his masterly effort." As for the president, he uttered "a few brief, but most appropriate words" to dedicate the cemetery.[13]

Newspapers apportioned far less space to Lincoln's remarks than to Everett's two-hour oration. Advance copies of the latter went to papers in some large cities, which allowed them to publish the entire text accompanied by editorial comment. "The few lines of Lincoln's speech," explains one historian, "received late in the evening by telegraph, and because of their brevity, were hastily set in type and commanded little attention." For example, the *New York Times* printed Lincoln's remarks without analysis, preceded by "The President then delivered the following dedicatory speech" and followed by "Three cheers were then given for the President and the Governors of the States." *Frank Leslie's Illustrated Newspaper* handled the text similarly, placing it deep inside the issue under the headline "The Gettysburg Celebration"—just after "To My Little Brother," a forgettable poem, and an article titled "A Japanese Legend." *The Times* of London cruelly compared Lincoln's "luckless sallies" at Gettysburg to Sancho Panza's conduct as governor of Miguel de Cervantes's fictional Isle of Barataria.[14]

Soldiers manifested virtually no interest in Lincoln's words. Gabor S. Boritt, whose exploration of contemporary reaction to the address is unrivalled in its thoroughness, quotes a Pennsylvania sergeant who pronounced Everett's speech "elegant" but said nothing about Lincoln's. "Nor did most other soldiers—anywhere," adds Boritt, who speculates that the "silence of the soldiers about Lincoln's speech may have been the most hurtful" element of public reaction for the president. Lieutenant Frank A. Haskell, a member of Brig. Gen. John Gibbon's staff in the Army of the Potomac's Second Corps, attended the program at Gettysburg on November 19. The author of a detailed and famous account of the battle written immediately after Lee's retreat from Pennsylvania, Haskell tersely dismissed events at the dedication in a letter to his brother on November 20: "We had little interest in the ceremonies, and I shall not attempt to describe them."[15]

Many who did pay attention to Lincoln's speech would not apply key phrases about equality and freedom to the slavery question. Lincoln reached out to a broad spectrum of the loyal citizenry by avoiding any direct mention of emancipation. He recalled the Founders and, echoing his message to Congress in July 1861, expressed his hope that the shining American example of "government of the people, by the people, for the people" would endure in a restored Union. When he spoke of "a new birth of freedom," many listeners (and later readers) would have conjured images not of ending slavery but of guaranteeing and extending their own liberty and freedom, through political action and economic promise, to shape and benefit from a Union where the cards were not stacked against common people.

Almost exactly five months after his visit to Gettysburg, Lincoln discussed how crucial words held different meanings. Speaking to an audience at a fair in Baltimore sponsored by the U.S. Sanitary Commission, he suggested that the "world has never had a good definition of the word liberty, and the American people, just now, are much in want of one." Both Union and Confederate supporters claimed to fight for liberty but clung to antithetical definitions. Turning first to one widely applied in the free states, Lincoln remarked that "the word liberty may mean for each man to do as he pleases with himself, and the product of his labor." For slaveholders, in contrast, it "may mean . . . to do as they please with other men, and the product of other men's labor." Each side claimed to protect liberty while ascribing tyranny to the other. In Lincoln's time, both of his definitions would have been associated mainly with white people. "Freedom" and "equality" could be added to a list of politically charged words that included "liberty," which had variant nineteenth-century meanings that changed across ensuing decades.[16]

Senator Charles Sumner of Massachusetts offered a retrospective judgment about the importance of the Gettysburg Address in a eulogy titled "Promises of the Declaration of Independence, and Abraham Lincoln." Delivered in Boston on June 1, 1865, it applauded how "grandly, and yet simply" Lincoln had announced a new nation "with the Equality of All Men as its frontlet!" The president had given his life to make good on the promise of the Declaration of Independence, and his speech, "uttered at the field of Gettysburg, and now sanctified by the martyrdom of its author, is a monumental act . . . The world noted at once what he said, and will never cease to remember it." Sumner was only partly correct—the world had not taken much notice in late 1863. But United States victory in the war, the accomplishment of emancipation as part of that victory, and Lincoln's assassination and civic apotheosis all helped elevate the speech to a position that warranted the kind of analysis Garry Wills and countless others have provided.[17]

That long-term importance should not obscure the fact that neither the speech, nor any other factor, led most loyal citizens to place emancipation alongside Union as a principal goal in the conflict. Yet that perception has become common. In a widely cited essay, Edward L. Ayers stresses what he sees as the profound impact of James M. McPherson's books and Ken Burns's PBS documentary in the late 1980s and 1990s.

"These historians celebrate the outcome of a war that put the country on the long path to the civil rights movement and greater equality," argues Ayers, in "powerful histories" that tell "a story of freedom emerging through the trial of war, or a great nation becoming greater through suffering." In print and on film, the pair dramatize how "antislavery, progress, war, and national identity intertwined at the time of the Civil War so that each element became inseparable from the others . . . The story has become common sense to Americans; emancipation, war, nation, and progress all seem part of one story, the same story." A historian of film anticipated Ayers's comments about Burns, asserting that the production cast the war "as essentially a struggle for freedom" that "dealt with the fundamentally important question of the future status of African Americans." Others have seconded Ayers's characterization of McPherson's work, including one who labels it civil rights generation scholarship that "led the effort to turn the Civil War into an emancipation event."[18]

Director Edward Zwick's *Glory,* a splendid film about the 54th Massachusetts Infantry, has promoted a popular understanding of the war as primarily a crusade for black freedom. Premiering in 1989, *Glory* introduced millions of viewers to the fact that African American soldiers fought in the Civil War. Well acted and staged, it features memorable scenes that deal with the meaning of the war. Probably the most powerful depicts the night before the regiment's famous assault against Fort Wagner on July 18, 1863. Gathered around a campfire, the soldiers take turns singing and explaining why they are fighting. A sergeant who ran off and left his family in bondage hopes to prove his manhood and strike a blow at slavery. "Heavenly Father, we want you to let our folks know that we died facing the enemy," he says in the rhythmic cadence of a church service: "We want them to know that we went down standing up. Amongst those that are fighting against our oppression, we want them to know, Heavenly Father, that we died for freedom. We ask these blessings in Jesus' name, Amen."[19]

Freedom's Unfinished Revolution: An Inquiry Into the Civil War and Reconstruction, a volume intended to shape secondary school curricula, also situates emancipation and race at the center of the conflict. Published in 1996 as part of the American Social History Project based at the City

University of New York, it features a foreword by Eric Foner that terms
it "an up-to-date account" that highlights "the key role played by African
Americans in bringing about emancipation, securing the Union's victory, and establishing the agenda for the nation's first postwar attempt to
create a truly interracial democracy." The authors encourage students "to
make connections between the past and the present" regarding "civil
rights, questions of freedom and equality, the power of racial tensions,"
and other topics. A long section on "War Aims: Union or Freedom" juxtaposes excerpts from Lincoln's letter of August 22, 1862, to Horace
Greeley with a letter from Harriett Tubman to Lydia Maria Child and
passages from three editorials by Frederick Douglass. The authors supply
no explanation of what Union meant in the mid-nineteenth century but
pose a basic question to students: "Which war aim would you support:
'union' or 'freedom'? After reading the documents below, write a paragraph explaining your stand." That any student would give Union serious consideration within this framework seems highly unlikely. The book
also attributes military victory to African American participation. After
defeats in 1861 and the first half of 1862, "new laws encouraged even
more slaves to escape, and . . . the number of black men and women employed by the Union Army increased. First slowly, then dramatically, the
balance of military power on the front lines changed between North and
South."[20]

Any consideration of emancipation and black military service should
reject the idea of inevitability. However difficult to imagine in the
twenty-first century, the United States could have achieved victory with
slavery intact and no African American units in its armies. It also could
have lost the war with emancipation on the table and black men composing approximately 10 percent of all loyal forces. More than twenty
years ago, James M. McPherson urged readers to respect "the dimension
of *contingency*—the recognition that at numerous critical points during
the war things might have gone altogether differently." That advice has
lost none of its relevance, and it most often applies to military campaigns
that wielded enormous influence over political, economic, and social dimensions of the war.[21]

The late spring and early summer of 1862 and the summer of 1864 prove the fallacy of imagining emancipation as an inevitable result of the conflict. The most striking example of emancipation-related contingency occurred in June and early July 1862. The first half of that year witnessed a remarkable series of Union successes. In the Western Theater, United States military forces in Tennessee won victories at Forts Henry and Donelson and Shiloh, captured Nashville and Memphis, seized control of hugely important logistical areas, and edged into northern Mississippi to occupy the vital rail junction of Corinth. Farther south, combined naval and land operations compelled the surrender of New Orleans, which closed the Mississippi River as a vital economic artery for the Confederacy. Facing an imminent shortage of manpower, the Confederate Congress passed a conscription act in mid-April that triggered widespread southern desertion as George B. McClellan's Army of the Potomac mounted a powerful threat against Richmond. By the end of May, "Little Mac" had pressed Gen. Joseph E. Johnston's army to the outskirts of the Rebel capital. Two scenarios seemed most likely—abandonment of the city by Johnston, whose retreat toward Richmond with relatively little fighting had infuriated many Confederate soldiers and civilians, or a siege that almost certainly would have ended with Richmond's capture. Either of those outcomes, when added to catastrophic Confederate losses in the West, likely would have ended the war. Union victory would have come with slavery largely untouched in most places, no record of military service for black men, and the politically ambitious McClellan, a Democrat and opponent of forced emancipation, recognized as the victors' preeminent hero.

Military contingency shaped events, including the future of emancipation, in seismic fashion after Johnston was wounded on May 31 at the battle of Seven Pines. That incident opened the way for Jefferson Davis to place Robert E. Lee in command of what would become the Army of Northern Virginia. Lee launched an offensive at the end of June, driving McClellan away from Richmond in the Seven Days battles. Over the ensuing eight weeks, Lee reoriented the war in Virginia to the Potomac River, winning another major victory at Second Bull Run on August 28–30 and crossing the national frontier into the United States in early September. Although the Army of Northern Virginia retreated to Virginia after the battle of Antietam, a sea change had occurred on both sides. Confederate morale rebounded from an abysmal low in mid-June, while the loyal citizenry in the United States braced for a protracted conflict.[22]

A longer war increased the likelihood that slavery would not survive. Abolitionists understood this from the beginning, as evidenced by a letter from Radical Republican senator Charles Sumner to Wendell Phillips in the wake of First Bull Run. "Be tranquil," Sumner counseled on August 3, 1861, "Never did I feel so sure of the result. The battle & defeat have done much for the slave . . . I told the Presdt that our defeat was the worst event & the best event in our history; the worst, as it was the greatest present calamity & shame,—the best, as it made the extinction of Slavery inevitable." Shortly after McClellan fell back from Richmond in July 1862, the Congress, Lincoln, and some Federal commanders took important steps. Two pieces of legislation enacted on July 17 held great potential. The Second Confiscation Act freed slaves of all people loyal to the Confederacy, and the Militia Act approved, though it did not require, employment of "persons of African descent" in "any military or naval service for which they may be found competent." On July 22, the president informed his cabinet that he intended to issue a proclamation of emancipation. The following month, Maj. Gen. Benjamin F. Butler began recruiting black men in New Orleans, and the War Department authorized similar efforts in the Union-controlled Sea Islands off South Carolina. Ironically, a single Confederate victory had provided a powerful impetus to emancipation and the ancillary enrollment of African American soldiers.[23]

The summer of 1864 raised the specter of Union defeat despite emancipation and the presence of scores of thousands of men in USCT units. After a spring of ebullient hope arising from Ulysses S. Grant's promotion to general in chief of the Union armies, the people of the United States eagerly focused on campaigns in Virginia and northern Georgia. May and early June unfolded with Sherman making progress toward Atlanta and Grant closing in on Richmond, but by mid-July the overall strategic picture deeply troubled most loyal citizens. Union offensives orchestrated by Maj. Gens. Nathanial P. Banks, Benjamin Butler, and Franz Sigel had failed along the Red River in Louisiana, between Petersburg and Richmond, and in the Shenandoah Valley. Sherman had crossed the Chattahoochee River but then stalled outside Atlanta, and a small Rebel army under Lt. Gen. Jubal A. Early marched rapidly down the Shenandoah Valley, crossed the Potomac, and shelled the northernmost defenses of Washington before slipping back into Virginia. Most important by far, Grant's forces suffered massive casualties in the Overland campaign, which included a brutal setback at Cold Harbor and no clearcut battlefield successes. A few Democratic newspapers labeled Grant a butcher who wasted lives to no effect. During the third week of June, Grant and Lee settled into a siege along the Richmond-Petersburg front that promised to grind on indefinitely. Lincoln shared the general population's growing pessimism, as indicated by his blind memorandum to the cabinet predicting Republican defeat in 1864 and raising the possibility of Confederate independence should the Democrats carry the elections.[24]

More than three years into the conflict, freedom for the mass of African Americans remained a fragile proposition. Anyone who believed in emancipation might well dread the prospect of Democratic success. In early December 1863, Lincoln had announced as part of his plan for reunion a requirement that former Rebels take an oath of allegiance and accept all proclamations and legislation then in force regarding slavery. George B. McClellan, the Democratic presidential candidate in 1864, specifically omitted any mention of emancipation in his letter accepting the nomination. "The preservation of our Union was the sole avowed object for which the war was commenced," he wrote to members of the Democratic National Committee on September 8. "To restore and preserve it," he affirmed, "the same spirit must prevail in our Councils, and in the hearts of the people. The reestablishment of the Union in all its integrity is, and must continue to be, the indispensable condition in any settlement ...The Union is the one condition of peace. We ask no more." Under a Democratic administration, even one that might insist on prosecuting the war to a successful end, the status of freedpeople in the Confederate states immediately would become clouded. Moreover, among the four loyal slave states, only Maryland had made significant progress toward emancipation.[25]

Military contingency intervened again when Sherman captured Atlanta on September 1–2 and General Sheridan won three smashing victories in the Shenandoah Valley between September 19 and October 19. News from these battlefields electrified the loyal home front and sent ripples of despair across much of the Confederacy. They also secured a second term for Lincoln and fueled a Republican landslide in Congress— political outcomes that kept emancipation in place as an official war aim. "The dark days are over," observed the editor of the Republican *Chicago Tribune* about Atlanta, "Thanks be to God! The Republic is safe!" Greatly relieved by the news from Sherman, Lincoln issued a "Proclamation of Thanksgiving and Prayer" on September 3, noting "the glorious achievements of the Army under Major General Sherman in the State of Georgia" and crediting God's "mercy in preserving our national existence against the insurgent rebels who so long have been waging a cruel war against the Government of the United-States, for its overthrow."[26]

Apart from their importance in buttressing emancipation as a war aim, the victories in Georgia and the Shenandoah Valley help explain why white citizens believed black military contributions to be of secondary value. USCT units played no combat role with either Sherman's or Sheridan's armies, which was typical of a broader policy of relegating black regiments to a variety of supporting tasks. That policy, rooted in prejudice and other factors, frustrated many African American soldiers who wanted a chance to prove themselves in battle. Most USCT regiments performed valuable but not decisive service. Their work received positive notice in the northern press and among white citizens, but the biggest battles, not one of which featured black soldiers, garnered the most attention during and after the war.[27]

This focus on grand battles contributed to the exuberant atmosphere in Washington for the Grand Review. Spectators welcomed the opportunity to see the Army of the Potomac, whose soldiers had contested nine of the twelve fields that extracted the most Union blood, and Sherman's veterans, who had captured Atlanta and gutted the interior of

Georgia and South Carolina. Black or white units whose résumés boasted more guard duty than active campaigning would not have summoned emotional images of the type associated with the celebrated Irish Brigade, the infantry that marched with Sherman to the sea, or the men who turned back Lee's invasions of 1862 and 1863.[28]

The degree to which much of the loyal white population supported emancipation and praised black soldiers revealed an ability to moderate racist attitudes in pursuit of Union. Most Republicans quite readily agreed that slavery must go and saw the utility of adding black regiments to the army—though they usually linked emancipation to saving the Union and often evinced deep-seated prejudice. A number of moderate Republicans joined the party's Radicals in calling for the extension of political rights to black veterans and perhaps to literate African American men more generally. Yet the war also exposed fissures among those who would have described themselves as unionists and embraced a war against secession in 1860–1861. Some Democrats, precisely how many is beyond knowing, recoiled from both forced emancipation and any semblance of basic rights for black people. They favored "the Union as it was" and in some cases veered close to supporting the Confederacy. Most soldiers hated these "peace Democrats" or Copperheads, equating their statements and actions with treason and demanding they be punished. Other Democrats reluctantly accepted emancipation and the enrollment of black soldiers as necessary to save the Union, while voicing unrelievedly vicious opinions about African Americans as people. A sizeable percentage of white citizens undoubtedly hoped freedpeople would not migrate north after the war, and many spoke of some kind of enforced relocation abroad.[29]

The two leading American illustrated newspapers provide a lens through which to examine mainstream attitudes toward emancipation and black military service. *Frank Leslie's Illustrated Newspaper* and *Harper's Weekly*, established respectively in 1855 and 1857, combined articles, woodcuts of sketches by artists in the field, cartoons, and other pictorial material. Both were published in New York City and often printed more than 100,000 copies per issue, each of which probably passed through many hands.[30] Hoping to reach the widest possible readership, neither pursued a strong ideological agenda—though on the whole Republicans, much more than Democrats, would have found coverage of emancipation and enrollment of black soldiers in both papers to their taste. The two weeklies reflected, and perhaps helped shape, a moderate approach to emancipation and African American military participation based on a desire to muster all resources to restore the Union. Both welcomed anything that discomfited slaveholders during the war and envisioned a stronger Union in the absence of slavery-related sectional stress. Negative racial stereotypes pervaded their articles and illustrative material, and black people as human beings only occasionally engaged the editors. Yet the weeklies demonstrated that war had wrought changes regarding forced abolition and related topics that would have been unimaginable just a few years earlier.

Almost from the beginning, the newspapers approved of efforts to deny enslaved labor to the Confederates. In September 1861, *Leslie's* praised Maj. Gen. John C. Frémont's effort to liberate slaves owned by pro-Rebel owners in Missouri and called on Congress to broaden the previous month's First Confiscation Act, which freed slaves directly involved in supporting Confederate military operations. "By December, it is to be hoped," wrote the editor, "the Administration and Congress will have become aroused to the reality of the present struggle." *Harper's Weekly* already had predicted that Benjamin F. Butler's contraband policy, first applied in May 1861 at Fort Monroe in Virginia, would inevitably spread. "That negro slavery will come out of this war unscathed is impossible," insisted an article titled "Slavery and the War." "The mere escape of slaves," stated the piece with considerable prescience, "will weaken the institution irrevocably in the States where the war is waged; for Government must obviously act upon the principles of General Butler's letter." In January 1862, *Harper's* optimistically affirmed that people of the North were willing to see slavery end as a result of the war—but added that they already had grown tired of "those eternal discussions in Congress about the disposal of negroes . . . It is widely felt that nothing can prevent our ultimate success except divisions among ourselves such as these discussions seem calculated to provoke."[31]

Lincoln's preliminary proclamation received quick support from the illustrated weeklies. "The proclamation of the President . . . practically abolishes slavery throughout the United States after next New-Year's Day," announced *Harper's* on October 4, 1862. A "large majority" in the North would have objected to Lincoln's action earlier in the war, and even now "a mortal antipathy for the negro is entertained by a large class of persons at the North." Yet the conflict had "produced a remarkable change in the opinions of educated and liberal men," who would back Lincoln. Demagogues might seek to incite working-class opposition by raising the specter of free black men flooding north to compete for jobs, but the only serious opposition to Lincoln's action would appear "in circles whose loyalty to the country may well be questioned." *Leslie's* took a more cautious approach, stressing connections between the measure and the war for Union. "The President's Proclamation . . . has been promulgated as a war measure," the paper informed its readers, "and as a logical necessity from the various confiscation bills adopted by Congress. On the *right and power* of the President to issue such a Proclamation (we are not discussing its *policy*) there can be no doubt." To commemorate the final proclamation, which it described as "the great event of the day," *Harper's* published a two-page drawing by Thomas Nast that contrasted the lives of slaves and freedpeople and featured a domestic scene of a family in their "free and happy home."[32]

Emancipation's practical application to the war for Union formed a strong leitmotif in *Harper's* and *Leslie's* articles and images. In dozens of issues, readers saw or read about African American teamsters, drovers, cooks, washerwomen, blacksmiths, stevedores, pioneers, river pilots, and laborers building fortifications, cultivating cotton under Union management, and improving roads. On December 21, 1861, *Harper's* placed vignettes of contrabands near Beaufort, South Carolina, on the front page. Between January and March 1863, it emphasized the connection between Lincoln's final proclamation and the swelling force of black labor supporting the war effort in a series of woodcuts depicting contrabands entering Union lines. Occasionally names would accompany stories or illustrations, as when *Leslie's* identified Robert Smalls, William Morrison, John Smalls, and A. Gradine in a woodcut titled "Heroes in Ebony—The Captors of the Rebel Steamer *Planter*." *Harper's* also noted Smalls and his exploit: "We publish herewith an engraving of the steamer *Planter,* lately run out of Charleston by her negro crew, and a portrait of her captain, Robert Smalls." An accompanying account, clipped from the *New York Herald,* deemed Smalls's exploit "one of the most daring and heroic adventures since the war commenced." For the most part, however, regular readers of the two weeklies gained an impression of a disparate mass of nameless black contributors to the Union cause.[33]

Each paper quickly established a pattern of publishing racist cartoons and illustrations of contrabands and other African Americans. *Leslie's* offered a cruel example captioned "Dark Artillery; Or, How To Make Contrabands Useful" in late October 1861. It depicted grotesque black men with cannon tubes strapped to their backs, one of them on all fours as a gunner pulled the lanyard and a projectile exited the barrel. *Harper's* had run a cartoon titled "Contraband of War" in late June featuring two black men in front of a fortification, one wearing a military kepi and uniform jacket and the other, much older, clad in plantation garb. The dialogue conformed to typical white representations of black speech patterns: "First Contraband Article. 'Why, Julius, what's goin' to become ob de cullud pop'lation in dis War? Heah's dis chile been mor'n sebenty yeahs one ob de cullud race, an' been called a *niggah,* a *chattels,* an *institution,* an' now he's a *contraban'.* I s'pose de out-cum will be dis niggar will lose his position on de face ob de airth altogedor—dat's so!'" In June 1862, a *Harper's* article on "Our Black Friends Down South" employed a lightly scornful tone before concluding, "These poor creatures realize plainly enough that we are their friends, and they have never let slip an opportunity of showing us that their friendship is worth having." Accompanying the article was an unflattering woodcut of a large, grinning black woman with small children to her left and right, greeting Union soldiers: "Oh! I'se so glad you is come. Massa says he wish you was in de bottom ob de sea—but you aint in de bottom ob de sea, you is he'yar & Oh! I'se so glad to see yer."[34]

The illustrated weeklies also touted the wisdom of deploying black soldiers to assist the Union war effort. In January 1863, *Harper's* criticized opponents of African American recruitment. Rebels used their slaves "in any capacity in which they may be found useful. Yet there are people

here at the North who affect to be horrified at the enrollment of negroes into regiments." Later that spring, *Harper's* followed up with a pair
of woodcuts—"Teaching The Negro Recruits The Use Of The Minie
Rifle" (on the front page) and "A Negro Regiment In Action" (a two-
page illustration). A short article titled "Negroes as Soldiers" also sought
to counter "ignorant prejudice" against black military service.[35]

Both papers used the Militia Act of 1862 to make a case for recruitment of black soldiers. *Harper's* printed a cartoon titled "A Consistent
Negrophobist," in which an African American offered a line to a drowning white man whose head barely remained above water. The caption
targeted anyone who preferred the possibility of Confederate independence to black recruitment: "Drowning Gentleman: 'Take that Rope
away, you darned Nigger!' What decent White Man, do you suppose, is
going to allow himself to be saved by a confounded Nig——"(*Goes
down, consistent to the last.*)" *Leslie's* resorted to racist language (as well as
ethnic slurs) and focused entirely on the need for Union manpower
rather than any sense of helping black men, arguing that "men with black
skins are to be used in whatever way available; that a cubic yard of earth
shoveled by a negro is worth as much as if thrown up by a white man;
and that a bullet fired by Sambo is just as deadly as if fired by Jonathan,
Patrick, or any Teuton whatever."[36]

Black troops in battle garnered attention as well. Assaults by the 1st
and 3rd Louisiana Native Guards at Port Hudson, Louisiana, on May 27,
1863, marked the initial large-scale deployment of African Americans in
combat, an event *Leslie's* covered in some detail on June 13. A large
woodcut showed the "Assault of the Second Louisiana (Colored) Regiment on the Rebel Works at Port Hudson, May 27." Although the paper
got the regiment wrong, it offered a short front-page tribute to the black
men who mounted the assault and included a long poem dedicated to
them. *Harper's* noted African American units in the battle of Milliken's
Bend, Louisiana, fought on June 7, 1863. A double-page woodcut of the
action placed a black color bearer in the foreground, flanked by comrades fighting hand-to-hand with Confederates. A brief article called it
"the sharp fight at Milliken's Bend, where a small body of black troops
with a few whites were attacked by a larger force of rebels." The artist

added a brief account of the action that mentioned a moment of humiliation for a slaveholder—something that surely resonated with many readers. "A rebel prisoner made a particular request that *his* own negroes not be placed over him as a guard," observed Theodore Davis: "Dame Fortune *is* capricious! His request was *not* granted." Later issues included text and illustrations related to other engagements where USCT units fought, among them various clashes during the siege of Petersburg, as well as the entrance of black troops into Richmond and Charleston.[37]

Atrocities against black soldiers galvanized the editors at *Harper's* and *Leslie's* to print strong denunciations of the slaveholding class. The execution of African American prisoners at Fort Pillow, Tennessee, by troops under Maj. Gen. Nathan Bedford Forrest in April 1864 inspired famous woodcuts in both publications. *Leslie's* placed "The War in Tennessee—Rebel Massacre Of The Union Troops After The Surrender At Fort Pillow, April 12" on the front page. "The annals of savage warfare nowhere record a more inhuman, fiendish butchery than this," observed *Harper's*, "perpetrated by the representatives of the 'superior civilization' of the States in rebellion." A month later, the paper revisited the issue with a two-page group of vignettes illustrating "Rebel Atrocities." These included "Genl Forrest Shooting a Free Mulatto," "Negro Teamsters Tied To a Tree and Shot," and executions of black soldiers at Fort Wagner, Fort Pillow, and Milliken's Bend. The vignettes "represent only a few of the sad facts which rebel inhumanity has forced into the history of the time," averred the editor, all of which stemmed from Jefferson Davis's policy of defining captured black troops as runaway slaves rather than as legitimate soldiers.[38]

Most coverage of black military service in the illustrated press dealt with noncombat roles and probably reinforced public perceptions of USCT units as rear-echelon rather than front-line troops. *Harper's Weekly*, for example, published a woodcut of Brig. Gen. Edward A. Wild's African Brigade liberating slaves in eastern North Carolina, adopting a somewhat dismissive tone in the accompanying text. "The scene in our sketch represents the colored troops on one of these plantations freeing the slaves," it read: "The morning light is shining upon their bristling bayonets in the back-ground, and upon a scene in front as ludicrous as it is interesting. The personal effects of the slaves are being gathered together from the outhouses on the plantation and piled, regardless of order, in an old cart, the party meanwhile availing themselves in a promiscuous manner of the Confiscation Act by plundering hens and chickens and larger fowl." The piece closed with a jab at the slaveholder on the scene, who watched his former slaves and his possessions depart, "leaving 'Ole Massa' to glory in solitude and secession." *Harper's* also ran a woodcut of USCT troops digging trenches in front of Fort Wagner, opposite Charleston. A third example, in *Leslie's,* dealt with "Pickets of the First Louisiana 'Native Guard' Guarding the New Orleans, Opelousas and Great Western Railroad" in 1863. Deep in the woods and seemingly far from danger, four of five figures stood or sat around campfires while the fifth, leaning on his musket, gazed into the distance.[39]

In early 1864, *Leslie's* devoted two pages to a group of eleven woodcuts that underscored the noncombatant roles of USCT men. Titled "The Negro In The War—Sketches Of The Various Employments Of The Colored Men In United States Armies," the group included just two sketches depicting combat—a large one of Milliken's Bend that occupied the central position and a smaller one of soldiers firing "In The Trenches." Another pair presented armed soldiers—"On Picket" (three men resting along a palisade and one on watch) and "Scouts" (two men crouching behind a tree and gazing toward a Confederate camp). The remaining seven, all of which portrayed unarmed African Americans, were titled "Building Roads," "Cooking in Camp," "Unloading Govt. Stores," "Driving Govt Cattle," "Washing in Camp" [women], "Teamster of the Army," and "Govrnt. Blacksmiths' Shop." The message these woodcuts conveyed to a typical reader would have been clear. Black soldiers had carried muskets in some minor battles, but the bulk of their service took place far from bloody fields of action.[40]

A cartoon published in *Leslie's* less than a month after "The Negro In The War" further compromised the idea of African American men as first-rate Union soldiers. The newspaper undoubtedly approved of black military service—in fact had urged it long before it became government policy—but nonetheless often deployed race in cruel fashion. In the cartoon, two bounty brokers contended for the attention of a possible recruit. Posters to the right and left promised "Highest Bounty Paid Here. Colored Men $375" and announced "300,000 Good Recruits Wanted!!!" The conversation unfolded: "1st Broker—'Now, then, yer know I spoke to yer first.' 2nd Ditto—'Can't you let the gentleman decide for himself.' Bewildered Man and Brother—'You bofe very kind gemmin, but I'se afraid dey's waiting up dere for me to finish up dat whitewashin'.'"[41]

Passage of the Thirteenth Amendment in the House of Representatives on January 31, 1865, made the pages of *Harper's* and *Leslie's*. For some reason, *Harper's* offered little commentary, though a poem about the amendment titled "Free America" followed a woodcut that took up the entire front page on February 18. In the preceding issue, the paper had reported, again without comment, that in "the House, the proposition was passed to submit to the Legislatures of the several States the following amendment to the Constitution." *Leslie's* devoted its lead article on February 18 to the event, and a two-page woodcut of the tumultuous scene in the House appeared inside the issue. Once ratified in a reunited Union, the paper reminded readers, the amendment would increase the South's power in Congress. Black people would henceforth count as a full person rather than three-fifths of one. Delaware, New Jersey, and Kentucky likely would refuse to ratify, but popular approval meant "that it will be hard for the Legislatures of these States long to resist." Choosing language that spoke to the power of emancipation to safeguard the Union from future threats, *Leslie's* affirmed that "public sentiment is for the extirpation of slavery, 'the evil cause of all our woes.'"[42]

Harper's ran a cartoon in February 1865 that captured some of the unanticipated, and quite striking, consequences of the conflict. In "A Man Knows A Man," two one-legged veterans, one black and one white, looked each other in the eye. "Give me your hand, Comrade!" said one. "We have each lost a Leg for the good cause; but, thank God, we never lost HEART." Very few people in 1860 could have guessed that a huge biracial army would end the war victorious over a republic established by a powerful slaveholding class. Fewer still probably could have imagined a bond of true comradeship across the racial divide. Moreover, the cartoon raised the possibility of equality beyond the military sphere for black men who had risked their lives, and suffered horrible wounds, in national service.[43]

Although illustrative of how the war shattered some antebellum racial conventions, the cartoon should be used carefully. It implied that the two soldiers shared a single vision of "the good cause," but white men in the United States Army, in contrast to their black comrades, seldom valued emancipation as much as Union. As with soldiers' testimony regarding Union, a few examples from letters and diaries reveal patterns relating to emancipation and black soldiers.

The initial reaction to Lincoln's final proclamation included a great deal of opposition, some of which remained strong through the end of the war. A well-educated Illinois soldier stationed in North Carolina, Valentine C. Randolph recorded on February 10, 1863, that "the soldiers, generally have a bitter enmity towards the negroes. Any, that plead for even the most common rights of the negro, do so at the risk of their popularity with their comrades. 'Damned nigger' is a very common epithet and coupled with 'Damned Abolishionist.' This is true, not of any particular regiments only, but generally so far as my observation extends, which has by no means been limited." Much later in the war, a member of the 16th New York Heavy Artillery fulminated against those who would alter the old Union "by proclamations and suspensions of the safeguard of human liberty" and ruin "the country with their absurd notions of negro equality." An Ohioan writing from Louisiana in December 1864 conveyed a chilling sentiment. After Confederates "came in and killed some of the U.S. Soldiers of African decent," the 114th Ohio Infantry was "ordered back in quick time to save their black pates the only pitty it is that they did not kill all of them for they are fit for nothing but to eat up rations."[44]

Some soldiers worried that Lincoln's proclamation would compromise the war for Union by exacerbating political fractures in the North and solidifying Confederate determination. John Chipman Gray, a lawyer and officer who later supported the Thirteenth Amendment as "better than a thousand of your juggling emancipation proclamations," decried Lincoln's action on January 5, 1863. Moreover, Radical Republican agitation on emancipation, he believed, "has united the South and has divided the North, it has induced to vote with the democrats many men as patriotic as any in the country and who would have fought as long as any for the proper object of the war." A veteran of Shiloh in the 70th Ohio Infantry, Samuel Evans worried about news of widespread unhappiness with emancipation on the home front. "I am very fearful there [is] so much opposition to the war upon the Side of the Union," he confessed to his father on February 8, 1863, "that the lives of all the brave soldiers already lost, the enormous expense The Nation is already gone to, will be a sacrifice without bettering our condition." Attacking Ohio's Copperheads, who used emancipation to attract support, Evans argued that denying slaves' labor to the Rebels helped the Union: "My doctrine has been anything to weaken the enemy." Peter Vredenburgh, Jr., a major in the 14th New Jersey Infantry, had mixed feelings about the proclamation but predicted it would weaken enthusiasm for the war. "Men here, who were good Union sympathizers before are now on the other side," he informed his father: "I have met a good many intelligent men here and they all say that to carry out the Proclamation will ruin them . . . Strictly it may be right, but it was unwise to enforce it, because there are so many ignorant and prejudiced people who say, 'well, if they are going to take our niggers away we won't stand it,' etc."[45]

A small minority of soldiers enthusiastically greeted news of emancipation as a moral accomplishment. Deployed to Minnesota after the Sioux uprising in the summer of 1862, James Madison Bowler of the 3rd Minnesota Infantry learned on October 8 of the preliminary proclamation. He read the news "with great pleasure . . . I now feel that we are upon the right road at last." A Republican during the war, Bowler began his service as a corporal in the 3rd Minnesota and closed it as a major in the 113th USCT Infantry. He mentioned the final proclamation in August 1863, detailing how he had lectured a fellow soldier named Will Govette "for his foolish pro-slavery notions. He is opposed to Lincoln's proclamation of Freedom." Bowler pronounced himself "conceited enough to believe that I shamed him if nothing more." A physician with the Army of the Potomac went much further in his exuberant response. "I would rather be a beggar all my days," wrote James Oliver in his diary, "than to see this war close with slavery still within the boundaries of the U.S. Thank heaven it is being swept away. What songs will be sung by future generations." George W. Snell described the impact of coming face-to-face with slavery and numbers of black people. Stationed in New Orleans with the 15th New Hampshire Infantry, he wrote on March 18, 1863: "I am a stronger aberletionist, since I came out here than I was in New Hampshire." He hoped God would assist the Union army to "whip out Rebeldom and slavery both together."[46]

By far the most common soldiers' response accepted emancipation, sometimes more grudgingly than others, as a useful or even necessary tool to achieve victory over the Rebels. For Jacob Behm of the 48th Illinois Infantry, who fought in the Western Theater, "the necessity of Emancipation is forced upon us by the inevitable events of the war . . . and the only road out of this war is by blows aimed at the heart of the Rebellion." Slaveholders had rebelled to protect their human property in the long term, and "if Slavery should be left undisturbed the war would be protracted untill the loss of life and national bankruptcy would make peace desireable upon any terms." Behm expressed certainty about one thing, "that when Slavery is removed this Rebellion will die out and not before during the war." An officer in the 123rd Illinois Infantry, who described himself as "a conservative young Democrat," summarized his thinking in mid-May 1863: "While in the field I am an abolitionist; my government has decided to wipe out slavery, and I am for the government and its policy whether right or wrong, so long as its flag is confronted by the hostile guns of slavery." George H. Mellish of the 6th Vermont Infantry adopted a similar stance. From camp near Danville, Virginia, in early May 1865, he wrote that he favored emancipation but was "getting so I hate the sight of a darkey." "We have a large supply of niggers around here," he said disdainfully, "and such darkys. They go clear beyond all nigger novels you ever heard of." Mellish wanted freedpeople "sent to their proper residence—Africa." A corporal in the 15th Connecticut Infantry minced no words: "I dont care how many Negroes he [General Benjamin Butler] arms or how many get their heads broak if it will help to end the war."[47]

The *New York Sunday Mercury* included a popular feature titled "Our

War Correspondence," which earned wide popularity among soldiers who enjoyed sampling opinions from comrades serving in all theaters of the conflict. A piece titled "The Negro Soldiers Bill" ran on February 8, 1863. Predictions that Lincoln's proclamation would bring disaster had proved incorrect, stated the author, who then laid out a Union-based plea for the enrollment of black troops. "Negroes should be allowed to fight and made to fight," he stated, "The North has sacrificed hundreds of thousands of her brave and generous sons. No further drain can be made on the white population without withdrawing from society its chief pillars of support, and leave the social fabric to topple into ruins. It would be preposterous to draft white men to fight, while hosts of the sable sons of Africa are ready to be transformed into soldiers, and whose services the Government has a right to claim."[48]

Many soldiers who first opposed emancipation came to see it as a boon to the Union war effort. Their conversions seldom had anything to do with extirpating slavery on moral grounds or overcoming racial prejudice; rather, motivation typically stemmed from a search for weapons to weaken Confederate military resistance, a desire to have black soldiers perform noncombatant labor, and a willingness to let USCT units absorb battle casualties. The overriding goal of Union almost never changed.

William Bluffton Miller's diary illuminates the complexity of attitudes toward abolition and race among white soldiers. Miller's 75th Ohio Infantry campaigned with the armies of the Ohio and the Cumberland, service that brought him into considerable contact with slavery and contrabands. In February 1863, he wrote: "We were discussing the Emancipation Proclimation and I find others as well as my self who are afraid of the effect in the north and fear it will cause a war there. A great many soldiers condemn it on that account." Five months later Miller heartily endorsed emancipation because "it gives us advantage of them in this. That they must run their Slaves south to help eat up their Supplies which are Scarce at best or we will make Soldiers of them and I am not very particular if they put them in the front rank as they can stop a Rebbel Bullet as well as a white Soldier." Miller loathed Copperheads, hotly debated the war with Democratic friends in Indiana in 1863, and took pride in fighting "for the Union one and inseperable and that Freedom might live to the Abolition of Slavery and all men regardless of collor may be free." Miller sometimes expressed sympathy for the plight of contrabands but always saw them as inferior to white people. On February 25, 1865, with his regiment operating along the Charleston and Augusta Railroad, he deprecated "the poorest country I ever seen . . . The Slaves here are more monkey than human. I cant understand half they say."[49]

Two infantrymen from Iowa and Maine touched on another common theme, speaking for countless white soldiers happy to see black soldiers perform thankless tasks unrelated to combat. Benjamin F. McIntyre advanced from sergeant to lieutenant while the 19th Iowa Infantry operated in the Trans-Mississippi and the Deep South. Stationed near Brownsville, Texas, in late 1863, he mentioned that several "Corps d' Afrique regiments . . . have been employed in unloading vessels, assisting the Pioneers in constructing pontoon bridges, and various other arduous duties that would have compelled our own boys to have performed had no negro regiments been in the service of the government." McIntyre returned to the topic five months later, detailing the many tasks that required "the labor of hundreds of men for months . . . this is work of a very disagreeable character and for one I thank the originators of the Corps d' Afrique for taking from us such labor as belongs to menials." Despite their blue uniforms, McIntyre assigned the USCT men to a category separate from white soldiers. "While our soldiers pride themselves on the nice condition of their arms," he wrote, "the Corps d' Afrique are proud of the fine condition of their picks and spaids." Daniel W. Sawtelle, an enlisted man in the 8th Maine Infantry, praised the fighting capabilities of black soldiers during a skirmish in South Carolina, closing with, "So much for the nigger regt. I say bully for them if they can make the negroes fight their own masters. I am willing for one but don't want to be made a nigger of anyway. I come out here to fight not work."[50]

Two leading generals articulated a final connection between emancipation and a successful war for Union. Ulysses S. Grant and Maj. Gen. William Starke Rosecrans addressed the need to remove slavery as a corrosive agent in the hands of selfish slaveholders. "I never was an Abolitionest, [n]ot even what could be called anti slavery," Grant stated to Congressman Elihu B. Washburne in late August 1863, "but I try to judge farely & honestly and it become patent to my mind early in the rebellion that the North & South could never live at peace with each other except as one nation, and that without Slavery." Although anxious for the reestablishment of peace, Grant "would not therefore be willing to see any settlemen[t] until this question is forever settled." Rosecrans unburdened himself regarding slaveholding oligarchs in a conversation with Frederick Law Olmsted in March 1863. "They are so set upon being little nigger aristocrats," fumed the general, "that they will sacrifice everything else to it. What is their spirit of chivalry? It's the same spirit which loves to bully niggers." Slaveholders delighted in boasting about their honor, he continued, but "What does it amount to? They reverence it just so long as it keeps ahead of their self interest and passions, but as soon as their passions or self interest comes in play, honor falls behind." The loyal citizenry possessed "a wonderful patriotism standing opposed to the selfish pride of those little nigger-tyrants . . . I do not believe that as much pure patriotism—pure patriotism, without mixture of self interest—was ever found in the common run of any people on earth before. Men, common men in the ranks deliberately make offering of their lives for the sake of the nation."[51]

Although some have placed emancipation at the heart of the presidential election of 1864, soldiers' comments left no doubt that saving the nation, to use General Rosecrans's language, easily trumped killing slavery as a motivation to vote for the Union ticket of Lincoln and Andrew Johnson.[52] Most states permitted their soldiers to vote in the field—though Delaware, Illinois, Indiana, New Jersey, and Oregon did not. Democrats complained vociferously, and perhaps with some merit, that Republicans conspired to suppress the anti-Lincoln military vote. Only twelve states counted soldiers' ballots separately. Those that can be identified favored Lincoln by a margin of 119,754 to 34,291—78 percent compared to 55 percent among the electorate as a whole. For soldiers, votes for Lincoln ensured that the war would be prosecuted vigorously until Rebels capitulated and the Union prevailed.[53]

Three soldiers from New York, Maine, and Ohio recorded widely held opinions about the election. Edward King Wightman, a Democrat and noncommissioned officer in the 3rd New York Infantry, held "no very great respect" for Lincoln or McClellan and pronounced both parties' platforms "contemptible." He cast a ballot for Lincoln because the "main question seems to be whether we shall continue the war until the rebellion is subdued." The integrity of the Union could "be restored only by force of arms and . . . such a course is necessary in order to vindicate the honor and establish the power of the Republic." Another noncommissioned officer, Abial Hall Edwards of the 29th Maine Infantry, believed the two parties in 1864 were "Unionists & Dis Unionists and I think as much of a war Democrat as I do of a Lincoln man." The Democratic platform called for a cessation of hostilities short of victory, which would "disgrace the memory of our fallin brothers[.]" Edwards craved peace but would vote for Lincoln, "remain here and if it need be lay down my life before we give up one iota of the victories we have gained to the Rebel hords." After Lincoln's victory, he explained to his future wife, "No Anna I do not desire the war to last 4 years longer. Neither do I want a peace that would disgrace us as a nation." John Marihugh of the 21st Ohio Infantry shared Edwards's sentiments. Deployed to Camp Butler near Springfield, Illinois, he summed up his ideas in one long sentence: "Wall a bout the election I think that Old Abe will be Electid with out mutch truble & if the Cop[perhead]s try too make truble down here we shall give them hell & that is whats the mater & I say three chears for Old Abe & the union."[54]

Innumerable letters mirrored Marihugh's dislike of Copperheads and silence about emancipation as an issue in the election of 1864. Major Henry E. Richmond of the 4th New York Heavy Artillery touched on the nation, citizen-soldiers, and Copperheads in letters to his wife. He thought anyone who voted for McClellan would be "aiming a blow at & stabbing our National life to the heart." Pronouncing his military service "the noblest cause that a loyal citizen can do—the suppressing of the Rebellion against . . . our country & the best government that God ever vouchsafed to his children," Richmond insisted that "none but a copperhead or traitor" would support the Democrats or embrace peace short of Union victory. He considered any man who cast a ballot against Lincoln "no better than the enemy 100 yds in front, who fires his *bullets at us.*" A second lieutenant in the 76th Ohio Infantry used fewer, though equally inflammatory, words to make the same point. "The peace sneaks of the north should know by this time," wrote Lyman U. Humphrey from near Chattanooga, "that their damnable cause must go down to nothingness and their names be forever damned to eternal infamy." The soldiers "burn indignantly at the doings of the traitors behind us." Asa M. Weston, another Ohioan serving in Georgia, hoped Lincoln would be reelected but worried that men in Kentucky units "will vote for Mc-Clellan ... so much the more willingly I suppose because he suits [Copperhead politician Clement L.] Vallandigham."[55]

Early Union regimentals contain excellent material on emancipation and its consequences—though just more than a third of the sixty-four examined here ignore the end of slavery as a noteworthy outcome of the war. The ideas, arguments, and descriptive narratives published in the conflict's immediate aftermath conform closely to wartime soldiers' testimony about war aims, black military service, and the ways in which racial attitudes affected behavior and political opinions. These opinions regarding emancipation should not obscure the very widely held belief among Union soldiers that slavery had caused the war.

Taken as a group, these regimentals underscore the degree to which emancipation figured in most soldiers' minds primarily as a means to achieve and uphold Union. Four examples from Ohio, New York, and Illinois illustrate this point. Chaplain Thomas M. Stevenson of the 78th Ohio Infantry observed that "to suppress the rebellion without interfering with slavery, is an absurdity which would be only taking the effect and leaving the cause." A restored Union could be safe only with emancipation. No other course would "make a loyal people in the South ... As well make a mocking-bird out of a moccasin snake, or make the substance of opposite affinities unite." Lincoln understood this, and his proclamation "was the key that turned all our efforts into success, and opened the doors of victory and complete success to our arms." The wartime regimental of the 23rd New York Infantry reprinted a letter about Lincoln's proclamation, which, asserted its author, "does not seem to offend any one in this part of the army." The letter took Benjamin Butler's pronouncement about runaway slaves literally: "It is pretty well settled in these military circles that negroes during the continuance of this war are as clearly contraband as cannon, 'hard tack,' quinine, saltpeter, or mercurial ointment."[56]

Wales Wood, adjutant of the 95th Illinois Infantry, flatly denied that emancipation had been the principal goal of the war. "It was claimed by some people, and there are probably those who still adhere to the opinion," he wrote in the autumn of 1865, "that the war against secession was carried on by the Government from the beginning with the prominent idea on the part of the Administration of abolishing slavery . . . , and that the incipient plan of emancipating the slaves was fully illustrated and carried into practice by the Proclamation of President Lincoln." That interpretation misconstrued the president's intent to offer the proclamation "only as a *war measure* to hurt traitors and kill rebellion." Although emancipation hurt the Rebel military effort, Wood believed the "negro question at all times during the progress of the war, was an annoying subject to military commanders, in endeavoring to carry out the policy of the Government." Wood also mentioned General Frémont's plan to seize slaves of Rebel owners in Missouri as a policy designed to help fight the war for Union, as did David Lathrop of the 59th Illinois Infantry. "General Fremont was far in advance of the nation's representatives, either in the field or cabinet," asserted Lathrop, "He realized that the only way to stop rebellion was to chastise rebels with the rod of justice."[57]

Ovando J. Hollister of the 1st Colorado Volunteers detailed a lively discussion about emancipation among men in Company I of the 2nd U.S. Dragoons in September 1862. This group, who differed from the vast majority of Union men under arms because they were professional soldiers, "contained representatives of every shade of the idea, from the opposer of slavery on principle, to the tolerator of slavery on the ground of expediency, and the worshiper of slavery from long association and habit." Few Americans embraced fanatical devotion to any idea, mused Hollister, manifesting instead a very practical approach to life. Although motivation to fight the war against Rebels did not spring from a love of "*Liberty for all,*" true patriots "will rejoice that the destruction of chattel slavery in the United States, is an inseparable adjunct of the present upheaval of society.""Adjunct" was the crucial word for these men—though Hollister himself stood ardently against slavery on moral grounds—and set up the summary sentence. "We finally concluded," wrote Hollister with a swipe at slaveholders, "that because slavery is aggressive, if not because it is wrong, we must necessarily war against it."[58]

Chastising slaveholders through forced emancipation proved widely popular in the units covered by the regimentals. Lieutenant Bartholomew B. S. De Forest, quartermaster of the 81st New York Infantry, developed this theme. He hoped Rebel leaders would be punished severely in the aftermath of a war for "the preservation of our glorious Union." Black soldiers could help achieve that end, which would be complete only if slaveholders who "ruled with the iron hand of despotism" and "sought to perpetuate the institution of Slavery at the sacrifice of a Republican Government" had been utterly vanquished. Once Rebel armies had been dispersed and slavery abolished, "tyranny, that bitter foe of free institutions and humanity," would have been eradicated from American soil.[59]

Regimental historians reached disparate conclusions about black military contributions. Very few perceived USCT regiments as decisive in any major battles, though several expressed admiration for black courage in smaller actions. Almost all welcomed the labor of African American soldiers because it freed white men from the kinds of noncombatant work they detested. A handful endorsed full citizenship for black soldiers based on their military service, though several drew a sharp line between the idea of equality within the wartime military sphere and in postwar society. Prejudice pervaded nearly all of the regimentals—often providing a jarring contrast to even the most appreciative accounts.

The chroniclers of the 117th and 115th New York Infantry acknowledged superior performances by USCT units at Petersburg and Olustee. Surgeon James A. Mowris of the 117th described the costly action outside Petersburg on June 15, 1864, where USCT men made their initial appearance on a big Virginia battlefield. The "brave fellows" had carried the outer line of Rebel works and then assaulted and captured a second line: "These black soldiers, were highly elated, even those who were severely wounded, greeted their white compatriots, with, 'Tell you boys, we made um get;' 'We druv em.'" The episode impressed white observers, noted Mowris with a touch of sarcasm: "Those who were politically the most conservative, suddenly experienced, an accession of respect for the chattel on this discovery of its 'equal' value in a possible emergency." Lieutenant James H. Clark of the 115th, a regiment that suffered heavy casualties at the battle of Olustee, described how one of the USCT regiments in that engagement "formed and maneuvered under fire, and suffered heavy losses." Although their colonel was killed, the black soldiers "preserved their line admirably and fought splendidly."[60]

George W. Powers of the 38th Massachusetts Infantry typified those who found things to praise and criticize about black soldiers in combat. A veteran of operations in Louisiana and Virginia, he wrote in detail about two "native Louisiana regiments" in a skirmish on May 25, 1863, during the Port Hudson campaign. "A great deal of romance has been spoken and printed about this affair," Powers observed, "but, without wishing to detract in the least from the really valuable services rendered by the colored troops during the siege, especially in the engineer's department, it may be doubted if the exaggerated accounts of their bravery were of any real benefit to the 'colored boys in blue.'" Because it long had been fashionable "to decry the courage of the colored man, and deny him all the attributes of manhood, . . . when he proved himself something more than a beast of burden, public opinion went to the opposite extreme" and "asserted that this new freedman was the equal, if not the superior, of the Northern volunteer soldier." White soldiers even heard that General Banks said black soldiers "went where the white ones dared not go." Powers dismissed this as an improbable story that nonetheless "injured the general's popularity, and increased the prejudice already existing against the colored troops." On the night of May 26, Powers added in a short passage that twice damned African American comrades, a black regiment panicked and mistakenly fired a volley toward the 38th Massachusetts, but their aim was so bad "the bullets whistled harmlessly over head, and the panic soon subsided."[61]

In his history of the 9th New Jersey Infantry, Hermann Everts ignored emancipation in the broader sense but inserted one comment critical of black soldiers. The 9th spent a good deal of time in proximity to USCT units, including in the trenches at Petersburg in the summer of 1864. Everts used a record of daily events in preparing the regimental, which included an entry for July 10, 1864, that suggested USCT soldiers lacked basic knowledge expected of veterans: "With the exception of the picket-firing, the night passed quietly. The picket-firing, so annoying, and so very unnecessary in most cases, was generally done by the negroes, as these troops need the sound of cannon-balls around their heads and ears to keep their eyes open." Everts's observation accorded with other evidence from the first phase of the siege at Petersburg that suggested many white soldiers even doubted positive reports about the 54th Massachusetts in the assault at Fort Wagner—though some men changed their minds when they witnessed USCT troops overrun Rebel positions on June 15.[62]

Black soldiers also emerged as less than exemplary in Col. W. W. H. Davis's narrative of the 104th Pennsylvania Infantry. Davis discussed the difficulty many white soldiers experienced with the idea of black enlistments, remarking that it took "some time to educate them up to this point." Deployed to South Carolina in early 1863, the 104th saw Col. Thomas Wentworth Higginson's 1st South Carolina Infantry (Union), the initial regiment of former slaves officially sanctioned by the War Department. "These African defenders of our national honor were lounging about camp and shore," recalled Davis with more than a hint of condescension, "clad in their blue dress coats and scarlet breeches. Our men gazed at them with strange interest, as it was the first time they had ever seen negroes equipped as soldiers. This sight carried me back to an earlier period in the history of the war, when arming the negroes to make soldiers of them dared not be talked about aloud." Davis also described how Brig. Gen. William Birney, son of the famous abolitionist James Gillespie Birney, detailed six men from the 104th to cook for a group of contraband laborers. This happened when two black regiments were posted near where the work was to be done and, insisted Davis, arose from Birney's wish "to degrade the white soldiers and insult the regiment . . . Is it then a cause of wonder that he was heartily despised by the white troops?"[63]

The regimentals suggest that white soldiers reached no consensus about the postwar fate of USCT veterans and other freedpeople. Joseph Grecian, who wrote his history of the 83rd Indiana Infantry during the last part of the war, thought they should be educated "so as to be competent to take care and govern themselves. Meanwhile, they will be afforded means of accumulating a sufficient amount of wealth to take them to, and establish themselves in the Old World, from which they were brought, and thus they may become a 'polished shaft' in the hand of Providence to enlighten 'poor dark Africa.'" Lieutenant De Forest of the 81st New York printed a letter that affirmed USCT men "should be recognized as equal with the white soldier, when they are engaged in one common cause." Once a black soldier returned to civilian life, however, and "he lays off the blue jacket, he is a negro still, and should be treated as God designed he should be, as an inferior, with kindness and sympathy, but not as an equal, in a social point of view."[64]

Henry T. Johns, a clerk in the 49th Massachusetts Infantry, presented deeply conflicting ideas about what the war would yield for African Americans. He presented his history in the form of letters to render the text "less didactic and stiff," signing his preface in early May 1864. Johns enthusiastically supported the Emancipation Proclamation and the enlistment of black soldiers, and in early 1863 predicted "Negro equality" but not "social equality" after the war. Talented black men would rise on their merits. Later in his text he envisioned a much bleaker future for freedpeople because they belonged to an inferior race. "Like the Indians," he prophesied, "they will disappear from before us"—perhaps returning to Africa. Yet at the end of the book he gave "all honor to our negro soldiers. They deserve citizenship. They will secure it." There would be much suffering in what he termed "the transition state," but a "nation is not born without pangs."[65]

A handful of regimental historians took an entirely positive stance. Pennsylvanian John C. Myers especially implored northern readers not to fear the effects of emancipation. Aware of shrill predictions of an influx of freedpeople into the northern states, he predicted they would remain in the South, "where cotton will be grown by free labor." Although denied education, the black man was as well informed as "his late master . . . Almost all of them have the marks, the mind, the courage, and the intellect of the Caucassian stamped upon their features. Trust him. Stand by him and see that he has fair-play. That is all he needs, even at this early period, the infancy of his birth-day to freedom."[66]

Two seemingly contradictory themes run through almost all of the regimentals—sympathy for the plight of contrabands and pointed racism. Indeed, the two came together in many passages. Throughout the war, slaves supplied information about Rebel military forces, identified crucial roads, assisted prisoners who escaped from Confederate control, and worked in many capacities with Federal armies. All of these actions impressed soldiers and regimental historians. For example, Chaplain John W. Hanson of the 6th Massachusetts Infantry spoke of a "universal desire for freedom among the colored people" near Suffolk, Virginia, in late 1862. "Simple-minded, good-natured, patient, and possessed of a certain natural shrewdness," he continued, "we generally found them as intelligent as, and every way the equals, and in ability to take care of themselves the superiors of, the white people left in our neighborhood." African Americans provided excellent information about Confederate movements and "never betrayed trust." Falling back on a racist cliché, Hanson also stated that a "volume could be filled with reminiscences of our sooty attendants."[67]

George Powers of the 38th Massachusetts and Lyman B. Pierce of the 2nd Iowa Cavalry, writing about operations in Louisiana and Mississippi, remarked appreciatively about how slaves shared their meager supplies of food with the invading Union soldiers. The overall demeanor of the slaves, noted Pierce, "left no room to doubt their loyalty to our cause." Thomas W. Stevenson remembered "pathetic scenes" along the track of Sherman's March to the Sea, as thousands of contrabands, many of them carrying small children and personal possessions, begged to accompany the army. "They cannot be made to understand that they must be left behind," he wrote sadly, "and they are satisfied only when General Sherman tells them—as he does every day, that we shall come back for them some time, and that they must be patient until the proper hour of deliverance comes." The Federal soldiers killed bloodhounds and other dogs along the route to Savannah, according to Stevenson, "determined that no flying fugitives, white men or negroes, shall be followed by track-hounds that come within reach of their powder and ball."[68]

A. F. Sperry devoted a long passage to a black family in Arkansas who worked in the camps of the 33rd Iowa Infantry. The husband performed various odd jobs while his wife and their two grown daughters "offici-ated as washer-women for the regiment." All four were "quiet, sensible, industrious folks; and in a little while a mutual friendship between the regiment and 'Uncle Tony and Aunt Lucy,' was firmly established." Sperry created a picture of mutual respect within a framework that observed "differences of color and tastes." How the black people felt about the situation cannot be recovered, but the Iowan perceived that they "were treated as civilly as white folks would have been in the same circum-stances. If all negroes were like them, the social problem need never pres-ent a difficulty."[69]

Limitations of space prevent anything like a complete catalog of racist passages in the regimentals, but a few should suffice to convey the overall tenor. An Ohio artillerist commented about slaves near Clarksville, Ten-nessee, in the spring of 1862: "Occasionally, a group of 'wooley heads' could be seen, displaying their 'ivories,' and swinging their old hats." Wil-liam Grunert of the 129th Illinois Infantry, who wrote compassionately about contrabands in some parts of his regimental, gave a cruel descrip-tion of black observers at a parade of Sherman's Fifteenth Corps in Sa-vannah just before Christmas in 1864. "Only those that were eye wit-nesses can form a correct idea about the capers the darkies cut," he began. As the soldiers passed, "Like pillars the astonished darkies stood, some-times breaking out in a terrible laughter, such as only darkies can, sur-prised at the regular step of the men and the regularity of the endless column, . . . The music commences again, and like a flock of frightened sheep, the black crowd rushed after the music, dancing, hopping and slapping their hands."[70]

Evan M. Woodward, an adjutant in the 2nd Pennsylvania Reserves, found himself and the regiment in northern Virginia in April 1862. Many black people trailed the Union column, and one day what Woodward termed "an amusing scene" occurred. The regimental band began to play, whereupon "the negroes involuntarily broke forth into a dance, clapping their hands and singing." When the music stopped "a grand butting match took place, their heads crushing together like rocks, but producing no effect upon them." White soldiers threw some pennies into the crowd, which triggered a scramble—after which the black people "left for their homes, happy with their afternoon's sport."[71]

Like many other regimental historians, Lt. Solon W. Pierce of the 38th Wisconsin Infantry and W. H. Chamberlin of the 81st Ohio Infantry employed black dialect that they probably considered both humorous and appropriate for white readers. After Lee abandoned Petersburg on April 2, 1865, the 38th entered the city to the delight of a joyful African American population. "An old wench was descried across a common, hurrying toward us with all possible speed," stated Pierce, "shouting, 'Halleluyah! Glory to Jesus, de Linkum sogers am cum!'" She shook hands with numerous soldiers, "hopping and dancing with joy," and her "antics soon brought a crowd of 'Linkum sogers' around her, drawn there by her voluble and queer expressions." Shifting tone dramatically, Pierce closed on an empathetic note: "God grant that these poor, oppressed people may not have their hopes of freedom and happiness lost in the mazy labyrinths of 'Reconstruction.'" Chamberlin described slaves in northern Mississippi in the autumn of 1862. Unaware of Lincoln's proclamation, one of them informed the Union soldiers, "Massa tole us dat you all Yankees at Corinth would make we 'uns work on de big forts tell we died, an' den give us some beef on a cracker, an' throw in a hole alive an' bury us!" Why did he come to Union lines then, asked the Federals. "Oh, we knowed massa *lied!*" came the reply.[72]

General histories of the conflict published in 1865 and 1866 complement regimentals as sources regarding the importance of emancipation. The usual themes of Union, oppressive oligarchy (both European and slaveholding), and democratic self-government appeared prominently, but the authors also counted emancipation among the uplifting outcomes of the war. One book situated "restoration of the Union" at the center of the war but besought God to see that the "full fruition" of the conflict's "blessed fruit is realized by men of every name, color, and description in this broad land." Thomas P. Kettell employed the phrase "war against the American Union," celebrating "the unconquerable will of a free people" whose victory disappointed "the aristocratic governments of the Old World" and empowered all "struggling democracies." He also declared that "above all, perhaps, in the overthrow of the institution of slavery, the war furnished some compensating advantages."[73]

In his popular *Pictorial History of the Civil War in the United States of America,* Benson J. Lossing spoke first of Union before evaluating the importance of slavery's end. "The Republic has survived the strife within its bosom, and it now bears on," he observed with an eye toward the future, "in the great procession of nations, its precious burden of Free Institutions and Democratic Ideas, as nobly and vigorously as ever. The Union has been preserved, and its broad mantle of Love and Charity covers all its children with its ample folds." But emancipation figured prominently in his assessment of the war's meaning. Lincoln's proclamation, "considered in all its relations, was one of the most important public documents ever issued by the hand of man." Time would enhance the stature of the proclamation "as a consummation of the labors of the Fathers of the Republic, who declared the great truth, that '*all* men are created equal.'"[74]

Lossing's prose offered an image of Lincoln as the prime agent of liberation. That conception grew in the postwar years, enhanced by a martyrdom that could be applied both to the struggle for preservation of the Union and the effort to eradicate the stain of slavery. Thomas Ball's sculpture for the Freedmen's Memorial to Abraham Lincoln, funded by donations from free black people and dedicated in Washington, D.C.'s Lincoln Park in 1876, captured in bronze what would become widely accepted in American society. Ball's Lincoln towered over a semi-nude slave in the act of rising to his feet. Below the pair was the single word "EMANCIPATION." For most people who saw the sculpture, Lincoln bestowed and the passive African American man received the gift of freedom—something that distressed Frederick Douglass at the time and many others later. Over time, Lincoln the "Great Emancipator" eclipsed Lincoln the "Savior of the Union" in the national imagination. That fact not only obscured a great deal about the president's goals and actions during the war, but it also helped precipitate a debate about who was primarily responsible for emancipation. The debate heated up in the last quarter of the twentieth century among historians who analyzed the roles of Lincoln, the Congress, a few generals, and, most notably, the mass of enslaved people in the Confederacy. Often left out or consigned to the margins was the impact of the Union army as an agent of liberation—an omission that would have astonished soldiers and civilians of the wartime generation.[75]

Union general Benjamin F. Butler proclaimed in May 1861 that African Americans who reached Union military lines would be treated as "contraband of war" and not returned to Confederate control. "Contrabands" became an almost universally accepted term over the course of the war. This photograph, taken in May 1862 during George B. McClellan's Peninsula campaign, shows twenty-three black refugees near Cumberland Landing. (Library of Congress, Prints and Photographs Division, reproduction number LC DIG-cwpb-01005)

The illustrated press published a number of engravings of contrabands in various military theaters. In this example, a group of black men march to work at Fort Monroe. The accompanying text praised General Butler's actions but closed with a callous observation: "Doubtless the 'nigger band' have never had so pleasant an existence as under their new state of contraband existence." (*Frank Leslie's Illustrated Newspaper,* November 2, 1861)

William Morrison.   Robert Smalls.   A. Gradine.
John Smalls.

Most African Americans depicted in the illustrated weeklies were not identified. An exception was Robert Smalls, who gained modest fame for seizing the Confederate vessel *Planter* in Charleston harbor in April 1862. *Frank Leslie's* published small portraits of Smalls and three of his compatriots with the caption: "Heroes in Ebony— The Captors of the Rebel Steamer Planter, Robert Small, W. Morrison, A. Gradine, John Small." (*Frank Leslie's Illustrated Newspaper*, June 21, 1862)

Both *Harper's Weekly* and *Frank Leslie's* published demeaning cartoons relating to African Americans, though the frequency diminished as the conflict unfolded. One of the earliest, and cruelest, was "Dark Artillery; Or, How To Make the Contrabands Useful," which appeared in *Frank Leslie's* on October 26, 1861. (*Frank Leslie's Illustrated Newspaper,* October 26, 1861)

Harper's Weekly lampooned Democrats who opposed any use of African Americans to help win the war in "A Consistent Negrophobist." The cartoon, which appeared during a period of severe Union manpower shortages, depicts a drowning man refusing help proffered by a young African American he addresses as "you darned Nigger!" (*Harper's Weekly,* August 16, 1862)

Most loyal citizens accepted black military service—some more readily than others—as a factor that would help save the Union. Thousands of USCT troops fought in the battle of the Crater at Petersburg, Virginia, on July 30, 1864. This photograph shows black soldiers in the works at Petersburg eight days later. (Library of Congress, Prints and Photographs Division, reproduction number LC DIG-cwpb-01232)

Most black combat duty came at engagements of small or middling size, several of which were covered by the illustrated press. *Frank Leslie's* published this illustration of the 1st and 3rd Louisiana Native Guards in action at Port Hudson, Louisiana, on May 27, 1863. Maj. Gen. Nathanial P. Banks, the Union army commander, wrote in his report that "no troops could be more determined or more daring." (*Frank Leslie's Illustrated Newspaper,* June 27, 1863)

Atrocities against black soldiers received a great deal of attention in the loyal states. None inflamed public opinion more than Fort Pillow, where Confederates under Maj. Gen. Nathan Bedford Forrest killed a number of African American prisoners. *Harper's Weekly* published "The Massacre At Fort Pillow," a full-page engraving, eighteen days after the battle. (*Harper's Weekly,* April 30, 1864)

The illustrated press consistently covered African Americans serving with United States armies in noncombat roles. In "Pickets of the First Louisiana 'Native Guard' Guarding the New Orleans, Opelousas and Great Western Railroad," five black soldiers, four of them in relaxed poses, await arrival of an approaching train. (*Frank Leslie's Illustrated Newspaper,* March 7, 1863)

EXCITING SCENE IN THE HOUSE OF REPRESENTATIVES, JANUARY 31st, 1865, ON THE PASSAGE OF THE AMENDMENT TO THE CONSTITUTION ABOLISHING SLAVERY FOR EVER.

Both *Harper's Weekly* and *Frank Leslie's* supplied readers with large engravings of the scene in the House of Representatives when the 13th Amendment passed on January 31, 1865. *Leslie's* caught the sense of wild celebration on the floor and in the packed galleries. (*Frank Leslie's Illustrated Newspaper,* February 18, 1865)

A MAN KNOWS A MAN.

"Give me your hand, Comrade! We have each lost a Leg for the good cause; but, thank God, we never lost Heart."

In "A Man Knows A Man," *Harper's Weekly* presented maimed veterans, whether black or white, as equals in the struggle for "the good cause." (*Harper's Weekly,* April 22, 1865)

4

....

THE ARMIES

*A*braham Lincoln and Ulysses S. Grant stated the obvious
in attributing to armies of citizen-soldiers the salutary
outcomes of a vastly disruptive and costly war. The president's two most famous speeches affirmed the centrality of military campaigns to the conflict's core purposes. At Gettysburg, he reminded listeners that soldiers who engaged in fierce combat amid the surrounding
fields and hills had struggled with nothing less at stake than survival of
the Founders' representative government. The world, he predicted, "can
never forget what they did here." Just more than fifteen months later
in the Second Inaugural Address, Lincoln, well aware that most in the
large audience paid close attention to military affairs, invited them to
join him in gratitude for what the armies had accomplished. "The progress of our arms, upon which all else chiefly depends," he said, "is as well
known to the public as to myself; and it is, I trust, reasonably satisfactory
and encouraging to all." The "all else" included emancipation, to which
the president devoted some of the most quoted sections of his speech.
Grant's congratulatory General Orders No. 108, addressed to "Soldiers of
the Armies of the United States" on June 2, 1865, seconded Lincoln's

sentiments. "By your patriotic devotion to your country in the hour of danger and alarm—your magnificent fighting, bravery and endurance—," stated an admiring Grant, "you have maintained the supremacy of the Union and the Constitution, overthrown all armed opposition to the enforcement of the Law, and of the Proclamations forever Abolishing *Slavery,* the cause and pretext of the rebellion." Also like Lincoln, Grant expressed certainty that these achievements would be celebrated "in all time to come."[1]

Reaction to the Grand Review demonstrated how seriously the loyal public took the ideas expressed by Lincoln and Grant. The crowds in Washington on May 23–24, 1865, believed the soldiers embodied what was best about the American republic. They had saved the Union and ensured its future solvency by destroying slavery. Lacking the wealth and power conveyed by their slave property, a defanged southern aristocracy never again could rend the national fabric. Although triumphant on storied battlefields, Sherman's and Meade's veteran armies did not represent militarism poised to fuel nationalistic aggression but just the opposite— an aggregation of citizens who, in Grant's words, had manifested a "patriotic devotion" and would put aside martial trappings and return to peaceful pursuits. In a war beset by deep divisions in the loyal states, the army stood as a powerful national symbol and the largest and most important unifying institution, one that brought together men from all parts of the nation and both major political parties. Soldiers clad in their dark blue jackets and light blue trousers, unless in regimental formations with their state flags, could not be identified by region or political ideology but only as citizens under arms in the service of the Union cause.

The Union dead continued as a nationalizing force for many decades. They received unprecedented treatment by the federal government and the loyal citizenry. Nearly 300,000 of the 360,000 soldiers who perished in the war were reinterred in a new system of national cemeteries, many of them located on or adjacent to battlefields. Long rows of markers recalled the conflict's magnitude and served as a source of national unity for visitors, who periodically gathered at the sites to hear speeches and honor the slain men's service that had preserved the republic. Decoration Day, formally proclaimed by Illinois congressman and former general

John A. Logan in 1868 and later known as Memorial Day, promoted the "strewing with flowers or otherwise decorating the graves of comrades who died in defense of their country during the late rebellion." Logan, commander-in-chief of the Grand Army of the Republic, the preeminent organization of Union veterans, charged his comrades to "Let no neglect, no ravages of time, testify to the present or to the coming generations that we have forgotten as a people the cost of a free and undivided republic." By 1890, every northern state had designated Decoration Day as an official holiday. Monuments also soon graced countless town squares, local burying grounds, and battlefields, often topped by the figure of a common soldier and bearing texts that recalled the level of loss sustained by the Union armies.[2]

The centrality of what the armies accomplished and the resonance for those on the home front of their self-sacrificing example have been largely forgotten in recent publications about the conflict.[3] Two very different Civil Wars await readers seeking to understand our transforming national trial—both of which often do little to illuminate the relationship between military affairs on the one hand and the goal and meaning of Union and the process of emancipation on the other.

Popular historians have created a body of work overwhelmingly focused on armies and generals that routinely neglects, or ignores altogether, the larger political and social implications of military campaigns. They describe strategic maneuvering by generals seeking to place their opponent at risk. Once combat begins, officers and soldiers shed blood profligately for supremacy on previously insignificant bits of the American countryside. Union troops fall by the thousands in a small cornfield owned by farmer D. R. Miller close to Antietam Creek in Maryland, set a ghastly standard of slaughter near a backwoods Methodist church in Tennessee called Shiloh, and leave a harvest of bodies in a jumble of rocks named Devil's Den by local residents in southern Pennsylvania. Some of the most celebrated commanders in American military history dominate much of this Civil War. Ulysses S. Grant mounts a dazzling campaign against Vicksburg, reducing that Rebel stronghold overlooking the Mississippi River on July 4, 1863. Fourteen months after that pivotal event, William Tecumseh Sherman, who owes his success almost entirely to Grant's reassuring influence, delivers a powerful body blow to the Confederacy when he captures Atlanta. Hard on the heels of Sherman's success, Philip H. Sheridan rides to the battlefield at Cedar Creek to reverse an earlier tide of defeat and demoralization. Told and retold by every generation since the Confederate surrender in the spring of 1865, this Civil War—marked by honor and hubris, triumph and failure, and gallantry and perfidy on an epic scale—comes closer to serving as an American *Iliad* than any other element of our national past.[4]

The second of these two Civil Wars emanates, for the most part, from scholars in an academic setting. Here the focus is on the home fronts, on the ways in which the conflict affects, or does not affect, the daily rhythms of life on farms and in cities. Compelling political issues stand out sharply, such as how and when will emancipation be accomplished? And who should get credit for removing the stain of slavery? And does the Republican agenda anticipate the emergence, later in the century, of a capitalist behemoth en route to world-power status in the twentieth century? In this Civil War, anthracite coal miners in Pennsylvania's northeastern regions grow disenchanted with a government that seems to favor the wealthy, and the United States Sanitary Commission opens opportunities for some middle- and upper-class northern women to engage in public activity. Other women struggle to find their roles amid changing conceptions of what it means to be a patriotic mother, and politicians and the courts grapple with questions of loyalty, civil liberties, and belligerent property rights. This war offers a cacophonous jumble of advocates and victims, all of whom act out parts in a drama largely devoid of armies, battles, and generals. For readers drawn to a gripping narrative played out against the boom of cannons and the rattle of musketry, this is not the Civil War to fire the imagination or to evoke comparisons with Homer. Other readers, however, will find a slave's successful escape to freedom or a family's struggle amid the turbulence of war as powerfully moving as anything on the battlefield.[5]

Both strains of this literature obscure Lincoln's meaning when he declared that "all else" chiefly depended upon the armies. Neither elucidates how the two Civil Wars intersected and influenced one another. The root of the problem lies in the fact that far too many popular historians care for little beyond generals and soldiers on battlefields, while many academic historians nourish a dismissive attitude toward military history in general and Civil War campaign history in particular. The latter too often associate military history with militarism or write off interest in generals and armies as antiquarianism rather than serious scholarly endeavor.[6]

In testimony before Congress in 1990, for example, Deputy Executive Director James B. Gardner of the American Historical Association (AHA), the largest professional organization of its kind in the United States, spoke against any assumption of "special historical significance of Civil War battlefields." Giving such attention to battlefields, he insisted, would perpetuate "narrow, antiquated views of the past" rather than responding to "the challenging new topics and perspectives of contemporary scholarship" that interpreted the conflict as "a combat of societies" rather than "a struggle of armies." Gardner relied on an AHA volume titled *The New American History,* which includes the essay "Slavery, the Civil War, and Reconstruction" by Eric Foner that mentions military history only in passing. "Apart from works primarily military in orientation," it observes, "recent studies of the Civil War carry forward themes dominant in the new interpretation of antebellum history." Those themes include, among others, slavery and emancipation as central to understanding the war. The essay lacks any mention of what "works primarily military in orientation" might argue or reveal.[7]

Other instances of this approach to military history abound. In 1995, the *Harvard Gazette* ran a piece on a Civil War class being offered that summer. The professor stressed that he shunned military history. "Not a course in military history," he advised prospective students: "I make every effort to head off the would-be colonels who think the course is going to be a study of the battles. If you want to go up one hill and down the next, this course is not for you." Whoever wrote the article apparently found no irony in the fact that the professor was photographed in Harvard's Memorial Hall against a backdrop of names of graduates, including Robert Gould Shaw of the 54th Massachusetts Infantry, who had been killed or mortally wounded in action during the Civil War. The distinguished southern historian C. Vann Woodward almost certainly had academic colleagues in mind when he explained, as editor of the series in which the book appeared, why James M. McPherson's *Battle Cry of Freedom* had allocated a good deal of attention to military events. After quoting from McPherson's section on Antietam, Woodward observed, "[I]n the final reckoning, American lives lost in the Civil War exceed the total of those lost in all the other wars the country has fought added together, world wars included. Questions raised about the proportion of space devoted to military events of this period might be considered in the light of these facts."[8]

Apart from conveying a sense of massive human carnage, attention to military topics is absolutely necessary to grasp the larger meanings of the conflict. Engaging military events—how they were experienced by the troops, covered by the press, and understood by the public—illuminates critical issues such as how civilians identified soldiers and armies with the nation, how they praised certain commanders as exemplars of the republican ideal so important to the concept of Union, and how the armies accomplished what Lincoln and Grant attributed to their labors. Before developing some of those connections, it is crucial to reiterate that soldiers thought of their service as temporary and directed toward a clear goal. They were not professional warriors, as their West Point officers often observed and sometimes lamented, and Union armies cannot be put forward as evidence of an expanding, militaristic state. They fit comfortably within an American tradition of relying on citizens mobilized to meet a particular crisis with no expectation of long-term military service.[9]

A few basic numbers and testimony from soldiers at the time they mustered out illustrate the antimilitaristic nature of the armies that saved the Union and destroyed slavery. "When the Civil War ended in the spring of 1865," reckon the authors of the standard work on mobilization in American history, "the Union Army was the most powerful military force in the world, but its strength was soon dissipated in a rapid demobilization." On July 28, 1866, Congress passed legislation fixing the peacetime regular army at 54,302, a number reduced in 1869 to 37,313 and in 1876 to 27,472. During those years, soldiers carried out duties related to Reconstruction and conducted operations against Native Americans west of the Mississippi River. The regular army fluctuated between a low of 24,864 and a high of 28,953 between the end of Reconstruction and the outbreak of war with Spain in 1898. Apart from the small complement of regulars, the Union army on May 1, 1865, numbered 1,034,064 volunteers, 801,000 of whom mustered out by the end of November. One year later, just 11,043 of the volunteers remained in service. Secretary of War Stanton aptly said of the demobilization: "No similar work of like magnitude regarding its immensity and the small limit of time in which it has been performed, has . . . any parallel in the history of armies." France and Otto von Bismarck's recently unified Germany, both of which had smaller populations than the United States, offer a useful comparison. The Prussian army numbered almost 425,000 in 1880 and more than 600,000 in 1890, and the French army had an effective strength of approximately 550,000 in 1890.[10]

A picture of citizens in transition from temporary military duty to prior civilian pursuits emerges in evidence from the immediate aftermath of the war. Farewell addresses from officers often commented on this passage. Brevet Brigadier General Edward F. Winslow, one of Sherman's cavalry commanders, issued a representative order to his veterans on August 7, 1865. "Comrades: The war is ended," he began when reading his order to the assembled men in Atlanta, Georgia, "The last order you obey directs your return to your homes . . . Your career as soldiers is over. You go home as citizens, to reap the reward of your campaigns. Your country will always cherish the memory of her brave defenders." Winslow's final paragraph caught the essence of an army of citizen–soldiers. "I rejoice with you that our country is intact and united, our government stronger than ever," he remarked, "and that the necessity for our armed service no longer exists."[11]

Six soldiers wrote comments indicative of the larger body of testimony. Private John W. Haley of the 17th Maine Infantry enlisted in the summer of 1862 and fought throughout the war with the Army of the Potomac. On June 5, 1865, his brigade commander addressed the men of the 17th, offering "a glowing tribute for our good conduct" and expressing the wish that "we will make as good citizens as we have soldiers . . . In conclusion he said he hopes we will long live to enjoy the benefits of the government we risked so much to save." By June 8, the regiment had returned to Portland, where they received a warm reception from

"Virgins fair and matrons grave" who showered the men with flowers. Haley reached his hometown of Saco, a few miles southwest of Portland, the next day, experiencing strong emotions as he "neared the place I left nearly three years before." He thought about the dead and maimed from his regiment and hinted at his own psychological wounds, commenting that "*My* bruises are inward. It is all over now, and I can only regard it as a hideous dream—the smoking ruins, the sodden field, the trailing banner, the slaughtered thousands and wailing families, the roar of cannon, the Rebel yell and the Yankee hurrah have all passed away and we return again to peace." The formal mustering out occurred on June 10 in Portland, and the veterans, "a happy set of mortals," returned to Saco in the early hours of the following day. On June 19, Haley was working at the Saco Water Power Shop in the same job, in the same room, under the same boss as when he left for the army in August 1862.[12]

William Wiley of the 77th Illinois Infantry also entered the army in August 1862 but unlike Haley spent most of his active service in Louisiana and Mississippi. The 77th mustered out at Mobile, Alabama, on July 10, 1865. "This was a day that we had long looked forward to when we could feel that our work for which we had enlisted to do was done," wrote Wiley in a rather subdued entry in his diary, "and we could lay down our arms and return to our homes." The regiment had done its part "in atchieving a glorious victory in preserving and strengthening our institutions and restoring peace to our land and felt hapy in the thought of soon returning to our homes and friends from whom we had been separated for 3 long and weary years." The men arrived in Peoria, Illinois, on the morning of July 29 and promptly consumed "a sumptuous breakfast" prepared by "the ladies national Liegue." The flag presented to the regiment by Peoria's women in 1862 was returned, "badly soiled and torned riddled by shot and shell and stained with patriotic blood." Those marks of hard service, affirmed Wiley, "only added to its glory." After dinner that evening, "the old 77 Regiment disbanded each going their several ways to meet and greet their loved ones . . . and to take up civil life and it duties where they had laid it down three long years before." A farmer before the war, Wiley resumed that pursuit in Logan Township, west of Peoria.[13]

Surrenders of the principal rebel armies raised men's hopes of ending their service early. For most, the close of fighting signaled completion of their obligation as citizen-soldiers. Second Lieutenant Josiah H. Sturtevant of the 80th USCT requested permission on May 29, 1865, to leave the army. "Having nearly served the term for which I originally enlisted—viz. 3 years—the war being over, and not being desirous of making the profession of arms a business of life," Sturtevant urged a superior to accept his letter of resignation. A dozen officers in the regiment expressed support for his request. "You have felt it your duty," they wrote, "now that the armies of the rebellion are subdued, to resign your commission in our regiment, to attend the duties incumbent upon the husband and father." They would miss his company, "yet, when the immediate need of men is past with our country, we honor the man who flies to the society of his family."[14]

Iowan Charles O. Musser, of his state's 29th Infantry, was among the white troops deployed to Texas under Philip Sheridan in May and June 1865. By the middle of July, the twenty-three-year-old sergeant bridled at what he considered unfair treatment. Nearly all the regiments raised in the summer of 1862 except the 29th Iowa seemed to be mustering out. Only "a set of Ambitious villains—undermineing, Scheming officers," he sputtered, kept the 29th on duty. "We offered our services to our country to help put down the rebellion," Musser wrote home with reference to his conception of a citizen's military obligation, "that object has been accomplished, and our time is out, and we are no longer needed." The regiment soon boarded vessels for a journey to Iowa. Mustered out on August 10, Musser returned to his family's farm near Council Bluffs.[15]

William Garrigues Bentley's testimony demonstrates how soldiers shifted from a military to a civilian focus while still in uniform. A nineteen-year-old farm boy living fifty miles east of Cincinnati when war erupted, Bentley joined the 104th Ohio Infantry, campaigned with western armies, and finished the conflict under Sherman in North Carolina. In May 1865, he discussed his future in a letter to his mother. Expecting to be mustered out soon, he expressed an interest in working as a mechanic. "I was glad to hear from the boys that business is still flourishing in the old shop," he wrote, adding that he foresaw little "difficulty about getting into business after I get home." His uncle's shop was a possibility, but if nothing was open there other options likely would be available. The regiment left service on June 17, took a week to reach Cleveland, and was discharged on the 27th. Bentley entered the machinist's trade in Salem, Ohio. Forty-nine years later, his obituary described him as a "most highly respected citizen" whose life as a civilian matched "the three years during which, in Union blue he defended his country's integrity and honor."[16]

One last witness spoke to the bonds of military comradeship as well as the relationship between soldiers and civilians at the end of the war. John Bennitt, a surgeon with the 19th Michigan Infantry, wrestled with the idea of resigning before his regiment mustered out but, unlike Lieutenant Sturtevant, decided against it. He learned in mid-May 1865 that "all troops whose term of service would have expired before the first of October next are to be mustered out as soon as the proper muster-out papers can be made." As a surgeon, he could leave even earlier, he told his wife, and "I do not see it as my duty to remain any longer now that there is almost certainly prospect that hostilities will soon cease throughout the whole land." Yet he opted to stay, as honor dictated waiting until all of the 19th Michigan left service. When he did get home, he would "settle again to regular business." On June 13, he wrote his wife from Detroit, where the regiment, mustered out on the 9th, had received a "splendid reception, and feasted as sumptuously." The response from civilians during the trip to Detroit touched Bennitt, who savored the ties between loyal citizens and soldiers about to return to their peaceful lives. "I could not restrain tears," he confessed, "to see the real earnest warm hearted greeting given to the men who had borne the burden of the war—given by the people of our own state here, and all along the way." It suggested that "the people have some appreciation of the toils and dangers these men have endured for their country's sake."[17]

Although they show civilian appreciation of what their men in uniform had accomplished, comments such as Bennitt's should be considered alongside wartime grousing among soldiers who believed they sacrificed far more than those behind the lines. Present in all wars, this phenomenon has been examined by numerous scholars interested in common soldiers. Many men particularly resented Copperheads and others who manifested strong antiwar sentiment, often dismissing them as traitors equivalent to Rebels who had taken up arms against the Union. Two soldiers from Indiana and Minnesota serving in Louisiana evinced typical sentiments. Jake Hart, whose 93rd Indiana Infantry camped at Berwick on October 3, 1864, used one of Lincoln's best-known phrases in complaining about dissension on the home front. "We the people of the North could if we were all of one opinion suppress this rebellion in six months," he wrote, "but a house divided against its self can not stand . . . [I]f the North does not join in mass . . . we surely will fail in putting down this present rebellion but I hope there is not traitors enough to accomplish it. However I fear they are prolonging this war years." Harrison Washburn of the 1st Minnesota Light Artillery, at Lake Providence in February 1863, wondered if people were "suppressing the news" on the home front. "I should like to know what is going on in the North," he stated pointedly. He found it "strange that the people can not be more united in our cause for it is certainly a just cause."[18]

Arnold Yeckley, a member of the 126th New York Infantry writing from Union Mills, Virginia, reacted comparably to reports of growing antiwar sentiment in the spring of 1863. Peace would come only via "the bloody road to victory," he insisted, something "[e]very sensible & honest man knows" and only "a coward & a tory" would dispute. Admitting he had lost some of the enthusiasm that originally led him to enlist, Yeckley nonetheless drew a stark line between himself and civilians who spoke of brokering a peace with the Rebels. "I fail to see what attraction there is at home," he wrote bitterly, "in association with 'copperheads' & men (who can) but are too cowardly to aid in the suppression of the rebellion . . . I sometimes wish that I could be at home for a short time. I solemnly think that I would shoot some of these men who would be traitors if they are not cowards.[19]

People on the home front followed the activities of their citizen-soldiers very carefully throughout the war—something that might seem obvious but bears closer attention. Expectations about Union victory ebbed and flowed according to the armies' fortunes, which millions of people traced though accounts in the newspapers. Whatever else drew their attention each day, the loyal populace could not escape news from the battlefronts. During the course of the war, *Harper's Weekly* devoted all but a handful of its covers to military operations, commanders, or topics directly related to the war effort.[20] Editors from across the nation routinely provided coverage of all theaters, with emphasis on those where the largest armies operated or the most prominent operations were in progress. Moreover, years of sanguinary warfare scarcely eroded the public's appetite for news about military campaigns. Those on the home front grew weary of the war and wished for it to end (as did the soldiers), but they hungered for news and opinions about military affairs. Whatever their politics, editors and readers maintained steady support for soldiers and consistently described the armies as congregations of men at arms who carried the nation's hopes on their bayonets.

Reading through newspapers day by day reveals just how much the war dominated attention behind the lines. A close examination of a half-dozen dailies—the *Albany Evening Journal* (Republican), *Chicago Tribune* (Republican), *New York Herald* (Democratic), *New York Times* (Republican), *New York Tribune* (Republican), and *Philadelphia Daily Evening Bulletin* (Republican)—during the first six months of 1864 serves to make this point. These and other newspapers, often read aloud or passed around, carried news from the military front to a huge swath of the loyal population.

On April 15, for example, the principal field armies had not commenced their spring campaigns. Yet readers found a bountiful array of stories and reports about military topics. The *Philadelphia Daily Evening Bulletin* covered action in Alabama, Louisiana, Kentucky, North Carolina, Mississippi, Tennessee, and Arkansas—with details regarding Maj. Gen. Nathaniel P. Banks's Red River campaign in Louisiana and the Confederate massacre of black and white unionist soldiers at Fort Pillow garnering a good deal of space. In Chicago, the *Tribune* dealt with Fort Pillow and the Red River campaign as well as activity in Arkansas, Florida, and Virginia. The *New York Herald* printed a long account from Louisiana together with reports from Tennessee and Virginia. Horace Greeley's *New York Tribune* featured North Carolina, while Henry Raymond's *New York Times* included a piece on morale within the Army of the Potomac. Later in the spring, as Grant's operations in Virginia and Sherman's in Georgia got under way, the papers printed even more military news.

The editors frequently reminded readers—both in and out of uniform—that the nation appreciated what the armies were doing. As the time approached for the Army of the Potomac to break camp and engage Robert E. Lee's veterans for a third season of operations, the *New York Times* spoke of it as a national institution in which all Americans had a heavy emotional investment: "The interest and affection and prayers of the country begin once again to go out for our army. It has the love and admiration of the whole land." More than five weeks and 40,000 Union casualties later, the *Times* praised the army's rank and file as "the noblest soldiers in the world, fighting in a cause as noble." As for U. S. Grant, he had proved himself in the gruesome Overland campaign in every way worthy of the "martial ardor and self-sacrificing enthusiasm" of his citizen-soldiers. The Democratic *New York Herald* similarly tied together the Army of the Potomac, the Union, and the people. "The army goes forward strong in a just cause," stated the editor in early May, "in its own valor, in the skill of its leader, and in the confidence of the people."[21]

In the third week of May, with the relentless nature of the Overland campaign already apparent, the *Chicago Tribune* discussed Grant and his soldiers in pieces that captured how much depended on military actions. The president, the Congress, and the people eagerly awaited additional news from the front, remarked the editor, who also linked the price of gold to military events because the "antennae of Wall Street are extended out over the field in Virginia, feeling, testing, and touching every point in the situation." All depended on Grant's operations, while "the nation behind him, whose destinies he is shaping under Providence," too often did no more than "gape, eager for more news; believe in Grant; make buncombe speeches; pass buncombe resolutions, and keep close watch of prices current to the end that they may get gain." The army, in contrast, manifested "patriotic inspiration" and if asked to perish in the nation's "agonizing struggle, it would . . . ask to be turned where it might 'die with its face toward the enemy.'" The *Tribune* mentioned horrific losses in the campaign, including one Michigan regiment reduced to seventeen able-bodied men, connecting them directly to the cause of Union. Be-

cause of the soldiers' heroism and sacrifice, "a rescued country will treasure up gratitude for the Army of the Potomac."[22]

Editors often identified Union armies with the entire country, as an
armed projection of the nation's determination to crush the slaveholders'
rebellion. Before Grant launched the Overland campaign, the *New York
Herald* described how great a burden Union soldiers would bear in the
next round of fighting. "Our own institutions, the integrity of the 'great
republic,' whose requiem has been already chanted in monarchical Europe," announced the paper, "and even the question of the ability of an
intelligent people to govern themselves, are at stake on the great battle
that is soon to be fought in Virginia." Heavy fighting at the Wilderness
on May 5–6—the initial clash of the Overland campaign—inspired a
good deal of such analysis. The *New York Times* ran a piece titled "The
Nation's Triumph" casting the Army of the Potomac—"More gallant
soldiers, the world never saw"—as a vital national institution. The *Philadelphia Evening Bulletin* marveled that soldiers remained undaunted despite "fearful fatigue and exposure." "Their countrymen look to them as
the saviors of the nation," added the editors, knowledge of which helped
the men sustain "their *morale* in all this fearful struggle."[23]

These articles in 1864 regarding the army as a national institution
continued a leitmotif that extended back to the beginning of the conflict. In early November 1861, for example, *Frank Leslie's Illustrated Newspaper* ran a piece titled "The National Army" that "estimated, from reli-
able data, that the National troops now in the field, or on their way to
the seat of war, number 512,000." A table gave totals for enlistments from
all the free states, the border slave states, and the District of Columbia,
and the editor observed, "We ought soon to see some result commensu-
rate to this grand armament." *Harper's Weekly* published a large woodcut
in April 1862, titled "The Great Uprising of the North," that showed a
mass of men rallying to the cause under various state flags. Artist Charles
Parsons explained the scene: "The hardy sons of New England swarm
over the hills, joining their brothers of the Middle States—swelling, as
they meet, the mighty current setting in from the far-off States of the
Pacific and glorious West—bearing aloft in irrepressible might the Stars
and Stripes in defense of Liberty and Union!" Robert Gould Shaw, then

a member of the 7th New York State Militia, created a similar image in prose for his mother on April 18, 1861. "The Massachusetts men passed through N. York this morning," he wrote from Staten Island just before leaving for Washington, "Won't it be grand to meet the men from all the States, East and West, down there, ready to fight for the country, as the old fellows did in the Revolution?"[24]

The loyal population increasingly identified U. S. Grant—who commanded all the armies of citizen-soldiers after March 1864—with the nation as well, looking to him, more than to anyone else, to produce results on the battlefield sure to guarantee the viability of the American republic. Grant's fellow citizens saw him as "a true hero," observes a study of the general's stature in the nineteenth century, "celebrated for his strength, his resolve, and his ability to overcome severe obstacles, banishing the possibility of failure." His path to preeminence began in the Western Theater, where victories in early 1862 at Fort Donelson and Shiloh, in July 1863 at Vicksburg, and in late 1863 at Chattanooga solidified his reputation as the nation's best military leader. Congress paid the republic's ultimate compliment for a soldier when it reinstated the rank of lieutenant general, held previously only by George Washington, and conferred it on Grant in the aftermath of his success at Chattanooga.[25]

At first wary of a military hero who might hold presidential aspirations, Lincoln supported the congressional action when assured that Grant, in the general's own words, wanted no part of "politics either as an aspirant for office or as a partizan." In early March 1864, Grant journeyed to Washington, where he met Lincoln for the first time, received his commission as lieutenant general, and took up duties as general in chief of all United States armies. Lincoln told Grant in presenting the commission that it represented the "nation's appreciation of what you have done and its reliance upon you for what remains to do in the existing great struggle . . . I scarcely need to add that with what I here speak for the nation goes my own hearty personal concurrence."[26]

The nation's appreciation rested not only on Grant's celebrated victories but also on a widespread belief that he personified the best of American virtues. An Iowan who saw Grant at Vicksburg mentioned his unassuming character, which appealed to both soldiers and civilians. "Gen

Grant has passed around the lines several times," Benjamin F. McIntyre wrote in his diary on June 28, 1863, "but in his old white hat and unpretending appearance we seem to forget such a man could be the very man we love to honor & he passed by seemingly indifferent to things around him and scarcely observed by us." Unlike the aristocratic Lee, whose gifts as a commander most loyal newspapers and soldiers grudgingly acknowledged, Grant represented the mass of persevering northern citizens. In a piece titled "Grant and Lee," the *Chicago Tribune* spoke to Grant's unswerving strength as a feature of the larger Union cause: "He understands Northern character, and reposes entire confidence in the pluck and endurance of his soldiers." Possessing "cold, imperturbable tenacity," Grant would "adhere to a grip with the vigor of a mastiff. It is Grant's lion heart that wins. Lee is a valiant man; but his courage is not perfectly awful like that of his opponent." The *New York Herald* pegged Grant's "characteristic of staunchness" as identical to that of Union soldiers. He was of "the same caliber as his troops—an imperturbable Northern man." Turning to a poetic fragment, the paper asserted that soldiers, had they known the exact qualities of all their commanders, would have chosen Grant:

> For choice, being the mutual act of all our souls,
> Makes merit her election, and doth boil
> As 'twere from forth us all a man distilled
> Out of our virtue.[27]

Another newspaper highlighted Grant's refusal to seek praise for his accomplishments. Under the headline "Honors To Grant," it described him as "truly modest, as are all great men, and despises the flunkeyism that tries to crowd honors on a military man before he has finished the work assigned to him." Published on June 7, 1864, this piece stressed that Grant and the loyal population shared crucial characteristics. The "sound, steady, practical common sense of the Americans" showed in their failure to rejoice before Grant delivered the knockout blow—and his belief that the government and people had showered him with more praise than he deserved demonstrated the degree to which he mirrored their attitude. As it stood, with the armies nearly at the end of the Overland campaign, the relationship between the loyal population and their general in chief was evident: "No one is more beloved by them than he is."[28]

The *New York Tribune* summarized the many ways in which Grant suited the loyal citizenry's ideal of a soldier. Blessed with the "genius of common sense," he also possessed the "power and determination to get ahead." Perhaps most important in a republic at war, no lurking ambition for political power motivated him. "Grant has thus far worked for the good of the country," observed the author, and each "battle has been for it without ulterior view. If God sends honest fame as the reward, he does not disdain it; but it must be a sequel, not an aim."[29]

Because Grant had no partisan political identity, Democrats and Republicans could support him with equal enthusiasm. Boosters for both parties saw in him a future presidential candidate—though the Copperhead wing of the Democratic Party, with its increasing call for an armistice short of victory, harbored many critics who considered Grant too willing to sacrifice his soldiers. Yet the breadth of Grant's appeal was enormous. On July 25, 1863, Senator Henry Wilson of Massachusetts, a Republican and ardent abolitionist, approvingly quoted Charles A. Dana's evaluation of Grant. Sent to observe Grant at Vicksburg by Secretary of War Edwin M. Stanton, Dana had found much to praise. "He tells me that Grant is modest, true, firm, honest and full of capacity for war," noted Wilson, who especially liked that Grant "is in favor of destroying the cause of this civil war—of overthrowing Slavery and that his army is deeply imbued with the same feeling. I am glad to hear from so good a judge such an account of Grant and his noble army." Seven and a half months later, the Democratic *New York Herald* cheered the elevation of Grant to the post of general in chief. "General Grant in Washington represents the people and the people's policy," insisted the *Herald,* and "represents that policy which looks to the downright and earnest prosecution of the war as the only means to restore peace and save the country from the absolute ruin that faction and debt are likely to bring upon it." He would counter, thought the editor, "the virulent and unscrupulous" Radical Republicans and "the incompetency of the President."[30]

Unlike George B. McClellan, an undeniably talented soldier who habitually crossed the line between politics and military affairs, Grant accepted that he must always defer to civilian superiors. He thus stood steadfastly in the tradition of George Washington, something his fellow citizens recognized and applauded. *Frank Leslie's Illustrated Newspaper* sounded this theme in March 1864: "Gen. Grant is the only man, except Gen. Washington, who has been honored with the full rank of Lieut.-General in the United States . . . We have now one responsible military head to which the people can look for the guidance of our armies, and he is worthy of the trust." At about the same time, the *New York Herald* compared Grant favorably to Caesar, Napoleon, and Oliver Cromwell, suggesting that "he may equal the achievements of those three men and keep within the constitution. He may do all the good that they did and none of the harm." No one conversant with Grant's record, stated the *Herald* in language sure to please all who believed in civilian supremacy over the military in their republic, "could for a moment suppose General Grant capable of any interference with the liberties of the country." Two months later, after the first ten days of the gruesome Overland campaign, the *Herald* placed Grant above selfish politics. The people knew only that "he has saved the nation, and that is enough to know. Having saved it, he is not likely ever to betray it . . . His politics—they are the constitution and the Union." Should Grant ever run for president, the *Herald* expected "his election to be as unanimous as that of General Washington and as beneficial to the welfare of the republic."[31]

Grant's popularity certainly exceeded that of Lincoln as the war entered its final months. Although the assassination would affect Lincoln's reputation in profound ways, it did nothing to diminish Grant as a towering figure whose military stewardship proved essential to saving the Union. The loyal citizenry bonded with their general in chief, sad about the cruel casualties in the Overland campaign but trustful of his ability to crush the rebellion by implementing a strategic blueprint that involved not only the operations at Petersburg and Richmond but also those of Sherman and Sheridan in Georgia, the Carolinas, and the Shenandoah Valley.[32] Some in the United States believed Grant had wasted too many lives during the Overland campaign—a few likened him to a butcher. But the idea that Grant became widely known across much of the North as a callous officer unconcerned about casualties, which has made its way into much of the literature on the Civil War, does not hold up under close scrutiny. The peace movement gained support as casualty lists grew exponentially during the first seven months of 1864; however, victories in Georgia and the Shenandoah Valley undercut many of the arguments put forward by opponents of the war.[33]

Four quotations typify three categories of responses to Grant's generalship. Colonel Robert McAllister of the 11th New Jersey Infantry captured the attitude of the large majority—civilians, soldiers, and newspaper editors—who supported Grant despite heavy casualties in the Overland campaign. "This country is one vast graveyard—graves everywhere, marking the track of the army on the march and in battles," McAllister wrote three days after thousands of Union soldiers had fallen in failed assaults at the battle of Cold Harbor, "There have been many of our officers and men lost by so many charges . . . Notwithstanding this, we will have to charge sometimes. I am well satisfied that Genl. Grant understands his business and will eventually succeed. Everyone has confidence in him." The wife of a prominent Democratic judge in New York City took a similar stance. "Grant's success has been certain but slow," Maria Lydig Daly confided to her diary on June 8, 1864, "the enemy has been fighting every inch of the way . . . We have lost some of our best generals—[Brig. Gen. James S.] Wadsworth, [Maj. Gen. John] Sedgwick, [Brig. Gen. James Clay] Rice, and thousands of heroes whose names are known but to their sorrowing families. Our nationality will be born anew in blood and tears, but we trust it will rise purified and ennobled."[34]

Frank Wilkeson, an artillerist in the 11th New York Battery, discussed how Grant stood in the estimation of soldiers in the Army of the Potomac. His blunt thoughts underscored that Grant never completely won the hearts of the men in the ranks. Most of them greatly respected him and, more important, believed he would fashion a final victory, but he never matched George B. McClellan's charismatic hold on the troops. Similarly, Grant's western soldiers had withheld the kind of blind devotion they directed toward Sherman during the campaigns of 1864–1865. Although Wilkeson did not mention it, the fact that soldiers never bestowed on Grant an affectionate nickname—such as "Little Mac" for McClellan or "Uncle Billy" for Sherman—told a great deal. McClellan had been more beloved, yet veterans knew Grant was made of sterner stuff, and "the general opinion among them was; given Grant in command of the army in 1862, and the rebellion would have been crushed that year." The enlisted men "who put down the slaveholders' rebellion," concluded Wilkeson in a bit harsher estimate than many comrades would have rendered, "felt and talked and lived in hopes long deferred and never fulfilled, of the coming of a great commander whose military talent would command our unqualified respect. He never came."[35]

C. Chauncey Burr, who edited *The Old Guard, A Monthly Journal Devoted to the Principles of 1776 and 1787,* assailed Grant on behalf of the embittered Copperhead wing of the Democratic Party. "What is the difference between a *butcher* and a *general?*" he asked provocatively during the blood-soaked summer of 1864. His answer savaged both Grant and Lincoln: "A butcher kills animals for food. A general kills men to gratify the ambition or malice of politicians and scoundrels. To the eye of sense and religion the profession of the butcher is far more respectable than that of a general." With the presidential election approaching in August, Burr described a failed war effort. The army had lost confidence in Grant, he said, quoting an unnamed officer wounded "in one of the last of Grant's disastrous defeats" who complained of "the useless and horrible waste of life." Feigning pity for Grant, "the most unfortunate and the most to be pitied" of all Union generals, Burr prophesied: "Curses will follow his head to his grave . . . Never more can he go into a town or village in the whole North where his name will not excite horror in the breasts of numberless widows and orphans. He is the death's head of a whole people."[36]

Burr's prediction of a thoroughly discredited Grant missed the mark spectacularly. Just after Appomattox, *Harper's Weekly* caught the nation's temper in a tribute headed simply "GRANT." The Overland campaign had broken Lee's army, something Grant understood to be necessary, no matter the horrific casualties, if the Union were to triumph. "The whole career of Lieutenant-General Grant," read the piece, "shows the most profound comprehension of the rebellion, and the most absolute mastery of the means necessary to suppress it. An earnest, faithful, silent man, he understood both the spirit and the resources of the enemy. Conse-

quently he struck heavily at both." Timid and traitorous critics had called
Grant a butcher, but he "knew that to reduce the rebellion it was necessary to kill men and destroy provisions." Celebrating Grant's personal
reserve and modesty, *Harper's* ventured its own prediction: "The country
pays now, and will forever pay, the homage of its unqualified gratitude
to his genius and his spotless character." The article exuded a feeling of
republican triumph, highlighting virtuous leadership that had preserved
the Union and praising a free citizenry and its two principal heroes: "It is
not the least of 'the crowning mercies' of these days that our political and
military chiefs are men upon whose simple, earnest, unselfish devotion
to their country no taint of suspicion was ever breathed; and our children will be forever grateful that our national salvation was achieved by
the people under two such leaders as ABRAHAM LINCOLN and ULYSSES S.
GRANT."[37]

   Grant remained a powerful symbol of national affirmation throughout
the rest of the nineteenth century and into the twentieth, his central
role in saving the Union unaffected by the political scandals that swirled
around his presidency. Armies under his leadership had extinguished
Confederate military resistance and removed slavery as a future disruptive force, after which Grant welcomed the defeated white South back
into a nation whose citizens enjoyed more economic and political opportunity than any others in the western world. "Let us have peace,"
he wrote in accepting the Republican presidential nomination in
1868—peace based on the democratic, free-labor model of the North. A
medallion struck in 1870 grouped busts of Grant, Lincoln, and Washington side by side as "Defender, Martyr, Father"—a telling indication of
Grant's place in the American pantheon. In a marketplace "shaped by the
demands of Northern nationalism," observe the leading students of the
Union image in popular prints, "Ulysses S. Grant reigned supreme," ex-
celling even the martyred Lincoln. His funeral in New York City in 1885,
the largest in American history, attracted more than a million and a
half spectators, and another million turned out for the dedication of his
monument and tomb on Riverside Drive twelve years later. Obituar-
ies, remarks Joan Waugh in her analysis of Grant's death and funeral,
"linked Grant's idealized individual characteristics with the traits that ev-

ery American might possess—simplicity, honesty, and devotion to democracy."[38]

The nation preeminently remembered him as the century's greatest
warrior, whose citizen-soldiers had placed all Americans forever in their
debt. One funeral broadside, perhaps with an echo of *The Battle-Cry of
Freedom* in mind, printed Grant's portrait under "The Union For Ever,"
with smaller engravings of Sherman and Sheridan in the top left and
right corners. The veterans of a G.A.R. post in Tacoma, Washington, issued a touchingly warm statement after his death. The fame of the Union
army and its volunteer soldiers had "become the wonder and admiration
of the world" due largely to Grant. "In the interests of human freedom
and perpetuation of our glorious union," stated members of Custer Post
No. 6, "his memory will remain with us, fragrant, bright and dear forever; and his name be engraved upon our hearts as the greatest, grandest
hero the world ever saw." Walt Whitman offered his own tribute in a
stanza from "As One by One Withdraw the Lofty Actors," first published
in *Harper's Weekly* on May 16, 1885:

> Man of the mighty days—and equal to the days!
> Thou from the prairies!—tangled and many-
> vein'd and hard has been thy part,
> To admiration has it been enacted![39]

Considering the ubiquity of pertinent evidence, it is quite remarkable that neither the Union army nor Grant has gotten much sustained
attention in scholarship on wartime national sentiment. Two British historians briefly address the subject. In a perceptive survey of the conflict,
Peter Parish labels the Union army "one of the most potent agencies of
American nationalism; it was, apart from anything else, by far the largest
national organisation which the United States had ever seen." The survivors took home a more expansive view of the nation, while the Union
dead contributed "that stock of heroes and memories which a sense of
nationality demands." Susan-Mary Grant's study of antebellum northern
nationalism also acknowledges the importance of the armies. Communi-
cations between the battlefront and the home front contributed to a collective sense of nation. Moreover, soldiers often fought "alongside men

from different units and other states," an experience that "intensified and made solid a nationalist perspective that many of them had in theory but, until the war, few had experienced in practice." As for General Grant, his image during and after the war provided easily the best indication of how he fit into popular conceptions of Union and nation.[40]

In a recent book-length treatment of wartime northern nationalism, Melinda Lawson selects six agents of "transcendent nationalism"— each indisputably important but none from the military sphere. Lawson discusses women who organized Sanitary Fairs (exhibitions sponsored by the United States Sanitary Commission that raised money to support Union soldiers), Philadelphia financier Jay Cooke and his bond drives, party battles between Republicans and Democrats, urban Union Leagues that pursued various projects to further the war effort, abolitionist orators such as Frederick Douglass and Anna Dickinson, and Abraham Lincoln's public statements. The book gives a nod to soldiers as one of several "'agents' without conscious nation-building agendas" who also "lent their voices to the construction of national identity," conceding that "battlefield activities regularly informed wartime patriotism." Yet military operations, easily the most dominant subject of interest on the home front, are virtually invisible in the text.[41]

The best example of slighting the importance of military factors relates to the process of emancipation. As both Lincoln and Grant observed, the armies largely determined how and where freedom arrived in the Confederacy. What the president and his general in chief realized also should be apparent in the early twenty-first century—namely, that among contributory elements including Lincoln's Emancipation Proclamation, congressional legislation, and the actions of hundreds of thousands of African Americans in Rebel states, the impact of United States military forces stood out as absolutely essential.

People at the time recognized the correlation between the arrival of Union military forces and the opportunity for slaves to escape from bondage. A few examples—including several from soldiers serving in the Eastern, Western, Trans-Mississippi, and Atlantic Seaboard Theaters— confirm this awareness. On May 4, 1861, nearly three weeks before Benjamin F. Butler first employed the term "contraband of war" at Fort Monroe, *Harper's Weekly* addressed the topic in prescient fashion. "The

Government troops will not march into the Southern States under an Abolition banner," the illustrated newspaper observed. "But if the South expect that our gallant volunteers are going to hunt the slaves who may run away as they approach, they labor under a delusion . . . Wherever the United States Army goes, local, municipal, and State laws will be superseded by martial law; and the Fugitive Slave Act is not to be found in the Army Regulations. Whatever may be the intentions of the Government, the practical effect of a war in the Southern States, waged by Northern against Southern men, must be to liberate the slaves. This should be well understood."[42]

A soldier in Company B of the 3rd New Hampshire Infantry anticipated Lincoln's proclamation by several months. Edward F. Hall and his comrades reached Hilton Head, South Carolina, in the spring of 1862, where they had considerable contact with African Americans. He observed that "what to do with the Negro is the chief trouble in the war policy," mentioning various proposals put forward by politicians, Lincoln, and others. The president seemed undecided, but "some are for making a clean sweep of Slavery—as far as our army can penetrate—and issue proclamations, declaring all Slaves free, as an inducement for them to escape from their masters." Hall took a stance adopted by large numbers of Union soldiers. "Now I don't believe in 'Abolition' but in the progress of the war," he informed members of his family, "as our army penetrates the Southern country—of course we shall find a great many Negros who have been left behind by their masters—and many more who have run away from their owners," all of whom could be put to work at various tasks the white soldiers loathed. The key, as Hall mentioned twice, lay in the ability of Union forces to move ever deeper into the Confederacy.[43]

Robert Gould Shaw, while a captain in the 2nd Massachusetts Infantry, wrote to his mother on September 25, 1862. Antietam lay just eight days in the past, and news of Lincoln's preliminary proclamation of September 22 had made its way to the home front and the Army of the Potomac. "So the 'Proclamation of Emancipation' has come at last, or rather, its forerunner," Shaw began. "I suppose you are all very much excited about it. For my part, I can't see what *practical* good it can do now. Wherever our army has been, there remain no slaves, and the Proclamation will not free them where we don't go." Ten days later, in response to a somewhat pointed reply from his abolitionist mother, Shaw sought to mollify her without backing off his original point. "Don't imagine, from what I said in my last," he began on a note of accommodation, "that I thought Mr. Lincoln's 'Emancipation Proclamation' not right; as an act of justice, and to have real effect, it ought to have been done long ago . . . but still, as a *war-measure,* I don't see the immediate benefit of it, . . . as the slaves are *sure* of being free at any rate, with or without an Emancipation Act."[44]

A self-described conservative Democrat in the 32nd Missouri Infantry, Josiah Bradford suggested to his wife in late December 1863 that political debates about emancipation served no purpose because the armies had decided the issue. "I believe that slavery is already dead and buried," he wrote, "and what is the use of keeping so mutch nuse about it." He cherished the right to vote as he pleased: "That is what I am fighting for but the radicals are wanting to grow verry popular over the death of slavery." Insisting he was not a Copperhead, Bradford said he had "proaved my loyalty in half a dozen battles and I think if some of them strong radicals would proave theirs the same way I would have better faith in them."[45]

The 85th New York Infantry campaigned along the North Carolina coast in the winter of 1863, advancing inland near Lake Mattamuskeet on December 12. Private Charles Mosher recorded an encounter with the slaves on a local judge's plantation. "We were the first yankey soldiers that had been seen in these parts," he stated, and a group of old men, women, and small children—the "able bodied ones had gone up the country to work" for the Rebels—welcomed them enthusiastically with shouts of "Glory Hallelujah" and "Bless the Lord my foks hab come." The Federals joined in the shouting, pleased to be seen as heroes. "Those old colored people had it in their minds that they were to be free some time," continued Mosher, "and the northern men were to free them. They were right." The 85th's colonel told them to pack their belongings and accompany the regiment back to a waiting vessel while Union patrols searched the area. By the end of the day, estimated Mosher, 250 African Americans had boarded a ship that would take them to Plymouth Island.[46]

A member of the 90th New York Infantry reported on a much larger operation in Louisiana during June 1863. Writing to the editor of the *New York Sunday Mercury,* this soldier gave details of how his regiment helped "to convoy a train of contrabands" to Union lines at Port Hudson. Initially almost four miles long, the column grew as "every few miles, teams of all descriptions fell in, so that, by the time we reached our destination, our procession of 'person of African descent' stretched out over seven miles, from front to rear." Along the way, when a Confederate force approached, the Federals engaged in a forced march. "We might have waited for and fought them," explained the correspondent, "but the immense train to our charge, consisting of nearly 3,000 men, women, and children, with a large drove of horses and mules, could not be risked, the object of the attack being mainly to recover them." A night march took the column to within a few miles of its destination, and the "mission was as good as accomplished."[47]

The words of some Illinois soldiers in 1864 typify a huge number of Union men describing the same phenomenon across the entire Confederate landscape. A member of the 129th Illinois Infantry devoted a good deal of attention to contrabands during the March to the Sea. For example, on November 17 he noted: "Negroes, both male and female, came to us to-day in masses, having heard near and far of our arrival . . . At 1 o'clock we reached the beautiful town of Madison, where the blacks welcomed us most kindly and sincerely . . . saying 'God bless the Yankees,' and swearing that this was the happiest day of their life." Another veteran of the March to the Sea wrote on December 1, 1864, that his "brigade is in the rear of the column, and we are therefore in close proximity to the contrabands who follow us. When we halt they continue on, in order to be more surely protected by our arms. A squad of six women, ten or twelve children and one man has just passed." A soldier in the 9th Illinois Infantry, writing of what he termed a "four-day scouting expedition near Florence, Alabama, in January 1864," said the regiment "brought in about 500 negroes, men, women and children." In the region overall, "large numbers of negroes came in."[48]

Confederates well understood how the arrival of Union forces promoted emancipation. The appearance of George B. McClellan's Army of the Potomac on the Virginia Peninsula in April and May 1862 disrupted old social patterns in the counties between Fort Monroe and Richmond. The *Richmond Enquirer,* in language repeated endlessly throughout the war in Confederate accounts, commented about how African Americans responded to the Federal forces: "They have not proven as faithful as we expected," the paper noted with some surprise, even those "who have been tenderly treated by kind mistresses have heartlessly deserted them to follow after strangers." Ardent southern rights advocate Edmund Ruffin, who lived near Richmond, recorded the movement of slaves from local plantations and farms to the Union army. His diary entry for June 18, 1862, mentioned that two planters north of the Pamunkey River "have lost all their slaves, except a very few very old—& two others nearly all. They there escape by land, to McClellan's camps in New Kent . . . I think it not unlikely that every negro now remaining will follow, if the Yankee vessels & troops continue in possession of the adjacent water & land."[49]

Public sentiment in the Confederacy regarding proposals to arm slaves in late 1864 and early 1865 is instructive. Where slavery was not under threat from Union armies—as in Texas—slaveholders saw no reason to consider the proposal seriously. Where Union armies represented a direct threat—as in Virginia—the proposal found far more support. Sending some slaves into Confederate military service to hold back the Union's martial tide, believed many Rebels including Robert E. Lee, would make it possible to stabilize their slaveholding society in the long run.[50]

A Union army's withdrawal, as much as its forward movements, could affect emancipation. Confederate military forces often took away freedom their opponents had made possible, something evident during the 1862 Maryland campaign. Just before the battle of Antietam, Maj. Gen. Thomas J. "Stonewall" Jackson's Rebel divisions captured Harpers Ferry, where hundreds of contrabands had gathered under the safety of 12,000 Union soldiers. Many Confederates noted approvingly that Jackson's force had recovered escaped slaves as well as making prisoners of the Federal garrison. Amanda Virginia Edmonds, a diarist who lived near Paris, Virginia, cheerfully reported on September 16, "quite a victory at Harper's Ferry yesterday—several thousand taken prisoner and several hundred contrabands." Another woman, who had lived under Union occupation in Fairfax County, Virginia, for a significant part of the war, seemed to derive special comfort from Jackson's seizure of large numbers of runaway slaves. "We have just heard of the recapture by the Confederates of Harper's ferry," wrote Anne S. Frobel on September 17, "with 12000 yankees, and immense quantities of ordnance, ammunition, commissary stores and a large number of Contrabands, which in yankee parlance means negro."[51]

The number of African Americans from each of the Confederate states who served in the USCT underscores the Union army's role in shaping the geography of emancipation. Federal soldiers exercised the greatest control for the longest time along stretches of the upper and lower Mississippi River and in parts of West and Middle Tennessee, while also seizing stretches of the Atlantic coast between Norfolk and the Sea Islands off South Carolina, the area around Washington, D.C., western Virginia (what became the new state of West Virginia in 1863), and the lower James River. Most black men in Federal service from Confederate states came from those bordering the Mississippi River. Louisiana sent 24,052, which constituted 31 percent of that state's black men between the ages of 18 and 45; Tennessee sent 20,133 (39 percent); and Mississippi 17,869 (21 percent). Arkansas, another state bordering the Mississippi, contributed 5,526 black men, 24 percent of its overall number.

No other Confederate state sent even 10 percent of its military-age African American men. Texas, which experienced almost no Union incursions, contributed 47 enlistees—a statistically insignificant .001 percent of its 36,202 black men in the crucial age group. With the second largest slave population in 1860 but relatively little long-term Union military presence, Georgia accounted for just 3,486 recruits—4 percent of its total pool. And Virginia, where the Army of Northern Virginia prevented Union forces from establishing firm control over most of the state until 1865, provided only 5,919, 6 percent of its 101,428 military-age black males (by far the largest number in any state). Among the remaining Confederate states, all of which avoided wide-scale Union military occupation, Florida contributed 1,044 men (9 percent of its pool); South Carolina 5,462 (8 percent); North Carolina 5,035 (8 percent); and Alabama 4,969 (6 percent).[52]

This pattern of enlistment strongly supports Robert Gould Shaw's observation that nothing could free slaves in the absence of United States military forces. Intention did not drive the process. Troops commanded by officers who cared nothing about black people—William Tecumseh Sherman comes immediately to mind—proved as destructive to slavery as those led by ardent advocates of emancipation. No matter how prejudiced their own attitudes, Union soldiers functioned as cogs in a grand military mechanism that inexorably ground down slavery. A. F. Sperry of the 33rd Iowa Infantry confessed a detachment that many Union veterans doubtless shared. As his regiment moved toward Mobile near the end of the war, an old black woman approached the marching column and shouted, "Glory Hallelujah! The Lord's heard our prayers . . . There's eight hundred of us praying for you at Mobile! Go on! Go on!" Sperry described how "the tears coursed down her worn and wrinkled cheeks as she beheld the army which to so great a portion of her race seemed the harbinger of jubilee, and almost as the coming of the Lord." "It was no new thing to us," he continued in a passage that combined descriptive and introspective elements, "to be hailed by these bondsmen as their deliverers; yet if we some times stopped to think of it, there would come a strange question, how much we really deserved their gratitude? But thinking is the very least of a soldier's business; and so the incident and its impressions passed out of mind altogether, as the important trivialities of the march succeeded."[53]

Over the past thirty years, historians have dealt with the Union army's role in destroying slavery in an odd way. Historical debates about how 4 million African Americans achieved freedom most often feature those who support the idea of self-emancipation—that enslaved people took the lead in forcing the president and Congress to act—and those who readily concede Lincoln should not get all the credit but insist he should get a good deal of it. Advocates of different positions regarding how to apportion credit for emancipation typically mention the importance of the Union army—and then ignore it in the bulk of their analysis. James M. McPherson's essay, "Who Freed the Slaves?" substantively discusses Lincoln and self-emancipation before offering these two sentences: "Slaves did not emancipate themselves; they were liberated by

Union armies. Freedom quite literally came from the barrel of a gun."
McPherson then immediately shifts credit back to Lincoln, concluding that it was the commander in chief who "called these armies into
being."[54]

Similarly, the editors of the Freedmen and Southern Society project,
who made the most sustained and powerful case for self-emancipation
in the 1980s and 1990s, offer this: "Freedom came to most American
slaves only through force of arms. The growing Northern commitment
to emancipation availed nothing without victory on the battlefield." But
the overriding theme in the project's five volumes of documentary evidence, as well as in the ancillary volumes co-written by the editors, is
this: once removed from the notion that the Emancipation Proclamation
and the Thirteenth Amendment are the keys to understanding emancipation, "the story of slavery's demise shifts from the presidential mansion and the halls of Congress to the farms and plantations that became
wartime battlefields. And slaves—whose persistence forced federal soldiers, Union and Confederate policy makers, and even their own masters
onto terrain they never intended to occupy—become the prime movers
in securing their own liberty." Leon F. Litwack's Pulitzer Prize–winning
study of slavery's aftermath had anticipated this argument, declaring that
the "various dimensions of slavery's collapse—the political machinations,
the government edicts, the military occupation—should not be permitted to obscure the principal actors in this drama: the four million black
men and women for whom slavery composed their entire memory."[55]

In the pictorial history that accompanies Ken Burns's documentary,
Barbara J. Fields grants African Americans primary responsibility for
gaining their freedom. "The deceptively simple first step in the process,"
she writes, "came when slaves ran away to seek sanctuary and freedom
behind Federal lines, something they began doing as soon as Federal lines
came within reach." Nothing could happen until Union military units
arrived on the scene, yet the remainder of Fields's essay passes over this
observation and lays out the contraband population's undeniable impact
on Union policymakers, who eventually added emancipation to Union
as a nonnegotiable condition of any peace following United States victory. Only the progressive military occupation of greater swaths of Con-

federate territory opened the way for perhaps one-seventh of the 3.5 million slaves in the Confederacy to grasp freedom by the final spring of the war. First came Union armies, followed by a swelling migration of enslaved people from farms and plantations to lines held by the invading Yankees.[56]

The self-emancipation argument owes much to W. E. B. Du Bois's idea of "The General Strike," most famously articulated in *Black Reconstruction in America, 1860–1880*. Published to a largely indifferent scholarly community in 1935, that landmark study includes a chapter in which Du Bois examines "How the Civil War meant emancipation and how the black worker won the war by a general strike which transferred his labor from the Confederate planter to the Northern invader, in whose army lines workers began to be organized as a new labor force." This idea has been carried forward most recently by Steven Hahn in *The Political Worlds of Slavery and Freedom,* which advances the notion of the war as an unacknowledged "massive rebellion of southern slaves" worthy of comparison with Saint-Domingue in the late eighteenth century. Hahn relies on an expansive definition of "rebellion," finessing the fact that approximately 3 million slaves remained under Confederate control at the time of Appomattox.[57]

Some Americans conditioned by elements of popular culture might still cherish the image of Lincoln as "The Great Emancipator," but it has scant currency in the academy. Even on the wider cultural stage, telling indications suggest Lincoln has lost much of his former stature in this respect. Neither the Lincoln stamp issued as part of the Civil War series in 1994 nor any of the United States stamps or pennies minted to commemorate his bicentennial in 2008 dealt with the sixteenth president as an emancipator. Instead, he appeared as a self-made man, lawyer, orator, and commander in chief.[58]

To slight Union armies—whether to emphasize the movement toward freedom of hundreds of thousands of black people, or Lincoln's continuing importance, or some other factor—prevents true understanding of one of the transformative moments in American history. Ample evidence leaves no doubt that enslaved African Americans played a crucial—and long overlooked—part in the drama of emancipation. Lincoln also must remain near the center of any discussion of the topic. So also should Congress, which passed the First and Second Confiscation Acts and other legislation that, well before the Emancipation Proclamation, proscribed slavery in the District of Columbia and the federal territories and otherwise weakened the institution. But without the United States Army, none of the other actors could have succeeded on a broad scale. No matter how desperately slaves wanted to be free (a wish that had been consistently powerful during more than two hundred years of bondage), the chance for successful escape was negligible unless Union military forces had reached their area. In the heartlands of Alabama and Florida, almost anywhere in Texas, and wherever else Union forces established no long-term presence, freedom remained a chimera. Similarly, without the projection of United States military power, the Emancipation Proclamation and the Second Confiscation Act represented mere words on paper to both slaves and slaveholders in the Confederacy.

Just as the Union army must be considered a bright thread in the tapestry of emancipation, so also should it figure in many of the conflict's other meanings. As a national institution of unmatched reach and influence, an expression of a free society's reliance on citizen-soldiers, and the principal instrument wielded to salvage and safeguard the Founders' constitutional handiwork, it earned a singular place in the population's imagination. Millions of loyal Americans followed military campaigns up and down both sides of the Mississippi River, into the logistical heartland of Tennessee, along the much-contested Rappahannock River frontier in Virginia, through the hills of North Georgia toward Atlanta, and across a broad swath of the Carolinas. Reading extensive coverage in newspapers, they gained or lost heart according to reports from ever-shifting battlefronts. In the end, they pondered the meaning of victory and found ways to thank veterans and mourn the dead. The wartime generation, as both Lincoln and Grant predicted, never forgot that all else indeed had depended on the progress of Union arms.[59]

The loyal populace celebrated citizen-soldiers who would resume peaceful pursuits after restoring the Union. In the minds of many on the home front, the nation owed everything to men who donned uniforms. As Mary Logan wrote after watching the Grand Review, "Our republic had been saved by our invincible army." *Frank Leslie's* sought to capture this sentiment in an engraving of New York veterans being welcomed home. The tattered regimental flags—which contrast strikingly with the captured Confederate standard—add greater emotional power to the scene. (Collection of the author)

THE VETERAN IN A NEW FIELD. —FROM A PAINTING BY HOMER.

Winslow Homer turned his considerable talent to the subject of citizen-soldiers returning to civilian life. He painted *The Veteran in a New Field* in 1865, and *Frank Leslie's* subsequently published this engraved version. "[W]e can well congratulate ourselves upon the
manner in which the veterans have returned to their old fields," read the accompanying
text, "since in this we find one of the surest proofs of the stability of our political system."
(*Frank Leslie's Illustrated Newspaper,* July 13, 1867)

Wounded soldiers from the battles of the Wilderness and Spotsylvania recuperate at the U.S. Sanitary Commission facility in Fredericksburg, Virginia, in May 1864. One of the commission's founders described it as a force to overcome "local prejudices" and promote "National ideas . . . the great Federal idea for which we are contending at such cost of blood and treasure." The point of the commission was to assist the most important expression of national purpose—the Union armies. (Library of Congress, Prints and Photographs Division, reproduction number LC DIG-cwpbh-03385)

A newspaper vendor with the Army of the Potomac in the autumn of 1863. The soldier on the left has purchased one of the illustrated papers. (Library of Congress, Prints and Photographs Division, reproduction number LC DIG-cwpb-01140)

In "A Veteran on Furlough," a soldier in a warm domestic setting gestures to make a point. The artist effectively conveyed a sense of soldiers who fought for a much larger civilian population. The presence of men and women from at least three generations underscores the war's implications for both the present and future of the Union. (*Harper's Weekly*, February 6, 1864)

Ulysses S. Grant came to personify the war for Union, earning that status through a series of landmark victories in the Western and Eastern Theaters that began at Fort Donelson and culminated at Appomattox. Thomas Nast created this tribute for the cover of *Harper's Weekly* just before Grant became general in chief. Columbia pins a congressional medal on the hero, who stands opposite the base of a flag-bedecked column inscribed "UNION." (*Harper's Weekly,* February 6, 1864)

Allowing soldiers to vote in 1864 struck many loyal citizens as proof of the American democracy's resiliency. In this illustration from *Frank Leslie's,* soldiers read handbills relating to the election. "Through our camps our regiment seem to be all of one mind in regard to the coming election," wrote one soldier, "nine-tenths of them being good Union-loving men, who are in favor of 'free speech,' 'free press,' and the 'Monroe Doctrine.'" (Paul F. Mottelay and T. Campbell-Copeland, eds., *The Soldier in Our Civil War: Columbian Memorial Edition. A Pictorial History of the Conflict, 1861–1865,* 2 vols. New York: Stanley Bradley Publishing Company, 1893, 2:349)

Military campaigns profoundly influenced politics in the loyal states. William Tecumseh Sherman's and Philip H. Sheridan's armies won victories in 1864 that re-elected Lincoln and guaranteed emancipation as an outcome of Union victory. *Harper's Weekly* featured General Sheridan twice on covers during his Shenandoah Valley campaign, including this engraving in the wake of the battle of Fisher's Hill. (*Harper's Weekly,* October 8, 1864)

The army's role in the process of emancipation often gets lost in discussions of Lincoln and African Americans. Yet its presence proved crucial throughout the war. This photograph shows a group of enslaved people—some of them looking at near-by soldiers—crossing the Rappahannock River into Union lines during Maj. Gen. John Pope's Second Bull Run campaign of August 1862. (Library of Congress, Prints and Photographs Division, reproduction number LC DIG-cwpb-00218)

ARRIVAL AT CHICKASAW BAYOU OF THE SLAVES OF PRESIDENT DAVIS FROM HIS MISSISSIPPI PLANTATION.

Frank Leslie's probably took special pride in publishing this illustration showing the "Arrival at Chickasaw Bayou of the slaves of President Davis from his Mississippi plantation." The artist's handling of the scene suggests interest on the part of some but not all of the Union troops. (Paul F. Mottelay and T. Campbell-Copeland, eds., *The Soldier in Our Civil War: Columbian Memorial Edition. A Pictorial History of the Conflict, 1861–1865,* 2 vols. New York: Stanley Bradley Publishing Company, 1893, 2:88)

James Fuller Queen's twelve-episode treatment of the passage from slavery to liberty, probably published in 1863, shows the importance of the Union army in scenes eight ("Free!") and nine ("Stand Up A Man!"). After overpowering his tormenter, the man hides in the swamp before finding freedom and encouragement at a Union military camp. (Library of Congress, Prints and Photographs Division, reproduction number LC DIG-ppmsca-05453)

National cemeteries established to accommodate the Union dead served as significant sites of remembrance through the postwar decades. The soldiers' cemetery in Alexandria, Virginia, depicted in this photograph holds nearly 3,600 of the 300,000 men interred in such sites. (Library of Congress, Prints and Photographs Division, reproduction number LC DIG–cwpb–01380)

Decoration Day (later changed to Memorial Day) provided an occasion to recall the service of citizen-soldiers. In this engraving from *Frank Leslie's,* a one-armed veteran instructs a young boy, whose mother and sister place flowers on the grave. A column of veterans dressed in their old uniforms and with battle-worn Civil War flags passes in the rear. (Paul F. Mottelay and T. Campbell-Copeland, eds., *The Soldier in Our Civil War: Columbian Memorial Edition. A Pictorial History of the Conflict, 1861–1865,* 2 vols. New York: Stanley Bradley Publishing Company, 1893, 2:392)

5

....

AFFIRMATION

*L*oyal Americans greeted the end of the war imbued with a sense of great accomplishment. Whether part of the throng lining Pennsylvania Avenue at the Grand Review, witnesses to more modest ceremonies in other cities and towns, or individuals in countless homes, they welcomed returning citizen-soldiers who had preserved the Union, vanquished slaveholding aristocrats, and removed slavery as a future source of sectional contention. Although opinions about various important questions remained in flux, most people in the loyal states favored punishment for a few Confederate leaders and expected the mass of former Rebels to accept defeat and reenter the Union on the victors' terms. Lincoln's assassination sparked a period of retributive fury, but the killing of John Wilkes Booth on April 26, 1865, as he fled from Union cavalry pursuers, and the expeditious trial, conviction, and sentencing of his conspirators slaked most people's desire to inflict widescale punishment on ex-Confederates. The execution of Capt. Henry Wirz, commandant of the infamous Andersonville prison, in November 1865 had a similar effect. The work of the war seemed fully accomplished—

though a few white citizens supported extending the franchise to black veterans and perhaps to all African American men of voting age.[1]

The actions of President Andrew Johnson and events in various southern states increased support for a harder type of Reconstruction. Johnson at first spoke of making treason "odious" but quickly demonstrated a willingness, some said eagerness, to grant pardons to former large slaveholders. He also opposed crucial Republican legislation relating to Reconstruction. Former states of the Confederacy passed Black Codes that severely circumscribed African Americans' freedom. Perhaps more controversially in the loyal states, the southern states elected some Confederate political and military leaders to local and national office. At the same time, Union soldiers on occupation duty reported evidence of what they considered widespread treasonous sentiment among the beaten Rebels. Loyal citizens concluded that the old slaveholding oligarchy had not been effectively crushed after all and that its members intended, with help from Johnson and Democrats in states that had not seceded, to reassert their political power. These developments undercut the war's noble effort to save the Union and punish those who had sundered it in 1860–1861.[2]

Johnson's aggressive opposition to congressional Republicans and the intransigence of ex-Rebels pushed the loyal white citizenry far beyond where they envisioned going in the first flush of military victory. The Fourteenth and Fifteenth Amendments barred states from abridging citizens' rights, made it harder for ex-Rebels to hold office, and guaranteed the vote to black men. These amendments and an array of other legislation sought to secure and extend the fruits of Union victory and emancipation. The increasing severity of governmental policy had far more to do with chastising ex-Rebels than with helping African Americans, though the latter surely were the immediate and longer-term beneficiaries. Many historians have detected a "lost moment" during Reconstruction, when far more could have been done to achieve true equality for freedpeople. If only the white North had followed through on the promise of the great Civil War–era amendments, runs this argument, the grim racial story of the late nineteenth and twentieth centuries could have been much different. Such a view runs aground on the profound prejudice that existed in the United States between 1860 and 1880. Far from a lost moment, the era of Reconstruction represented a rather miraculous period that yielded essential improvements to the Constitution that would have been unthinkable except as an outgrowth of the war. Although Jim Crow later blighted the American South, the amendments remained as unequivocal evidence of the transformative power of a massive military event.[3]

The wartime generation maintained continuity regarding their principal goals in the war. David W. Blight's immensely influential work on the memory of the war underscores ways in which many white people, North and South, reached out to one another in the postwar decades. "In the end," writes Blight, "this is a story of how the forces of reconciliation overwhelmed the emancipationist vision in the national culture, how the inexorable drive for reunion both used and trumped race." Almost all loyal citizens eventually welcomed ex-Confederates back into the national fold. The point of a war to suppress rebellion, after all, had been to reunite the nation. But they did so while insisting that defenders of the Union had held the moral high ground. What might be termed situational reconciliation most often obtained, wherein newspaper editors or speakers in certain public forums emphasized commonalities of valor and steadfastness among Union and Confederate soldiers. That stance seldom carried over into serious discussions of which side had been right. Thus could some Union veterans join former enemies on a battlefield, as survivors of the Philadelphia Brigade did with those of George E. Pickett's Confederate division at Gettysburg in 1887, while also asserting the absolute superiority of their cause.[4]

U. S. Grant's *Personal Memoirs* offered a perfect example of holding out the hand of reunion while condemning secession and the effort to establish a Confederate nation. Writing about Lee at Appomattox, the Union hero expressed sympathy for his beaten opponent but unmasked contempt for the Rebel cause. During the meeting with Lee in Wilmer McLean's parlor on April 9, 1865, explained Grant, "I felt like anything rather than rejoicing at the downfall of a foe who had fought so long and valiantly, and had suffered so much for a cause, though that cause was, I believe, one of the worst for which a people ever fought, and one for which there was the least excuse."[5]

Shortly after Appomattox, Grant had expressed what surely was a common sentiment at that moment. He described to his wife, Julia, a desperate situation in the Confederacy. Writing from Raleigh, North Carolina, he mentioned a populace who hoped "to see peace restored so that further devastation need not take place for the country. The suffering that must exist in the South the next year, even with the war ending now, will be beyond conception." The slaveholding leadership class might be subject to penalties, suggested Grant, but not all Confederates: "People who talk now of further retaliation and punishment, except of the political leaders, either do not conceive of the suffering endured already or they are heartless and unfeeling and wish to stay at home, out of danger, whilst the punishment is being inflicted."[6]

Union soldiers deployed across the South at the end of the war echoed Grant's description of a beaten population, but many soon detected an attitude of defiance that deeply offended them. Sergeant William Henry Redman of the 12th Illinois Cavalry, stationed at Memphis in May 1865, believed "all Southern *Leaders* should be disfranchised, or severely punished. It won't do to give these devilish traitors the scepter of Power again." Happily, he added, they seemed to "acknowledge to have received a *good whipping*." Common Confederate soldiers "are all at home," reported Redman, "and peaceable as whipped dogs. We hear nothing more of Guerillas. In fact, the war is over here and Peace reigns supreme." Later in the year, however, Redman's unit transferred to Texas, and he grew increasingly angry about hostile civilians. On December 21, he wrote his mother, "The citizens of this county are as bitter toward the Yankees (as they call us) as they ever were. I have told them several times since we came here that I could whip the whole county with my Company." Redman issued orders for his men to shoot anyone who directly insulted them, and his soldiers took pains to fly their colors every morning because the Texans "do not like to see the Red White and Blue floating over their town."[7]

Another sergeant found a similarly surly population in Pascagoula, Mississippi. Mathew Woodruff's 21st Missouri Infantry put up with a variety of pro-Confederate gestures from an openly hostile white citizenry. "One can walk the streets any night in the city here & hear the Ladies singing & playing the Bonnie Blue Flag & other Treasonable airs," he recorded in his diary on October 17, 1865, "& we are evry day subject . . . to the insults & tantalizeing boasts and that right in presence of the authorities, and dare not resist it." On all sides one could hear "barefaced Treason uttered in the strongest terms, even the Public Press does not hesitate to pitch its vile rebukes right into the teeth of the authorities . . . There is not 9 out of 10 of these so called 'Whiped' traitors that I would trust until I saw the rope applied to their Necks, then I would only have Faith in the quality of the rope." Among many galling aspects of his occupation duty, Woodruff singled out how former Rebels regained political rights. "[W]e see them evry day restored to all their former rights & privalidges," he wrote angrily, "put in office and other responsible positions in the North as well as South where the true patriot and loveing defender of his country and the only self deserving men of our country, is refused."[8]

Grant offered a perceptive discussion of how attitudes changed in the loyal states. At the end of the war, he observed in his memoirs, most of the citizenry favored a quick reintegration of the Rebels into the nation. Most also opposed black suffrage, believing it would come after "a time of probation, in which the ex-slaves could prepare themselves for the privileges of citizenship." Grant scorned Andrew Johnson as one who kowtowed to the old slaveholding oligarchy, "a President who at first wished to revenge himself upon Southern men of better social standing than himself, but who still sought their recognition, and in a short time conceived the idea and advanced the proposition to become their Moses to lead them triumphantly out of all their difficulties." This alienated those "who had secured to us the perpetuation of the Union . . . , and they became more radical in their views." White southerners acted as if they, in concert with northern Democrats, "would be able to control the nation at once." Congress and most northern state legislatures

believed it "became necessary to enfranchise the negro, in all his ignorance ... because of the foolhardiness of the President and the blindness
of the Southern people to their own interest." As his letter to Julia from
Raleigh indicated, Grant initially favored "the course that would be the
least humiliating to the people who had been in rebellion." But gradually he "worked up to the point where, with the majority of the people,
I favored immediate enfranchisement."[9]

Throughout the postwar decades, the loyal population's commemorative efforts focused on how citizen-soldiers saved the Union (or suppressed the rebellion) and democratic free government triumphed over
oligarchy. The Confederate cause took a severe beating in many forums,
and emancipation often received prominent mention. Far more than
anything else, Union dominated inscriptions on monuments, which
were designed to instruct future generations. Examples from New England, the mid-Atlantic, the West, and the Southwest offered typical sentiments. In 1889, Nashua, New Hampshire, dedicated a tall shaft surmounted by the figure of Liberty to honor the city's men "Who Served
Their Country On Land And Sea During The War Of The Rebellion,
And Aided In Preserving The Integrity Of The Federal Union." Fifteen
years earlier in Lancaster, Pennsylvania, a monument with many of the
same design elements sought "To Honor The Men And Women Who
Gave Their Lives To Preserve The Union." In September 1898, Junction
City, Kansas, unveiled a memorial arch, atop which stood an infantryman
flanked by a pair of mortars. It commemorated soldiers and sailors "Who
Inspired By Patriotism Freely Offered Their Lives For The Maintenance
Of An Undivided Country." Long before the ceremony in Junction City,
residents of Santa Fe had placed an obelisk in the city's plaza, erected
by the "people of New Mexico through their legislatures of 1866–7–8,"
that carried the words, "May the Union be Perpetual."[10]

Some monuments incorporated Lincoln's words, and a few celebrated
emancipation as well as Union. In Macomb, Illinois, in 1899, the Grand
Army of the Republic memorialized the men of McDonough County
who "Voluntarily And Freely Gave Their Lives That Government Of
The People, By The People, And For The People Shall Not Perish From
The Earth." Manchester, New Hampshire, selected a design featuring

a tall round shaft topped by "Lady Victory," around the base of which stood figures of a Union infantryman, artillerist, cavalryman, and sailor. Completed in 1878, the monument went up "In Honor Of The Men Of Manchester Who Gave Their Services In The War Which Preserved The Union Of The States And Secured Equal Rights To All Under The Constitution." In Enfield, Connecticut, an infantryman in winter uniform surmounted a monument, placed on Main Street in 1885, in memory of men "Who On Land And Sea Periled Their Lives For Union And Liberty 1861–1865."[11]

The inscriptions on such monuments carried forward into the later nineteenth century the sense of devotion to Union so evident in newspapers, letters, diaries, and other wartime evidence—a continuity often hard to detect in modern analysis. Thomas J. Brown's treatment of postwar commemoration and public art, for example, adopts a dismissive tone, observing that "most Union inscriptions simply stated the supposed motives of soldiers with the expectation that the reader would approve of them." In fact, most of the loyal citizenry almost certainly would have approved of inscriptions that recalled a war for Union or democracy fought by civilians who temporarily took up arms. Brown also virtually ignores how conceptions of Union and the importance of citizen-soldiers, which reinforced one another so dramatically during the war, found expression in regimental monuments and statues of officers erected after the war. Commemorative art dedicated to citizen-soldiers, women, Abraham Lincoln (with much attention to emancipation), Robert Gould Shaw and the 54th Massachusetts Infantry (Augustus Saint-Gaudens's beautiful work installed on Boston Common in 1897), and Robert E. Lee and the Lost Cause receive ample discussion, but Brown allocates no attention to the hundreds of Union regimental monuments on battlefields or to any statue or memorial featuring Grant (not even his tomb) or other Union generals. The decision to ignore Grant is especially surprising considering Brown's discussion of statues of Lee and Lincoln and Lincoln's burial site.[12]

The twenty-fifth anniversary of the victory at Gettysburg provided a perfect opportunity for the wartime generation to revisit the war's purposes and outcomes. A number of loyal states placed regimental monuments on the field between 1887 and 1889, most of which involved ceremonies with one or more speeches. The texts of those addresses, conveniently collected in volumes by several of the states, highlight continuity of purpose among those who fought against the Confederate rebellion. Many speakers alluded to reconciliation in some manner, but, more obviously, they celebrated the Union and its citizen-soldiers and deprecated the Confederacy and oligarchic slaveholders.

Joshua Lawrence Chamberlain participated in the dedication of the 20th Maine Infantry's modest marker on Little Round Top on October 3, 1889, recalling the powerful nationalizing force of the armies. "The organization of the army of the Union was a counterpart of that of the Union itself," he told the crowd with an eye toward the importance of the American democratic example, "Our thoughts were not then of States as States, but of the States united,—of that union and oneness in which the People of the United States lived and moved and had their being. Our hearts beat to that one high thought; our eyes saw but the old flag; and our souls saw it, glorious with the symbols of power and peace and blessing in the forward march of man." Conceding Rebel courage, Chamberlain left no doubt that advocates of Union had been right. "[T]he cause for which we fought was higher; our thought was wider," he affirmed before taking aim at the slaveholders' memory of the conflict: "The 'lost cause' is not lost liberty and rights of self-government. What is lost is slavery of men and supremacy of States."[13]

The previous year, a speech for the ceremony of the 83rd New York Infantry on Seminary Ridge echoed Daniel Webster's rhetoric about liberty and Union. Addressing veterans in the audience, Orland M. Potter pronounced their efforts "necessary to save American liberty for yourselves and your children . . . American liberty was the child of the American Constitution and the Union of these States, and had not before been known or enjoyed by man." The Constitution had been "rescued from destruction and burial in the abyss of secession," stated Potter, "by the valor of the Union arms on the battlefields of the war we in part review to-day. Higher service for country and mankind has never been and can never be rendered than was rendered in that rescue."[14]

Citizens only temporarily in uniform had performed that service, a fact much appreciated by speakers at Gettysburg. In 1889, Michigan governor Austin Blair spoke in the National Cemetery, which Lincoln had helped dedicate in November 1863, with both Union soldiers and their cause in mind. "Our men engaged here were not mere soldiers," he commented, "they were also fellow-citizens engaged in a mighty struggle, and with a definite purpose in view. They were volunteers who had enlisted in this great war with an intelligent sense of patriotic duty . . . We are here to-day to dedicate these monuments because we know that the men who fought and fell here in the splendid Union army under George G. Meade fought in a cause that was wholly right." Theodore A. Dodge made a similar point on July 3, 1888, in remarks at the 119th New York Infantry's monument along the line of the 11th Corps near the Carlisle Road. "From and after the first three days of July, 1863," said Dodge, "the tide of secession receded, until, after another two years, a million and a half soldiers melted back into the population from whence they came, and the Union was . . . pronounced one and indivisible."[15]

Many speakers gloried in the success of a democratic republic against an aristocratic enemy. Former lieutenant colonel Samuel H. Hurst of the 73rd Ohio Infantry spoke in September 1887 in a program at the National Cemetery devoted to a group of Ohio regimental monuments. Hurst deplored the Confederacy, with its "ambitious dream of the Southern Empire, of aristocratic government, founded upon caste and slavery as 'the chief cornerstone,' and coupled with this chivalrous ambition for the establishment of aristocratic government, that one race might be supreme at the cost of the brutal degradation of another." Arrayed against that wretched model "was pride in the glory of the Republic and in its free institutions . . . faith in the rights of manhood; faith in democratic government; faith in free civilization, and as the outgrowth of these, there was the living and sublime purpose that freedom, and not slavery, should be the ruling power in the future government of these United States." Hurst deplored the idea of erecting Confederate monuments at Gettysburg: "I do not believe there is another nation in the civilized world that would permit a rebel monument to stand upon its soil for a single day, and I can see neither wisdom not patriotism in building them here." A Pennsylvanian, speaking to veterans and friends of the 38th Pennsylvania Infantry in September 1889, asked his listeners to "Behold this nation of American Freemen! No title of nobility, but in its place true nobility of manhood and womanhood."[16]

Anti-Confederate blasts appeared regularly in the regimental orations. A New Jersey colonel characterized the nascent slaveholding republic as a "military despotism born amid the throes of war, overthrown by the shock of arms, without history save four years of bloody strife, impelled by the twin furies of slavery and treason." Governor Blair termed the Confederate cause one "we can never admire," while Rev. James H. Botts of the 6th Michigan Cavalry blamed the war, and by extension establishment of the Confederacy, on "the growing power of slavery, the anticipated glory of secession and the vauntings of personal ambition." The Union cause, insisted Botts, justified the soldiers' "valor and sacrifice . . . compared with which the 'lost cause' will ultimately be lost in contempt in the impartial verdict of future generations." A former captain in the 11th Pennsylvania Infantry remembered comrades who thought the Confederacy so evil "[t]hey were willing to wash out the footprints of the rebel foe with their blood, and count it a joy to die."[17]

Emancipation figured in many of the speeches at Gettysburg. Col. John Ramsey of the 8th New Jersey Infantry, a unit that fought in the Wheatfield on July 2, 1863, spoke of "these beautiful monuments to the memory of the brave men who died . . . for the safety and perpetuity of the Republic; died that four millions of human beings with their unborn generations should be free; died that a 'government of the people, by the people, and for the people should not perish from the earth.'" Union victory meant that "the shackles of the slaves should be sold for old iron. That the auction block should be burned. That all men should breathe the fresh air of heaven direct, and not by inhalation from a master." Brigadier General William Hobson addressed veterans of the 17th Maine Infantry in October 1888. The regiment had lost 38 percent of its men in the Wheatfield on July 2, experiencing the "thunders of artillery at Gettysburg" that proclaimed "none but free men should live in a free country, and that they all should have equal rights and power under the laws."[18]

It has become a commonplace that the war changed how Americans thought of their country. During the antebellum years, most people said "the United States are . . ." After the war, however, they said "The United States is . . ," revealing for the first time an understanding of the whole as greater than the constituent parts. As Shelby Foote put it in his avuncular way: "And that sums up what the war accomplished. It made us an 'is.'"[19] Whether or not 620,000 deaths transformed "United States" from a plural into a singular proper noun (and it is by no means clear that happened), no one should infer a sea change in attitudes toward the nation. Loyal Americans of the mid-nineteenth century used "United States," "Union," "nation," and "country" interchangeably—and never wrote "the Union are . . . ," or "the nation are . . ." They possessed a strong sense of their nation as a democratic republic unique in the world, bequeathed to them by the founding generation and destined for future greatness if poisonous questions relating to slavery could be settled.

Ulysses S. Grant personified this way of looking at the nation. Like Lincoln, his mastery of language enabled him to convey a great deal in economical, sometimes lyrical prose. His post-presidential speeches and writings discussed the war and its meanings with great clarity. He referred alternately to national armies, the army of the United States, and Union armies—but employed no chronological progression leading from a more parochial usage to an expansive, nation-based one. In a speech delivered to a group of Americans near Hamburg, Germany, during his world tour in the late 1870s, Grant distilled into five sentences what most loyal citizens would have said gave the most meaning to their great internecine conflict. "What saved the Union," Grant told the dinner guests, "was the coming forward of the young men of the nation. They came from their homes and fields, as they did in the time of the Revolution, giving everything to the country. To their devotion we owe the salvation of the Union. The humblest soldier who carried a musket is entitled to as much credit for the results of the war as those who were in command. So long as our young men are animated by this spirit there will be no fear for the Union." The nation's greatest living hero had pared the war's triumphal elements to a single salient point. Citizen-soldiers had saved a democratic republic invaluable not only to its own citizens but also as an example of popular self-rule for the rest of the world. The powerful resonance of this idea among the loyal populace established the foundation for understanding the Union war.[20]

NOTES

ACKNOWLEDGMENTS

INDEX

NOTES

....

Abbreviations

CW   Abraham Lincoln, *The Collected Works of Abraham Lincoln,* ed. Roy P.
           Basler, 9 vols. (New Brunswick, N.J.: Rutgers University Press, 1953–
           1955).

FL   *Frank Leslie's Illustrated Newspaper*

HEHL   Henry E. Huntington Library, San Marino, California

HW   *Harper's Weekly*

JLNC   John L. Nau III Civil War Collection, Houston, Texas

OR   U.S. War Department, *The War of the Rebellion: The Official Records of the*
           Union and Confederate Armies, 127 vols., index, and atlas (Washington:
           GPO, 1880–1901), ser. 1 (unless otherwise noted, all references are to
           series 1).

Introduction

1. Walt Whitman, *Memoranda During the War* (1875; reprint, Boston: Applewood
Books, 1990), 49. On casualties among U.S. soldiers, see E. B. Long, *The Civil War
Day by Day: An Almanac, 1861–1865* (Garden City, N.Y.: Doubleday, 1971), 710–
711, 715–716. Long estimated "the total Federal casualties in the Army and Navy,
including dead from all causes and wounded, came to 642,427." This number did
not include nonparoled prisoners of war who survived their captivity—another

164,525. Union casualties thus exceeded 800,000. This number, at best approximate, does not mean 800,000 different men became casualties. Some soldiers suffered more than one wound, others were wounded in one action and subsequently killed, and still others were both wounded and taken as prisoners of war.

2. John Hay, *Inside Lincoln's White House: The Complete Civil War Diary of John Hay,* ed. Michael Burlingame and John R. Turner Ettlinger (Carbondale: Southern Illinois University Press, 1997), 211–212. Hay heard Seward make this comment on June 24, 1864, to the artist Francis B. Carpenter, who was painting *First Reading of the Emancipation Proclamation of President Lincoln.* Seward insisted that "the formation of the Republican party destroyed slavery: the anti slavery acts of this administration are merely incidental." Carpenter should have painted the cabinet meeting at which Lincoln decided to relieve Fort Sumter, thought Seward, because it "determined the fact that Republican institutions were worth fighting for."

3. *CW,* 5:537. For a discussion of the fate of Union in popular culture, see Gary W. Gallagher, *Causes Won, Lost, and Forgotten: How Hollywood and Popular Art Shape What We Know about the Civil War* (Chapel Hill: University of North Carolina Press, 2008), especially chapters 1 and 3.

4. For a convenient graph depicting the population in 1860, see James G. Randall and David Donald, *The Civil War and Reconstruction,* 2nd ed. (Lexington, Mass.: D.C. Heath, 1969), 5.

5. Peter Welsh, *Irish Green and Union Blue: The Civil War Letters of Peter Welsh, Color Sergeant 28th Regiment Massachusetts Volunteers,* ed. Lawrence Frederick Kohl and Margaret Cossé Richard (New York: Fordham University Press, 1986), 65–66.

6. Scholarly opportunity beckons anyone willing to get beyond a binary approach to questions of pro- or antiwar sentiment and activity in both the United States and the Confederacy. The American Revolution presents a valuable comparative model in this respect, and historians would do well to keep in mind that many citizens fell into a category between the equivalents of Patriots and Loyalists. This nebulous group occupied "an ambivalent position," as one scholar working on the Confederacy has put it, exhibiting malleable loyalties while always trying to do "what was best for themselves and for their families." See David Brown, "North Carolinian Ambivalence: Rethinking Loyalty and Disaffection in the Civil War Piedmont," in Paul D. Escott, ed., *North Carolinians in the Era of the Civil War and Reconstruction* (Chapel Hill: University of North Carolina Press, 1999), 8. On enlistments among poor men, see William Marvel, *Mr. Lincoln Goes to War* (New York: Houghton Mifflin, 2006), 54–62.

7. For an introduction to the topic of American nationalism, see Peter J. Parish, "An Exception to Most of the Rules: What Made American Nationalism Different in the Mid-Nineteenth Century?" *Prologue: Quarterly of the National Archives* 27 (Fall 1995):219–229. Parish tellingly noted that many prominent scholars writing about nationalism ignored the mid-nineteenth-century United States. Still indispensable is David M. Potter's "The Historian's Use of Nationalism and Vice Versa," in Potter, *The South and the Sectional Conflict* (Baton Rouge: Louisiana State University Press,

1968), 34–83. On Kentucky's postwar embrace of the Confederacy, see Anne E. Marshall, *Creating a Confederate Kentucky: The Lost Cause and Civil War Memory in a Border State* (Chapel Hill: University of North Carolina Press, 2010).

8. Broadside titled "Think before you Vote!" item GLC08546, Gilder Lehrman Collection, The Gilder Lehrman Institute of American History, New York City.

1. The Grand Review

1. Frank J. Welcher, *The Union Army 1861–1865: Organization and Operations,* 2 vols. (Bloomington: Indiana University Press, 1989), 1:416–417, 40–41, 506–507 (for positions of Union corps in May 1865); George G. Meade, *The Life and Letters of George Gordon Meade, Major-General United States Army,* ed. George Gordon Meade, 2 vols. (New York: Scribner's, 1913), 2:279; *OR,* 47(3):531, 526. On May 16, Grant wrote Sherman: "A Review not yet determined on. You might send for Mrs. Sherman anyhow. You will probably be here for some time. There are no orders for you."

2. Frank Abial Flower, *Edwin McMasters Stanton: The Autocrat of Rebellion, Emancipation, and Reconstruction* (Akron, Ohio: Saalfield, 1905), 288–289, credits Secretary of War Edwin M. Stanton with initially conceiving of the Grand Review. In Charles Royster, *The Destructive War: William Tecumseh Sherman, Stonewall Jackson, and the Americans* (New York: Knopf, 1991), 408, Royster states that Quartermaster General Montgomery C. Meigs "first proposed holding a review of both armies."

3. Francis F. McKinney, *Education in Violence: The Life of George H. Thomas and the History of the Army of the Cumberland* (Detroit: Wayne State University Press, 1961), 443–445; Larry J. Daniel, *Days of Glory: The Army of the Cumberland, 1861–1865* (Baton Rouge: Louisiana State University Press, 2004), 433; Welcher, *The Union Army,* 1:417; Ulysses S. Grant, *The Papers of Ulysses S. Grant,* ed. John Y. Simon, 31 vols. to date (Carbondale: Southern Illinois University Press, 1967–), 15:43–44; Philip H. Sheridan, *Personal Memoirs of P. H. Sheridan,* 2 vols. (1888; reprint, Wilmington, N.C.: Broadfoot, 1992), 2:208–209. Soldiers in the Sixth Corps felt somewhat cheated. One noted in his diary on June 8: "President Johnson with other dignitaries was seated upon a platform in front of the White House. They received us very kindly, but the people with the exception of the ladies who waved their handkerchiefs were very quiet. We expected to meet with a warm reception, . . . but evidently reviews are played out with Washington people." Elisha Hunt Rhodes, *All for the Union: A History of the 2nd Rhode Island Volunteer Infantry in the War of the Great Rebellion, as Told by the Diary and Letters of Elisha Hunt Rhodes . . . ,* ed. Robert Hunt Rhodes (Lincoln, R.I.: Andrew Mowbray, 1985), 243.

4. Welcher, *Union Army,* 1:506–507; *OR* 46(3):1005, 990.

5. Grant, *Papers* 14:438–439, 15:53–55, 57; Joseph T. Wilson, *The Black Phalanx; A History of the Negro Soldiers of the United States in the Wars of 1775–1812, 1861–'65* (Hartford, Conn.: American, 1890), 460–462. For Grant's orders to Steele, which informed him of the impending arrival of the Twenty-Fifth Corps, see *OR* 48(2):525–526.

6. Noah Andre Trudeau, *Like Men of War: Black Troops in the Civil War, 1862–1865* (Boston: Little, Brown, 1998), 455.

7. R. J. M. Blackett, ed., *Thomas Morris Chester, Black Civil War Correspondent* (Baton Rouge: Louisiana State University Press, 1989), 289; George Templeton Strong, *The Diary of George Templeton Strong,* ed. Allan Nevins and Milton Halsey Thomas, 4 vols. (New York: Macmillan, 1952), 3:575; *FL,* April 29, 1865, 92–93; *HW,* April 22, 1865, 248–249, 241. Historians have debated which unit was first into Richmond. See, for example, Trudeau, *Like Men of War,* 417–424; Ernest B. Furgurson, *Ashes of Glory: Richmond at War* (New York: Knopf, 1996), 331–336. Black soldiers were also the first to enter Charleston, a hugely symbolic event. See *HW,* March 18, 1865, 165, for a woodcut depicting the event.

8. *FL,* March 18, 1865, 403; *OR* 46(3):797, 816, 807; Trudeau, *Like Men of War,* 434.

9. Estimates of the number of soldiers who participated typically vary from 150,000 to 200,000. The former figure almost certainly is more accurate. The key to the discrepancy lies in the strength of the Army of the Potomac, which some sources place at 100,000. The tri-monthly return for April 10, 1865, reported 49,778 men in the three infantry corps (the Second, Fifth, and Ninth), which together with the cavalry and assorted other units would yield a total of approximately 65,000. See *OR* 46(1):63; Ulysses S. Grant, *Memoirs and Selected Letters,* ed. Mary Drake McFeely and William S. McFeely (New York: Library of America, 1990), 768. For examples of the higher estimate, see David S. Heidler and Jeanne T. Heidler, eds., *Encyclopedia of the American Civil War,* 4 vols. (Santa Barbara, Calif.: ABC-CLIO, 2000), 2:860–861; *HW,* June 10, 1865, 358.

10. Robert K. Krick, *Civil War Weather in Virginia* (Tuscaloosa: University of Alabama Press, 2007), 158; *Oquawka (Ill.) Spectator,* June 1, 1865; *Huntingdon (Pa.) Globe,* May 31, 1865; Ernest B. Furgurson, *Freedom Rising: Washington in the Civil War* (New York: Knopf, 2004), 395; *New York Evening Post,* May 23, 1865; Royster, *The Destructive War,* 406–408; *Franklin (Pa.) Repository,* May 31, 1865; *Philadelphia Daily Evening Bulletin,* May 24, 1865.

11. William Ray, *Four Years with the Iron Brigade: The Civil War Journal of William Ray, Co. F, Seventh Wisconsin Volunteers,* ed. Lance Herdegen and Sherry Murphy (Cambridge, Mass.: Da Capo, 2002), 372–373; George Tate, Diary, May 23, 1865, Papers of George Tate, 1854–1908, HEHL.

12. John Hill Ferguson, *On to Atlanta: The Civil War Diaries of John Hill Ferguson, Illinois Tenth Regiment of Volunteers,* ed. Janet Correll Ellison and Mark A. Weitz (Lincoln: University of Nebraska Press, 2001), 130–133. Ferguson was typical of many western soldiers who seemed especially intent, as an Illinois infantryman put it many years later, on presenting "as good a military display as the far-famed Army of the Potomac." Lucius W. Barber, *Army Memoirs of Lucius W. Barber, Company 'D,' 15th Illinois Volunteer Infantry. May 24, 1861, to Sept. 30, 1865* (1894; reprint, Alexandria, Va.: Time-Life, 1981), 211.

13. Oliver Otis Howard, *Autobiography of Oliver Otis Howard, Major General United States Army,* 2 vols. (1907; reprint, Harrisburg, Pa.: Archive Society, 1997), 2:210–212.

14. William Tecumseh Sherman, *Memoirs of General W. T. Sherman,* ed. Charles Royster (New York: Library of America, 1990), 865–866; Jack Rudolph, "The Grand Review: 'They Marched Like the Lords of the World,'" *Civil War Times Illustrated* 19 (November 1980):42; Mary A. Livermore, *My Story of the War: A Woman's Narrative of Four Years' Personal Experience* . . . (1887; reprint, New York: Da Capo, 1995), 515–517. Carl Rohl-Smith's imposing equestrian statue of Sherman, dedicated in 1903, stands on the spot where the general watched the Grand Review. Kathryn Allamong Jacob, *Testament to Union: Civil War Monuments in Washington, D.C.* (Baltimore: Johns Hopkins University Press, 1998), 93–97.

15. Charles S. Wainwright, *A Diary of Battle: The Personal Journals of Colonel Charles S. Wainwright, 1861–1865,* ed. Allan Nevins (1962; reprint, New York: Da Capo, 1998), 529–530.

16. Grant, *Memoirs and Selected Letters,* 769.

17. Benjamin Brown French, *Witness to the Young Republic: A Yankee's Journal, 1828–1870,* ed. Donald B. Cole and John J. McDonough (Hanover, N.H.: University Press of New England, 1989), 478–479.

18. Mary Logan, *Reminiscences of the Civil War and Reconstruction,* ed. George Worthington Adams (Carbondale: Southern Illinois University Press, 1970), 125–127.

19. *Philadelphia Press,* May 27, 1865; *Baltimore American,* May 27, 1865; *Chicago Tribune,* May 24, 1865.

20. J. Cutler Andrews, *The North Reports the Civil War* ([Pittsburgh]: University of Pittsburgh Press, 1955), 12–13; *New York Herald,* May 24, 1865.

21. *HW,* June 10, 1865, 353, 356–358, 364–365; *FL,* June 10, 1865, 177–180.

22. *HW,* June 10, 1865, 358; *FL,* June 10, 1865, 180; Sherman, *Memoirs,* 869; Joseph T. Glatthaar, *The March to the Sea and Beyond: Sherman's Troops in the Savannah and Carolinas Campaigns* (New York: New York University Press, 1985), 122–123. Other newspapers also offered dismissive descriptions of the contrabands with Sherman's armies. According to the *Baltimore American and Commercial Advertiser* of May 25, 1865, "Between the Second and Third Divisions of the Twentieth Corps was a large number of pack horses and mules, led by colored soldiers, servants, etc. . . . two diminutive white donkeys, mounted by small darkeys, attracted the attention of all the multitude on the route of the procession. The grotesqueness of their costume and the small size of the animals excited the laughter of thousands." Benjamin Brown French labeled the African American civilians *"nondescripts"* who provided "the most laughable sight of the entire review." French, *Witness to the Young Republic,* 479.

23. Georg R. Sheets, *The Grand Review: The Civil War Continues to Shape America* (York, Pa.: Bold Print, 2000), 53, 63–65; Lois Bryan Adams, *Letter from Washington, 1863–1865,* ed. Evelyn Leasher (Detroit: Wayne State University Press, 1999), 263–

267; Noah Brooks, *Mr. Lincoln's Washington: Selections from the Writings of Noah Brooks, Civil War Correspondent*, ed. P. J. Staundenraus (New York: Thomas Yoseloff, 1967), 473, 475; *Daily National Intelligencer* (Washington, D.C.), March 25, 1865.

24. Andrews, *The North Reports the Civil War*, 10–11; *New York Times*, May 26, 1865.

25. *The Liberator*, June 2, 1865.

26. Blackett, ed., *Thomas Morris Chester*, 353. Wilson's *The Black Phalanx*, written by a veteran who had served with USCT regiments, similarly made no complaint about the Grand Review. "On the 24th of May the 25th Corps began embarking for Texas by way of Mobile Bay," it stated. "The troops, however, occupied Texas but a short time, the confederate forces there surrendering upon the same terms as those of General Lee" (460–462). In *Free at Last: A Documentary History of Slavery, Freedom, and the Civil War* (New York: New Press, 1992), 511–512, editors Ira Berlin, Barbara J. Fields, Steven F. Miller, Joseph P. Reidy, and Leslie S. Rowland mentions that USCT service often continued beyond the end of hostilities because "most black regiments had not been organized until relatively late in the war." Some unnamed "federal officials," the editors add, "welcomed the opportunity to ship many of the black troops to the Mexican border to counter the threat posed by the emperor Maximilian." I am indebted to Barbara Gannon, a scholar of USCT soldiers, who shared her well-informed views about the deployment of the Twenty-Fifth Corps.

A review of several hundred USCT veterans took place in Harrisburg, Pennsylvania, on November 14, 1865. Simon Cameron, who had served as Lincoln's first secretary of war, was among the speakers. On the original review and a 2010 reenactment of the event, see "Harrisburg Will Celebrate 1865 USCT Grand Review," *Civil War News*, November 2010, 8. A Pennsylvania state historical marker offers this text: "Excluded from a May 1865 'Grand Review of the Armies' in Wash., DC, U.S. Colored Troops from Penna. and Mass. regiments assembled here at State & Filbert Sts. on Nov. 14, 1865 for a parade honoring their courage during the Civil War. Grand Marshal T. Morris Chester led them through Harrisburg to Sen. Simon Cameron's Front St. home to be gratefully acknowledged. Octavius Catto, William Howard Day, Gen. JB Kiddoo, & the Rev. Stephen Smith spoke." Like the marker, coverage of the 2010 reenactment asserted that USCT men had been barred from the Grand Review in Washington.

27. *HW*, June 10, 1865, 358; *Baltimore American and Commercial Advertiser*, May 25, 1865; Charles A. Page, *Letters of a War Correspondent*, ed. James R. Gilmore (Boston: L. C. Page, 1899), 396–397 (dispatch dated May 24, 1865); Brooks, *Mr. Lincoln's Washington*, 473; [Georgeanna Woolsey Bacon and Eliza Woolsey Howland, eds.], *Letters of a Family during the War for the Union, 1861–1865*, 2 vols. (N.p.: n.p., 1899), 2:714; Whitman, *Memoranda During the War*, 52. On Sheridan's deployment to the West, see also the *New York Evening Post* of May 23, 1865.

28. Gideon Welles, *Diary of Gideon Welles, Secretary of the Navy Under Lincoln and Johnson*, ed. Howard K. Beale, 3 vols. (New York: Norton, 1960), 2:310; *Philadelphia Press*, May 24, 1865; *Baltimore American and Commercial Advertiser*, May 25, 1865.

29. *Baltimore American,* May 27, 1865; *FL,* June 10, 1865, 180; *Baltimore American and Commercial Advertiser,* May 25, 1865; *Franklin (Pa.) Repository,* May 31, 1865.

30. [Bacon and Howland, eds.], *Letters of a Family during the War for the Union, 1861–1865,* 2:715; Whitman, *Memoranda During the War,* 52; *Philadelphia Daily Evening Bulletin,* May 23, 1865; *FL,* June 10, 1865, 177–178. See Washington's *Daily National Intelligencer,* May 25, 1865, regarding the size of the crowds. On the impressive physiques of Sherman's soldiers and the smart appearance of Meade's men, see also the *Philadelphia Daily Evening Bulletin,* May 24, 1865, and the *Huntingdon (Pa.) Globe,* May 31, 1865. A sergeant in the 105th Illinois Infantry wrote on May 26, 1865, that most onlookers probably went to the parade thinking "Sherman's army was a pretty good army to march and perhaps could fight tolerably but that they were entirely unmilitary and undisciplined . . . we had some pride in surprising the people somewhat." George F. Cram, *Soldiering with Sherman: Civil War Letters of George F. Cram,* ed. Jennifer Cain Bohrnstedt (DeKalb: Northern Illinois University Press, 2000), 168.

31. *Baltimore American and Commercial Advertiser,* May 24, 1865; Elizabeth Bacon Custer, *The Civil War Memoirs of Elizabeth Bacon Custer,* ed. Arlene Reynolds (Austin: University of Texas Press, 1994), 159–160; *Philadelphia Press,* May 24, 1865; John Ryan, *Campaigning with the Irish Brigade: Pvt. John Ryan, 28th Massachusetts,* ed. Sandy Barnard (Terre Haute, Ind.: AST Press, 2001), 158–159; Adams, *Letter from Washington, 1863–1865,* 267.

32. Annie G. Dudley Davis, Diary, May 28, 1865, HEHL; Bliss Morse, *Civil War Diaries and Letters of Bliss Morse,* ed. Loren J. Morse (Tahlequah, Okla.: Heritage Printing, 1985), 205; Page, *Letters of a War Correspondent,* 394; *New York Evening Post,* May 24, 1865 (quoting the *New York Times*); *Daily National Intelligencer* (Washington, D.C.), May 25, 1865. For a discussion of the symbolic importance of flags, which summoned in loyal citizens "mingled feelings of admiration, pride, and sadness," see Livermore, *My Story of the War,* 17–65 (quotation p. 17).

33. *Baltimore Sun,* May 25, 1865; *Daily National Intelligencer,* (Washington, D.C.), May 25, 1865; Louise Barnet, *Touched By Fire: The Life, Death, and Mythic Afterlife of George Armstrong Custer* (Lincoln: University of Nebraska Press, 2006), 35–36.

34. Don Higginbotham's *George Washington and the American Military Tradition* (Athens: University of Georgia Press, 1985) remains an excellent introduction to Washington as the ideal American military figure.

35. Logan, *Reminiscences of the Civil War and Reconstruction,* 127–130. The address was dated July 13, 1865. One of the best nonprofessional commanders on the Union side during the war, Logan developed a keen dislike for West Pointers and subsequently published a lengthy tribute to citizen-soldiers titled *The Volunteer Soldier in America* (Chicago: R. S. Peale, 1887).

36. *Daily National Intelligencer* (Washington, D.C.), May 23, 1865; *Baltimore American and Commercial Advertiser,* May 27, 1865; Adams, *Letter from Washington, 1863–1865,* 265–266 (dispatch written on May 27, appeared in print on May 31, 1865).

37. Adams, *Letter from Washington, 1863–1865,* 265 (dispatch written on May 24,

appeared in print on May 29, 1865). For an article that explores the theme of civic virtue among loyal soldiers and civilians, see Frances Clarke, "'Let All Nations See': Civil War Nationalism and the Memorialization of Wartime Volunteerism," *Civil War History* 52 (March 2006):66–93. "Unlike modern historians who point to military factors to explain the war's outcome," states Clarke, "the vast majority of Unionists argued unequivocally that their success resulted from the superior morality and civic virtue of their people—a version of the war well suited to reasserting American exceptionalism at home and abroad" (p. 67). Clarke's unionists might well have stressed military factors—which included but certainly were not restricted to citizen-soldiers doing grand work—far more than she implies.

38. Worthington C. Ford, ed., *War Letters 1862–1865 of John Chipman Gray, Major, Judge Advocate, and John Codman Ropes, Historian of the War* ([Cambridge, Mass.]: Riverside Press for the Massachusetts Historical Society, 1927), 496.

39. Cecilia Elizabeth O'Leary, *To Die For: The Paradox of American Patriotism* (Princeton, N.J.: Princeton University Press, 1999), 30–33.

40. Melinda Lawson, *Patriot Fires: Forging a New American Nationalism in the Civil War North* (Lawrence: University Press of Kansas Press, 2002), 180; Stuart McConnell, *Glorious Contentment: The Grand Army of the Republic, 1865–1900* (Chapel Hill: University of North Carolina Press, 1992), 8–9. McConnell argues that black veterans were consigned to segregated Grand Army of the Republic (G.A.R.) posts and otherwise ill-treated by their white counterparts during the postwar decades. Scholars have challenged this interpretation, discovering many integrated posts and describing a shared comradeship among black and white veterans. See, for example, Andre Fleche, "'Shoulder to Shoulder as Comrades Tried': Black and White Union Veterans and Civil War Memory," *Civil War History* 51 (June 2005):175–201; Barbara A. Gannon, *The Won Cause: Black and White Comradeship in the Grand Army of the Republic* (Chapel Hill: University of North Carolina Press, 2011). For earlier treatments that do not emphasize exclusion, see Allan Nevins, *The War for the Union: The Organized War to Victory, 1864–1865* (New York: Scribner's, 1971), 364–366; Shelby Foote, *The Civil War: A Narrative,* 3 vols. (New York: Random House, 1958–74), 3:1013–1018.

41. William B. Holberton, *Homeward Bound: The Demobilization of the Union and Confederate Armies, 1865–1866* (Mechanicsburg, Pa.: Stackpole, 2001), 28; Larry M. Logue, *To Appomattox and Beyond: The Civil War Soldier in War and Peace* (Chicago: Ivan R. Dee, 1996), 84; Terry L. Jones, *The American Civil War* (Boston: McGraw-Hill Higher Education, 2010), 626; Harry S. Stout, *Upon the Altar of the Nation: A Moral History of the Civil War* (New York: Viking, 2006), 456; Walter A. McDougall, *Throes of Democracy: The American Civil War Era, 1829–1877* (New York: HarperCollins, 2008), 492; Noah Andre Trudeau, *Out of the Storm: The End of the Civil War, April–June 1865* (Boston: Little, Brown, 1994), 321; Michael Fellman, Lesley J. Gordon, and Daniel E. Sutherland, *This Terrible War: The Civil War and Its Aftermath,* 2nd ed. (New York: Pearson Longman, 2008), 296.

42. Donald R. Shaffer, *After the Glory: The Struggles of Black Civil War Veterans* (Lawrence: University Press of Kansas, 2004), 184–185; Elizabeth D. Leonard, *Men of Color To Arms! Black Soldiers, Indian Wars, and the Quest for Equality* (New York: W. W. Norton, 2010), 19, 21–22.

43. Royster, *The Destructive War,* 405–406. For two brief positive accounts of the review, see Doris Kearns Goodwin, *Team of Rivals: The Political Genius of Abraham Lincoln* (New York: Simon and Schuster, 2005), 745–746; and Jeffry D. Wert, *The Sword of Lincoln: The Army of the Potomac* (New York: Simon and Schuster, 2005), 411–413. For a popular account that emphasizes differences between eastern and western soldiers, see Thomas Fleming, "The Big Parade," in *The Civil War—A Special Issue,* which was published as *American Heritage* 41 (March 1990):98–105.

44. A number of general histories of the Civil War era either ignore or barely mention the Grand Review. Among examples of the former, see Russell F. Weigley, *A Great Civil War: A Military and Political History, 1861–1865* (Bloomington: Indiana University Press, 2000); and John Keegan, *The American Civil War: A Military History* (New York: Knopf, 2009). For an example of the latter, see David J. Eicher's *The Longest Night: A Military History of the Civil War* (New York: Simon and Schuster, 2001), which devotes less than a paragraph to the Grand Review in more than 850 pages of text.

2. Union

1. *CW,* 8:149; Special Field Orders No. 76, May 30, 1865, in Sherman, *Memoirs of General W. T. Sherman,* 869–871. Sherman referred to the Armies of the Cumberland, the Ohio, and the Tennessee, which composed the force he led against Atlanta in the spring of 1864.

2. Karl Marx and Frederick Engels, *The Civil War in the United States,* ed. Richard Enmale (New York: International Publishers, 1937), 279–280. For a thoughtful analysis of the accomplishments, promise, and weaknesses of the republic in 1848, see the last chapter of Daniel Walker Howe, *What God Hath Wrought: The Transformation of America, 1815–1848* (New York: Oxford, 2007). See also Sean Wilentz, *The Rise of American Democracy: Jefferson to Lincoln* (New York: W. W. Norton, 2005), which cautions that to "impose current categories of democracy on the past is to block any understanding of how our own, more elevated standards originated" (p. xviii). On Americans and the European revolutions of 1848, see Andre Fleche, "The Revolution of 1861: The Legacy of the European Revolutions of 1848 and the American Civil War" (Ph.D. diss., University of Virginia, 2006).

3. Orville Vernon Burton, *The Age of Lincoln* (New York: Hill and Wang, 2007), 5–6; David Williams, *A People's History of the Civil War: Struggles for the Meaning of Freedom* (New York: New Press, 2005), 498.

4. Walter A. McDougall, *Throes of Democracy: The American Civil War Era, 1829–1877* (New York: HarperCollins, 2008), 399–400, 545, 492–493.

5. Harry S. Stout, *Upon the Altar of the Nation: A Moral History of the American Civil War* (New York: Viking, 2006), 458; Adam I. P. Smith, *The American Civil War* (New York: Palgrave Macmillan, 2007), 229.

6. Mark R. Wilson, *The Business of Civil War: Military Mobilization and the State, 1861–1865* (Baltimore: Johns Hopkins University Press, 2006), 1, 4, 191–192, 225.

7. Stout, *Upon the Altar of the Nation,* 381.

8. Michael Fellman, *In the Name of God and Country: Reconsidering Terrorism in American History* (New Haven: Yale University Press, 2010), 3, 58, 236; Lee W. Formwalt, "An American Historian North of the Border: A Conversation with Michael Fellman," *OAH Newsletter* 36 (February 2008):18.

9. Melinda Lawson, *Patriot Fires: Forging a New American Nationalism in the Civil War North* (Lawrence: University Press of Kansas, 2002), 6–7; Peter Parish, *The North and the Nation in the Era of the Civil War,* ed. Adam I. P. Smith and Susan-Mary Grant (New York: Fordham University Press, 2003), 8–9.

10. Christopher Waldrep, *Vicksburg's Long Shadow: The Civil War Legacy of Race and Remembrance* (Lanham, Md.: Rowman and Littlefield, 2005), xiii, xv–xvi; Edward J. Blum, *Reforging the White Republic: Race, Religion, and American Capitalism, 1865–1898* (Baton Rouge: Louisiana State University Press, 2005), 3.

11. Geoffrey C. Ward, *The Civil War: An Illustrated History* (New York: Knopf, 1990), 178. Fields's essay in the book is titled "Who Freed the Slaves?"

12. James M. McPherson and James K. Hogue, *Ordeal by Fire: The Civil War and Reconstruction,* 4th ed. (New York: McGraw-Hill Higher Education, 2009), 1-20. For representative indexes without entries for the concept of Union see: Burton, *Age of Lincoln;* Eicher, *The Longest Night;* Fellman, Gordon, and Sutherland, *This Terrible War;* Jeffrey Rogers Hummel, *Emancipating Slaves, Enslaving Free Men: A History of the American Civil War* (Chicago: Open Court, 1996); Jones, *The American Civil War;* McDougall, *Throes of Democracy;* Charles P. Roland, *An American Iliad: The Story of the Civil War,* 2nd ed. (New York: McGraw-Hill Higher Education, 2002); Smith, *The American Civil War;* Weigley, *A Great Civil War.*

13. Scott Nelson and Carol Sheriff, *A People at War: Civilians and Soldiers in America's Civil War, 1854–1877* (New York: Oxford University Press, 2008), 70–73; Fellman, Gordon, and Sutherland, *This Terrible War,* 91, 388.

14. For Union enlistments, see Frederick Phisterer, *Statistical Record of the Armies of the United States* (New York: Scribner's, 1883), 2–11. The totals are: 91,816 in response to Lincoln's call on April 15, 1861, for 75,000 militiamen to serve three months; 700,680 during the rest of 1861 (657,868 of whom enlisted for three years, 30,950 for two years, 9,147 for one year, and 2,715 for six months); and 524,060 in 1862 (421,465 for three years, 87,588 for nine months, and 15,007 for three months). The grand total of 1,316,556 undoubtedly included men who enlisted more than once; 1.2 million seems a reasonable estimate of different men who responded to the various calls for troops. McConnell's comments about ethnicity quoted here in Chapter 1 are correct—though their pertinence is more difficult to pin down. Soldiers reflected the society from which they were drawn. On the topic

of ethnicity, see Ella Lonn, *Foreigners in the Union Army and Navy* (Baton Rouge: Louisiana State University Press, 1951), chapter 1 and Appendix A; William L. Burton, *Melting Pot Soldiers: The Union's Ethnic Regiments* (Ames: Iowa State University Press, 1988).

15. On constitutional issues, see Michael Vorenberg, *Final Freedom: The Civil War, the Abolition of Slavery, and the Thirteenth Amendment* (New York: Cambridge University Press, 2004); Garrett Epps, *Democracy Reborn: The Fourteenth Amendment and the Fight for Equal Rights in Post-Civil War America* (New York: Henry Holt, 2006); Mark E. Neely, Jr., *The Fate of Liberty: Abraham Lincoln and Civil Liberties* (New York: Oxford University Press, 1991); and Stephen C. Neff, *Justice in Blue and Gray: A Legal History of the Civil War* (Cambridge, Mass.: Harvard University Press, 2010).

16. For a probing analysis of how historians bring their own cultural and political assumptions to the task of investigating the past, see Gordon S. Wood, *The Purpose of the Past: Reflections on the Uses of History* (New York: Penguin, 2008), chapters 19–21.

17. Population figures in the following three paragraphs were compiled from Campbell Gibson and Kay Jung, *Historical Census Statistics on Population Totals by Race, 1790 to 1990, and by Hispanic Origin, 1970 to 1990, for the United States, Regions, Divisions, and States*, Working Paper Series No. 56 (Population Division, U.S. Census Bureau: Washington, D.C., 2002). www.census.gov/population/www/documentation/twps0056/twps0056.html (accessed December 2010). The figures do not include Native American and Asian populations.

18. Iver Bernstein, *The New York City Draft Riots: Their Significance for American Society and Politics in the Age of the Civil War* (New York: Oxford University Press, 1990), Appendix C, p. 267; Craig Steven Wilder, *A Covenant with Color: Race and Social Power in Brooklyn* (New York: Columbia University Press, 2000), Table 6.1, p. 118; Junius P. Rodriguez, *Encyclopedia of Slave Resistance and Rebellion*, 2 vols. (Westport, Conn.: Greenwood, 2006), 2:544; Laura Tuennerman Kaplan, *Helping Others, Helping Ourselves: Power, Giving, and Community Identity in Cleveland, Ohio, 1880–1930* (Kent, Ohio: Kent State University Press, 2001), 84.

19. Eugene H. Berwanger, *The Frontier Against Slavery: Western Anti-Negro Prejudice and the Slavery Extension Controversy* (Urbana: University of Illinois Press, 1967), 139–141; V. Jacque Voegeli, *Free But Not Equal: The Midwest and the Negro during the Civil War* (Chicago: University of Chicago Press, 1967), 1. For a recent treatment of race in three Midwestern states, see Leslie A. Schwalm, *Emancipation's Diaspora: Race and Reconstruction in the Upper Midwest* (Chapel Hill: University of North Carolina Press, 2009). Schwalm describes the Civil War–era increase in black population in Iowa, Minnesota, and Wisconsin as significant. Between 1860 and 1870, however, the number of African American residents grew by only 6,135—from 1,069 to 5,762 in Iowa (out of a total population in 1870 of 1,194,020), 259 to 759 in Minnesota (out of 439,706), and 1,171 to 2,113 in Wisconsin (out of 1,054,670), p. 45. Schwalm gives the numbers for increase but not the overall populations in the states.

20. Scholars interested in the concept of whiteness would identify the unselfcon-

scious application of white power as part of the problem—and by extension part of historians' problem in finding specific evidence to support their analysis. For early examples of what has become a burgeoning literature on "whiteness," see Alexander Saxton's *The Rise and Fall of the White Republic: Class Politics and Mass Culture in Nineteenth-Century America* (New York: Verso, 1990); and David R. Roediger's *The Wages of Whiteness: Race and the Making of the American Working Class* (New York: Verso, 1991). This literature engages the nineteenth-century United States primarily through a prism of race as it related to class, gender, social and economic standing, and culture. Constraints of space prevent a detailed engagement with an analytical approach that raises as many questions as it answers. For a thoughtful review of the literature as of a decade ago, see Peter Kolchin, "Whiteness Studies: The New History of Race in America," *Journal of American History* 89 (June 2002):154–173.

21. John Edward Young, "An Illinois Farmer during the Civil War: Extracts from the Journal of John Edward Young," *Journal of the Illinois State Historical Society* 26 (April–July 1933):77–78.

22. Calvin Fletcher, *The Diary of Calvin Fletcher,* ed. Gayle Thornbrough and others, 9 vols. (Indianapolis: Indiana Historical Society, 1972–1983), 7:ix, 3–6, 51, 55. During the war, Fletcher played an active role in efforts to support Union soldiers and their families and worked closely with Indiana's Republican governor Oliver P. Morton on a number of projects. He also sought to help freedpeople, including contrabands who made their way to Indiana.

23. Daniel Webster, *The Papers of Daniel Webster,* ser. 4, *Speeches and Formal Writings, 1800–1852,* ed. Charles M. Wiltse, 2 vols. (Hanover, N.H.: University Press of New England, 1986–88), 2:550–551; Mary-Susan Grant, *North Over South: Northern Nationalism and American Identity in the Antebellum Era* (Lawrence: University Press of Kansas, 2000), 61; Wilentz, *Rise of American Democracy,* 321.

24. Kenneth M. Stampp, "The Concept of Perpetual Union," in Stampp, *The Imperiled Union: Essays on the Background of the Civil War* (New York: Oxford University Press, 1980), 33–35. Jackson's quotations are from his Proclamation on Nullification dated December 10, 1832.

25. W. R. Brock, *Conflict and Transformation: The United States, 1844–1877* (New York: Penguin, 1973), 130; Elizabeth R. Varon, *Disunion! The Coming of the American Civil War, 1789–1859* (Chapel Hill: University of North Carolina Press, 2008), 4–5, 1–2. Varon's book argues "that 'disunion' was once the most provocative and potent word in the political vocabulary of Americans." This suggests a question: How could "disunion" be so powerful a word if "Union" were not an even more important one?

26. Nicholas and Peter Onuf, *Nations, Markets, and War: Modern History and the American Civil War* (Charlottesville: University of Virginia Press, 2006), 2–4.

27. John Niven, *John C. Calhoun and the Price of Union* (Baton Rouge: Louisiana State University Press, 1988), 172–173.

28. *CW,* 5:527.

29. Ibid., 4:264–265.

30. Ibid., 438–439. The best exploration of the free labor ideology remains Eric Foner, *Free Soil, Free Labor, Free Men: The Ideology of the Republican Party before the Civil War* (New York: Oxford University Press, 1970). A paperback edition from 1995 includes a new introduction that argues only entrepreneurs and farmers fit the definition of "free men" as deployed by the Republicans.

31. *CW,* 5:388–389. For examples of harsh judgments of Lincoln's reply to Greeley, see Thomas J. DiLorenzo, *The Real Lincoln: A New Look at Abraham Lincoln, His Agenda, and an Unnecessary War* (Roseville, Calif.: Forum, 2002), 34–35; Lerone Bennett, Jr., *Forced into Glory: Abraham Lincoln's White Dream* (Chicago: Johnson, 1999), 474–479. For a very appreciative reading of the letter, which emphasizes Lincoln's political acumen in placing opponents on the defensive, see Allen C. Guelzo, *Lincoln's Emancipation Proclamation: The End of Slavery in America* (New York: Simon and Schuster, 2004), 132–136.

32. *CW,* 5:433–436 (quotation p. 433), 6:29–30.

33. Ibid., 5:530, 537.

34. Michael F. Holt, "Abraham Lincoln and the Politics of Union," in Holt, *Political Parties and American Political Development from the Age of Jackson to the Age of Lincoln* (Baton Rouge: Louisiana State University Press, 1992), 338–340. See also Richard Carwardine, "'A party man who did not believe in any man who was not': Abraham Lincoln, the Republican Party, and Union," in William J. Cooper and John M. McCardell, Jr., eds., *In the Cause of Liberty: How the Civil War Redefined American Ideals* (Baton Rouge: Louisiana State University Press, 2009), 40–62.

35. Breckinridge quoted in James A. Rawley, *The Politics of Union: Northern Politics during the Civil War* (1974; reprint with new preface, Lincoln: University of Nebraska Press, 1980), 156. For a straightforward narrative of the election of 1864, see John C. Waugh, *Reelecting Lincoln: The Battle for the 1864 Presidency* (New York: Crown, 1997).

36. *CW,* 8:149–151; William Frank Zornow, *Lincoln and the Party Divided* (Norman: University of Oklahoma Press, 1954), 94–97 (for the platform's resolutions).

37. Melville first published *Battle-Pieces and Aspects of the War* with Harper and Row in 1866. For a modern edition, see Hennig Cohen, ed., *The Battle-Pieces of Herman Melville* (New York: Thomas Yoseloff, 1963).

38. On the song's popularity, see Willard A. and Porter W. Heaps, *The Singing Sixties: The Spirit of Civil War Days Drawn from the Music of the Times* (Norman: University of Oklahoma Press, 1960), 69–70; Paul Glass and Louis C. Singer, *Singing Soldiers: A History of Civil War in Song* (1964; reprint, New York: Da Capo, 1993), 36–37.

39. George F. Root, *The Story of a Musical Life: An Autobiography* (Cincinnati: John Church, 1891), 132–133.

40. *CW,* 5:296–297. The states furnished 421,465 men in response to this call (Phisterer, *Statistical Record,* 4–5). Congress passed legislation for a national draft on April 16, 1863. The Militia Act of 1862, signed into law by Lincoln on July 17, sought 300,000 nine-month volunteers and gave the president permission, but did

not require him, "to receive into the service of the United States, for the purpose of constructing entrenchments, or performing camp service or any other labor, or any military or naval service for which they may be found competent, persons of African descent." For a discussion of the debates surrounding the Militia Act, see James W. Geary, *We Need Men: The Union Draft in the Civil War* (DeKalb: Northern Illinois University Press, 1991), 22–31.

41. Heaps and Heaps, *Singing Sixties,* 69–70. On northern fears of the Slave Power, see Leonard L. Richards, *The Slave Power: The Free North and Southern Domination, 1780–1860* (Baton Rouge: Louisiana State University Press, 2000), especially chapter 1. Confederates admired Root's tune so much they adapted it to their own use (Heaps and Heaps, *Singing Sixties,* 71–72).

42. The following five paragraphs are based in large part on patriotic covers in "Civil War Envelopes," 2 boxes, Ephemera Collection; and John Page Nicholson, comp., *Envelopes Issued During the War of the Rebellion 1861–1865,* 2 vols. (Philadelphia: n.p., 1880), both at HEHL. For illustrations of thousands of envelopes, see William R. Weiss, Jr., *The Catalog of Union Civil War Patriotic Covers* (n.p.: published by the author, 1995). For a very useful overview of covers in the United States and the Confederacy, see Steven R. Boyd, *Patriotic Envelopes of the Civil War: The Iconography of Union and Confederate Covers* (Baton Rouge: Louisiana State University Press, 2010).

43. Richard Eddy, *History of the Sixtieth Regiment New York State Volunteers, from the Commencement of Its Organization in July, 1861, to Its Public Reception at Ogdensburgh as a Veteran Command, January 7th, 1864* (Philadelphia: Crissy and Markley, Printers, for the author, 1864), 97; John W. Busey and David G. Martin, *Regimental Strengths and Losses at Gettysburg,* 4th ed. (Hightstown, N.J.: Longstreet House, 2005), 143; *OR* 25(1):185; Phisterer, *Statistical Record,* 62. Louis N. Beaudry, chaplain of the 5th New York Cavalry, also mentioned the volume of mail in his wartime diary. "My time was almost wholly consumed in writing letters for myself and others and attending to the mail," he wrote on June 5, 1864, "The men are bringing in mail very rapidly. We shall mail out about 800 letters in less than 36 hours' time." Louis N. Beaudry, *War Journal of Louis N. Beaudry, Fifth New York Cavalry: The Diary of a Union Chaplain, Commencing February 16, 1863,* ed. Richard E. Beaudry (Jefferson, N.C.: McFarland, 1996), 127.

44. For scores of examples of Washington on envelopes, see Weiss, Jr., *Catalog of Union Civil War Patriotic Covers,* 30–49.

45. For examples of Scott on envelopes, see ibid., 76–83.

46. For examples of McClellan on envelopes, see ibid., 84–103. Unlike Scott, he often was depicted with other Union officers.

47. Other early-war figures who graced many envelopes included generals John E. Wool, Robert Patterson, and John Pope.

48. Wiley probably read as many individual letters as anyone else. For discussions of methodology among contributors to the literature on common soldiers, see James M. McPherson, *For Cause and Comrades: Why Men Fought in the Civil War* (New York:

Oxford University Press, 1997), vii–x; Chandra Manning, *What This Cruel War Was Over: Soldiers, Slavery, and the Civil War* (New York: Knopf, 2007), 8–11; Kenneth W. Noe, *Reluctant Rebels: The Confederates Who Joined the Army after 1861* (Chapel Hill: University of North Carolina Press, 2010), 12–14. For a perceptive discussion of the literature, see Aaron Sheehan-Dean, "The Blue and Gray in Black and White: Assessing the Scholarship on Civil War Soldiers," in Sheehan-Dean, ed., *The View from the Ground: Experiences of Civil War Soldiers* (Lexington: University Press of Kentucky, 2007), 9–30.

49. I am indebted to a number of scholars with whom I have discussed the state of scholarship on common soldiers, including William Blair, Peter S. Carmichael, Joseph T. Glatthaar, Caroline E. Janney, Peter S. Luebke, T. Michael Parrish, Carol Reardon, and Joan Waugh. For warnings about the danger of cherry-picking evidence to support a thesis, see Jason Phillips, "Battling Stereotypes: A Taxonomy of Common Soldiers in Civil War History," *History Compass* 6 (September 2008):1, 408; Noe, *Reluctant Rebels,* 13 (quoting Glatthaar in a roundtable discussion). Noe labeled the practice of selecting only evidence that sustains the author's argument "lamentably frequent." For a path-breaking use of a sound statistical sample to get at basic questions regarding wealth, age, desertion, illness, casualties, and other subjects, see Glatthaar's *General Lee's Army: From Victory to Collapse* (New York: Free Press, 2008), appendix I, and *Soldiering in the Army of Northern Virginia: A Statistical Portrait of the Troops Who Served under Robert E. Lee* (Chapel Hill: University of North Carolina Press, 2011).

50. For example, see McPherson, *For Cause and Comrades,* chapters 7–8; McPherson, *What They Fought For, 1861–1865* (Baton Rouge: Louisiana State University Press, 1994), chapter 2; Earl J. Hess, *Liberty, Virtue, and Progress: Northerners and Their War for the Union* (New York: New York University Press, 1988), chapter 1; Reid Mitchell, *Civil War Soldiers* (New York: Viking, 1988), chapter 1. Interestingly, none of the indexes in these books has an entry related to Union as a concept.

51. Wilbur Fisk, *Anti-Rebel: The Civil War Letters of Wilbur Fisk,* ed. Emil Rosenblatt (Croton-on-Hudson, N.Y.: by the author, 1983), 207–208, 266; Terry M. McCarty and Margaret Ann Chatfield McCarty, eds., *The Chatfield Story: Civil War Letters and Diaries of Private Edward L. Chatfield of the 113th Illinois Volunteers* (Georgetown, Tex.: n.p., 2009–2010), 64.

52. William Bluffton Miller, *Fighting for Liberty and Right: The Civil War Diary of William Bluffton Miller, First Sergeant, Company K, Seventy-Fifth Indiana Volunteer Infantry,* ed. Jeffrey L. Patrick and Robert J. Willey (Knoxville: University of Tennessee Press, 2005), 52, 162–163.

53. Ron Gancas and Dan Coyle, Sr., eds., *Dear Teres: Civil War Letters of Andrew Joseph Duff and Dennis Dugan of Company F, the Pennsylvania Seventy-Eighth Infantry* (Chicora, Pa.: Mechling Bookbindery, 2003), 258–259, 288.

54. Robert McAllister, *The Civil War Letters of General Robert McAllister,* ed. James I. Robertson, Jr. (Baton Rouge: Louisiana State University Press, 1965), 533, 608.

55. Luman Harris Tenney, *War Diary of Luman Harris Tenney, 1861–1865,* ed. Frances Andrew Tenney (Cleveland, Ohio: Evangelical Publishing House, 1914), 134; Thomas L. Waterman, ed., *Upon the Tented Field* (Red Bank, N.J.: Historic Projects, 1993), 139; William T. Shepherd, *To Rescue My Native Land: The Civil War Letters of William T. Shepherd, First Illinois Light Artillery,* ed. Kurt H. Hackemer (Knoxville: University of Tennessee Press, 2005), 5 (italics in original).

56. The Henry E. Huntington Library's splendid collections, which include John Page Nicholson's unmatched library, hold all but four of the early regimentals as well as almost all of the hundreds subsequently published. For the breathtaking scope of Nicholson's collection, see [John Page Nicholson], *Catalogue of Library of Brevet Lieutenant-Colonel John Page Nicholson . . . Relating to the War of the Rebellion, 1861–1866* (Philadelphia: n.p., 1914). The catalog is 1,022 pages long.

57. On how scholars have treated the genre as a whole, see Peter C. Luebke, "Union Regimental Histories, 1865–1866" (M.A. thesis, University of Virginia, 2007), 1–6. I am much indebted to Peter for directing me to early Union regimentals.

58. For statements about intended audience, see [William Penn Lloyd], *History of the First Reg't Pennsylvania Reserve Cavalry, from Its Organization, August, 1861, to September, 1864 . . .* (Philadelphia: King and Baird, Printers, 1864), 4; Hermann Everts, *A Complete and Comprehensive History of the Ninth Regiment New Jersey Vols. Infantry. From Its First Organization to Its Final Muster Out* (Newark, N.J.: A. Stephen Holbrook, Printer, 1865), [3]; George W. Powers, *The Story of the Thirty Eighth Regiment of Massachusetts Volunteers* (Cambridge, Mass.: Dakin and Metcalf, 1866), iv.

59. William F. Fox, *Regimental Losses in the American Civil War, 1861–1865* (1898; reprint, Dayton, Ohio: Morningside, 1974), 122–423. Of the eighteen "fighting regiments," seven served only in the Army of the Potomac, three only in the western armies, one only in the Trans-Mississippi, four in South Carolina and the Eastern Theater, two in the Eastern and Western theaters, and one in the Trans-Mississippi and Eastern Theaters.

60. See Luebke, "Union Regimental Histories," 17, for a tabular summary of authorship.

61. James A. Mowris, *A History of the One Hundred and Seventeenth Regiment, N.Y. Volunteers, (Fourth Oneida,) from the Date of Its Organization, August, 1862, Till That of Its Muster Out, June, 1865* (Hartford, Conn.: Case, Lockwood and Company, 1866), 224–225 (Mowris was the regimental surgeon); Elias P. Pellet, *History of the 114th Regiment, New York State Volunteers* (Norwich, N.Y.: Telegraph and Chronicle Power Press Print, 1866), 288; J. R. Kinnear, *History of the Eighty-Sixth Regiment Illinois Volunteer Infantry, during Its Term of Service* (Chicago: Tribune Company's Book and Job Printing Office, 1866), 122.

62. J. Newton Terrill, *Campaign of the Fourteenth Regiment New Jersey Volunteers,* 2nd ed. (New Brunswick, N.J.: Daily Home News Press, 1884), 131–132; Ephraim J. Hart, *History of the Fortieth Illinois Inf., (Volunteers.)* (Cincinnati, Ohio: H. S. Bosworth,

1864), 10; Harris H. Beecher, *Record of the 114th Regiment, N.Y.S.V. Where It Went, What It Saw, and What It Did* (Norwich, N.Y.: J. F. Hubbard, Jr., 1866), 504–505. Terrill's volume is a largely unrevised second printing of the first edition, published in 1866. A sergeant in Co. K of the regiment, Terrill wrote the account between September 1, 1865, and July 15, 1866 (p. 132).

63. Evan M. Woodward, *Our Campaigns; or, the Marches, Bivouacs, Battles, Incidents of Camp Life and History of Our Regiment during Its Three Years Term of Service* (Philadelphia: John E. Potter, 1865), 14; John C. Myers, *A Daily Journal of the 192d Reg't Penn'a Volunteers Commanded by Col. William B. Thomas in the Service of the United States for One Hundred Days* (Philadelphia: Crissy and Markley, Printers, 1864), 146–147; Fletcher W. Hewes, *History of the Formation, Movements, Camps, Scouts and Battles of the Tenth Regiment Michigan Volunteer Infantry . . .* (Detroit: John Slater's Book and Job Printers, 1864), 53.

64. M. D. Gage, *From Vicksburg to Raleigh; or, A Complete History of the Twelfth Regiment Indiana Volunteer Infantry, and the Campaigns of Grant and Sherman, with an Outline of the Great Rebellion* (Chicago: Clarke and Co., 1865), 274–275. For an argument that northerners feared the spread of wasteful slave-based agriculture could threaten the nation's economy and the viability of the Union itself, see Adam W. Dean, "An Agrarian Republic: How Conflict Over Land Use Shaped the Civil War and Reconstruction" (Ph.D. diss., University of Virginia, 2010), ch. 3.

65. Mowris, *History of the One Hundred and Seventeenth Regiment,* 205–206.

66. H. M. Davidson, *History of Battery A, First Regiment of Ohio Vol. Light Artillery* (Milwaukee: Daily Wisconsin Steam Printing House, 1865), 139–141; Edwin B. Houghton, *The Campaigns of the Seventeenth Maine* (Portland, Me.: Short and Loring, 1866), 277; Powers, *Story of the Thirty Eighth Regiment,* 222.

67. Gage, *From Vicksburg to Raleigh,* ix; Thomas G. Murphey, *Four Years in the War. The History of the First Regiment of Delaware Veteran Volunteers, (Infantry.) Containing an Account of Marches, Battles, Incidents, Promotions . . .* (Philadelphia: James S. Claxton, 1866), 19–20; David W. Judd, *The Story of the Thirty-Third N.Y.S. Vols: or Two Years Campaigning in Virginia and Maryland* (New York: Benton and Andrews, 1864), 341.

68. Osceola Lewis, *History of the One Hundred and Thirty-Eighth Regiment, Pennsylvania Volunteer Infantry* (Norristown, Pa.: Wills, Iredell and Jenkins, 1866), 143–144; *CW,* 8:141.

69. Anyone conversant with mid-nineteenth-century sources has read innumerable references to the "damned Dutch," as German-speaking immigrants often were labeled, or seen Irish men and women depicted as simians in *Harper's Weekly, Harper's Monthly, Frank Leslie's Illustrated Newspaper,* and elsewhere. For analysis of attitudes toward German and Irish immigrants, see Bruce Levine, *The Spirit of 1848: German Immigrants, Labor Conflict, and the Coming of the Civil War* (Urbana: University of Illinois Press, 1992); Christian B. Keller, *Chancellorsville and the Germans: Nativism, Ethnicity, and Civil War Memory* (New York: Fordham University Press, 2007); Dale T. Knobel, *Paddy and the Republic: Ethnicity and Nationality in Antebellum America* (Mid-

dletown, Conn.: Wesleyan University Press, 1986); Susannah Ural Bruce, *The Harp and the Eagle: Irish-American Volunteers and the Union Army, 1861–1865* (New York: New York University Press, 2006).

70. Fleche, "The Revolution of 1861," 2–8; Marx and Engels, *The Civil War in the United States,* 23–24, 79.

71. Frank Freidel, ed., *Union Pamphlets of the Civil War, 1861–1865,* 2 vols. (Cambridge, Mass.: Harvard University Press, 1967), 2:1,131. This collection reprints Lieber's *Lincoln or McClellan. Appeal to the German in America* (New York: Loyal Publication Society, 1864). The pamphlet was published in English, German, and Dutch by the Loyal Publication Society as numbers 67, 59, and 71 respectively. Lieber most famously drafted rules of war for United States forces fighting the Confederacy, published in 1863 as General Orders No. 100 and widely known as the Lieber Code.

72. David Power Conyngham, *The Irish Brigade and Its Campaigns* (1867; reprint, New York: Fordham University Press, 1994), 5–6. Lawrence Frederick Kohl's introduction to this reprint stresses that Irish support for the war declined markedly after 1863 and that many Irish people living in the slaveholding states cheerfully supported the Confederacy (pp. xii–xvii). See also Fleche, "Revolution of 1861," for discussion of pro-Confederate sympathies among the Irish.

73. *HW,* May 23, 1863, 322.

74. *New York Times,* December 1, 1864. For analysis of the theme of republican government threatened by oligarchs—European and slaveholding in the American South—during the late antebellum years, see Michael F. Holt, *The Political Crisis of the 1850s* (New York: Wiley, 1978).

3. Emancipation

1. *CW,* 7:506–507. The meeting took place on August 19. Lincoln had developed similar themes two days earlier in a letter to Charles D. Robinson, Democratic editor of Green Bay, Wisconsin's, *Advocate* (ibid., 499–500).

2. Ibid., 5:48–49 (Lincoln's quotation is from his first annual message to Congress); Mark Grimsley, *The Hard Hand of War: Union Military Policy toward Southern Civilians, 1861–1865* (New York: Cambridge University Press, 1995), 141.

3. According to Col. H. L. Scott's *Military Dictionary: Comprising Technical Definitions; Information on Raising and Keeping Service, Including Makeshifts and Improved Matériel; and Law, Government, Regulation, and Administration Relating to Land Forces* (1864; reprint, Yuma, Ariz.: Fort Yuma Press, 1984), 283, fatigue duty included "work on fortifications, in surveys, cutting roads, and other constant labor."

4. For the 1864 vote, see Joel H. Silbey, *A Respectable Minority: The Democratic Party in the Civil War Era, 1860–1868* (New York: W. W. Norton, 1977), 151, 161.

5. *CW,* 8:332; Dunbar Rowland, ed., *Jefferson Davis Constitutionalist: His Life and Letters,* 10 vols. (Jackson: Mississippi Department of Archives and History, 1923), 5:72. For examples of arguments that manipulate evidence to play down the impor-

tance of slavery, see DiLorenzo, *The Real Lincoln;* and Charles Adams, *When in the Course of Human Events: Arguing the Case for Secession* (Lanham, Md.: Rowman and Littlefield, 2000).

6. Ira Berlin, Barbara J. Fields, Steven F. Miller, Joseph P. Reidy, and Lesley S. Rowland, *Slaves No More: Three Essays on Emancipation and the Civil War* (New York: Cambridge University Press, 1992), 4; Ira Berlin, Barbara J. Fields, Steven F. Miller, Joseph P. Reidy, and Lesley S. Rowland, *Free at Last: A Documentary History of Slavery, Freedom, and the Civil War* (New York: New Press, 1992), 95; Fields, "Who Freed the Slaves?", 179.

7. Manning, *What This Cruel War Was Over,* 6–7, 11, 152–153, 89–90, 255n5. Manning's index includes 15 lines of entries for "emancipation" but none for anything such as "Union, concept of."

8. Ibid., 258n28. In *For Cause and Comrades,* 124, James M. McPherson reports that in his sample, "Forty-two percent of the officers, compared with 33 percent of the enlisted man [sic] . . . explicitly supported emancipation." Support "increased after the low point of early 1863 as many anti-emancipation soldiers changed their minds." In *The Life of Billy Yank, The Common Soldier of the Union* (Indianapolis: Bobbs-Merrill, 1952), 42–44, Bell I. Wiley writes, "For every Yank whose primary goal was emancipation were to be found several whose chief goal was the Union and the system of government that it represented." Reid Mitchell, in *Civil War Soldiers,* 126, sums up his reading of the evidence: "When the Emancipation Proclamation made the war an antislavery war, some soldiers were jubilant, others horrified, and still more accepted the war's transformation with troubled minds." On reaction within the Army of the Potomac, see George C. Rable, *Fredericksburg! Fredericksburg!* (Chapel Hill: University of North Carolina Press, 2002), 373–378.

9. D. Reid Ross, *Lincoln's Veteran Volunteers Win the War: The Hudson Valley's Ross Brothers and the Union's Fight for Emancipation* (Albany: State University of New York Press, Excelsior Editions, 2008), 34–35; Robert Hunt, *The Good Men Who Won the War: Army of the Cumberland Veterans and Emancipation Memory* (Tuscaloosa: University of Alabama Press, 2010), 3. See also Mark A. Lause, *Race and Radicalism in the Union Army* (Urbana: University of Illinois Press, 2009), which describes an unusual version of unionism on the Kansas frontier: "Some Unionists, at least, articulated a triracial dream of the nation's future that increasingly loomed larger as the only practical means of securing the Union's survival" (p. 4). Native Americans serve as the third component of Lause's triracial framework.

10. Garry Wills, *Lincoln at Gettysburg: The Words that Remade America* (New York: Simon and Schuster, 1992), 37–38, 145.

11. Ibid., 38–39, 146.

12. Weigley, *A Great Civil War,* xviii; James Oakes, *The Radical and the Republican: Frederick Douglass, Abraham Lincoln, and the Triumph of Antislavery Politics* (New York: W.W. Norton, 2007), 119; Douglas L. Wilson, *Lincoln's Sword: The Presidency and the Power of Words* (New York: Knopf, 2006), 233–236; Eric Foner, *The Fiery Trial: Abraham Lincoln and American Slavery* (New York: W.W. Norton, 2010), 266–268.

Although it did not refer to Wills, David Donald's *Lincoln* (New York: Simon and Schuster, 1995), 465–466, quoted from the *Chicago Times* and just one other Democratic paper to reach a broad conclusion: "The bitterness of these protests was evidence that Lincoln had succeeded in broadening the aims of the war from Union to Equality and Union." For another admirer of Wills's "eloquent and persuasive case" that the Gettysburg Address "revolutionized the relationship between the Declaration of Independence, the Constitution, and the American nation," see Manning, *What This Cruel War Was Over,* 255n5. Manning does not offer any quotations from soldiers about the address.

13. Salmon P. Chase, *The Salmon P. Chase Papers,* ed. John Niven and others, 5 vols. (Kent, Ohio: Kent State University Press, 1993–98), 4:191–202; James P. McClure, Peg A. Lamphier, and Erika M. Kreger, eds., *"Spur Up Your Pegasus": Family Letters of Salmon, Kate, and Nettie Chase, 1844–1873* (Kent, Ohio: Kent State University Press, 2009), 244–245; Welles, *Diary,* 1:479–480; Hay, *Inside Lincoln's White House,* 113; French, *Witness to the Young Republic,* 435.

14. Louis A. Warren, *Lincoln's Gettysburg Declaration: "A New Birth of Freedom"* (Fort Wayne, Ind.: Lincoln National Life Foundation, 1964), 142; Herbert Mitgang, ed., *Abraham Lincoln: A Press Portrait* (1971; reprint, Athens: University of Georgia Press, 1989), 356–357, 362–364; *FL,* December 5, 1863, 171. Secretary of State William Henry Seward and Horatio Seymour, New York's Democratic governor, also spoke on November 18 in Gettysburg, and the press devoted some attention to both of them (a few Democratic papers led with Seymour's speech). On these accounts, see Gabor Boritt, *The Gettysburg Gospel: The Lincoln Speech that Nobody Knows* (New York: Simon and Schuster, 2006), 138, 141, 145.

15. Boritt, *The Gettysburg Gospel,* 136–138, 147; Frank L. Byrne and Andrew T. Weaver, eds., *Haskell of Gettysburg: His Life and Civil War Papers* (1970; reprint, Kent, Ohio: Kent State University Press, 1989), 233–234. Haskell disapproved of the reinterment of the Union dead at Gettysburg: "The skeletons of these brave men must be handled like the bones of so many horses, for a price, and wedged in rows like herrings in a box, on a spot where there was no fighting—where none of them fell!" (p. 235).

16. *CW,* 7:301. See Boritt, *The Gettysburg Gospel,* 116–117, on this subject. "Lincoln needed the masses in the middle," writes Boritt: "Equating his use of Jefferson's words with the rights of black people was only one possible interpretation . . . Equality could carry civil, economic, social, or racial connotations. To middle-of-the-road folk, the liberty he spoke about could be the white man's liberty."

17. Charles Sumner, *Charles Sumner: His Complete Works. Statesman Edition,* 15 vols. (Boston: Lee and Shepard, 1900), 12:271–272.

18. Edward L. Ayers, "Worrying About the Civil War," in Ayers, *What Caused the Civil War?: Reflections on the South and Southern History* (New York: W. W. Norton, 2005), 106–107; Robert Brent Toplin, "Ken Burns's *The Civil War* as an Interpretation of History," in Toplin, ed., *Ken Burns's* The Civil War: *Historians Respond* (New York: Oxford University Press, 1996), 28; Hunt, *Good Men Who Won the War,* 1. For a

dissenting opinion that insists Burns gave far too little attention to African Americans and the process of emancipation, see Leon Litwack, "Telling the Story: The Historian, the Filmmaker, and the Civil War," in Toplin, ed., *Ken Burns's* The Civil War, 119–140.

19. Gallagher, *Causes Won, Lost, and Forgotten,* 96–97. *Glory* offers little hint of restoring the Union as a powerful motivating force during the war.

20. William Friedheim and Ronald Jackson, *Freedom's Unfinished Revolution: An Inquiry into the Civil War and Reconstruction* (New York: New Press, 1996), viii, x, 61, 76. Historian Gary B. Nash, perhaps the leading academic scholar involved in shaping historical pedagogy in secondary schools, contributes a blurb for the book: "The text is sound as Vermont granite, reflecting the best scholarship of recent decades. Don't call this a textbook; call it a gold mine." Nash's endorsement also can be found on the American Social History website at http://ashp.cuny.edu/who-america/freedom-book/ (accessed December, 2010).

21. McPherson, *Battle Cry of Freedom,* 857–858.

22. On the importance of the Seven Days and Lee's emergence in field command as a turning point, see Gary W. Gallagher, "A Civil War Watershed: The 1862 Richmond Campaign in Perspective," in Gallagher, ed., *The Richmond Campaign of 1862: The Peninsula and the Seven Days* (Chapel Hill: University of North Carolina Press, 2000), 3–27.

23. Charles Sumner, *The Selected Letters of Charles Sumner,* ed. Beverly Wilson Palmer, 2 vols. (Boston: Northeastern University Press, 1990), 2:74–75; Berlin, Fields, Miller, Reidy, and Rowland, eds., *Free at Last,* xxix–xxx, 59–60; *CW,* 5:336–338.

24. The *New York Herald,* a moderate Democratic paper edited by James Gordon Bennett, remained optimistic through mid-June but on the 28th of that month could no longer mask disappointment: "We do not believe that our hope for the fall of Richmond must be relinquished; but, apparently, it must be again deferred; and hope so many times deferred may sicken a nation as bitterly as it will the heart of any single person in it."

25. *CW,* 7:53–54; George B. McClellan, *The Civil War Papers of George B. McClellan: Selected Correspondence, 1860–1865,* ed. Stephen W. Sears (New York: Ticknor and Fields, 1989), 595; Berlin, Fields, Miller, Reidy, and Rowland, eds., *Free at Last,* xxxii. Unlike McClellan, the Democratic platform in 1864 did not insist on restoration of the Union as a precondition to a cessation of fighting. See Donald Bruce Johnson, comp., *National Party Platforms, 1840–1956,* rev. ed. (Urbana: University of Illinois Press, 1978), 34–35.

26. Waugh, *Reelecting Lincoln,* 297; *CW,* 7:533–534.

27. According to Fox, *Regimental Losses in the American Civil War,* 541, the twelve campaigns with the highest Union casualties were (in descending order): Gettysburg, Spotsylvania, the Wilderness, Antietam, Chancellorsville, Chickamauga, Cold Harbor, Fredericksburg, Second Bull Run, Shiloh, Stones River, and the assaults against Petersburg on June 15–18, 1864. Of the twelve, only the action at Petersburg witnessed any significant fighting by black soldiers. The Ninth Corps included one

black division during the Overland campaign, but it was relegated to guarding wagon trains and other comparable duty. See the division's reports in *OR* 36(1):987–991. Fox included three black units among his three hundred "fighting regiments"—the 8th USCT, 79th USCT, and 54th Massachusetts—and seven among the 240 regiments that lost at least fifty men killed in a single battle. Black units suffered the highest number of men killed in the battles of Olustee, Nashville, the Crater, Fort Gilmer, Chaffin's Farm (2), and Fort Wagner (pp. 17–22, 421–423). Although each was a relatively small contest, Olustee and Fort Wagner resulted in a high percentage of casualties among Union soldiers (black and white). According to Thomas L. Livermore, *Numbers and Losses in the Civil War in America, 1861–1865* (1900; reprint, Bloomington: Indiana University Press, 1957), 75–76, casualties at Olustee were 214 per thousand men and at Fort Wagner 214 per thousand. At Port Hudson, another field where black troops fought, the ratio was 267 per thousand. By comparison, Union losses at Gettysburg were 212 per thousand.

28. For evaluations of black military contributions, see Dudley T. Cornish, *The Sable Arm: Black Troops in the Union Army, 1861–1865* (1956; reprint, Lawrence: University Press of Kansas, 1987), 285–291; and Joseph T. Glatthaar, "Black Glory: The African-American Role in Union Victory," in Gabor S. Boritt, ed., *Why the Confederacy Lost* (New York: Oxford University Press, 1992), 133–162. Glatthaar compares USCT units to American soldiers in World War I: "Like the doughboys in World War I, blacks helped to make the difference between victory and stalemate or defeat. They arrived in great numbers at the critical moment, and their contributions on and off the battlefield, in conjunction with those of whites, were enough to force the enemy to capitulate" (p. 161).

29. On the Democratic Party during the war, see Silbey, *A Respectable Minority;* Jean H. Baker, *Affairs of Party: The Political Culture of Northern Democrats in the Mid-Nineteenth Century* (Ithaca, N.Y.: Cornell University Press, 1983); Mark E. Neely, Jr., *The Union Divided: Party Conflict in the Civil War North* (Cambridge, Mass.: Harvard University Press, 2002); and Jennifer L. Weber, *Copperheads: The Rise and Fall of Lincoln's Opponents in the North* (New York: Oxford University Press, 2006).

30. Andrea G. Pearson, "*Frank Leslie's Illustrated Newspaper* and *Harper's Weekly*: Innovation and Imitation in Nineteenth-Century Political Reporting," *Journal of Popular Culture* 23 (Spring 1990):81. *Harper's Weekly* reported a circulation of 120,000 copies in early 1862, which, suggested the editor, was "the *largest* circulation of any Journal in this country in which Advertisements are published." The previous year, the editor estimated that each issue was read by ten adults (*HW,* January 4, 1862, 2; June 15, 1861, 369). For compilations of the Civil War–related illustrations from *Leslie's,* see Paul F. Mottelay and T. Campbell-Copeland, eds., *The Soldier in Our Civil War,* 2 vols. (New York and Atlanta: Stanley Bradley Publishing Company, 1893); for *Harper's,* see Alfred Hudson Guernsey and Henry M. Alden, *Harper's Pictorial History of the Great Rebellion,* 2 vols. (New York: Harper and Brothers, 1866).

31. *FL,* September 21, 1861, 289–290; *HW,* August 24, 1861, 530; January 25, 1862, 50.

32. *HW,* October 4, 1862, 626; January 24, 1863, 56–57; *FL,* October 25, 1862, 66. In the Republican *New York Times,* editor Henry J. Raymond noted that the preliminary proclamation "was conceived and resolved upon as a military measure, the effect of which would be two-fold: *First,* to deprive the rebel armies of the means of subsistence; and *second,* to reduce their numbers by making home-guards universally necessary." Lincoln's action, Raymond's piece made clear, was designed to hurt Confederates more than to help black people: "It is because we hate the Confederacy, that we like the Proclamation." *New York Times,* October 29, 1862, 4.

33. For examples of this coverage, see *FL,* November 2, 1861, 375; June 21, 1862, 180 (Robert Smalls and his compatriots); August 16, 1862, 325; December 20, 1862, 201; January 31, 1863, 296–297; March 5, 1864, 369; *HW,* June 14, 1862, 372–373 (including Smalls and the *Planter*); January 10, 1863, 32; January 17, 1863, front and back covers; January 17, 1863, 33, 48; January 31, 1863, 68; February 21, 1863, 116; May 9, 1863, 293. For a later example of contrabands reaching Union lines, see *FL,* August 20, 1864, 340.

34. *FL,* October 26, 1861, 368; *HW,* April 27, 1861, 416; June 14, 1862, 373. See also *HW,* September 3, 1864, 576; *FL,* March 25, 1865, 16. As the war went on, racist illustrations appeared less frequently.

35. *HW,* January 10, 1863, 18; March 14, 1863, 161, 168–169, 174.

36. Ibid., August 16, 1862, 528; *FL,* August 16, 1862, 321. See also [no author], *Ye Book of Copperheads* (Philadelphia: Frederick Leypoldt, 1863), a collection of anti-Copperhead cartoons. One echoed "A Consistent Negrophobist," depicting a drowning white man who spurned a black soldier offering his musket:

There once was a Patriot whose rigor
reached such a remarkable figure,
That he'd rather go down
in the water and drown
Than be saved by the help of a nigger. (p. 19)

37. *FL,* June 27, 1863, 209–210; March 5, 1864, 369 (a skirmish in South Carolina); July 9, 1864, 241 (front page; bringing in captured guns at Petersburg on June 15, 1864); March 4, 1865, 373 (action at James Island, S.C.); April 29, 1865, 92–93 (entering Richmond); *HW,* July 4, 1863, 427–428; March 18, 1865, 165 (entering Charleston); April 22, 1865, 248–249, 241 (entering Richmond). For brief narratives of African American soldiers at Port Hudson and Milliken's Bend, see John David Smith, ed., *Black Soldiers in Blue: African American Troops in the Civil War Era* (Chapel Hill: University of North Carolina Press, 2002), 78–135.

38. *FL,* May 7, 1864, 97; *HW,* April 30, 1864, 283–284; May 21, 1864, 328–329, 334. On the reaction to Fort Pillow, see Andrew Ward, *River Run Red: The Fort Pillow Massacre in the American Civil War* (New York: Viking, 2005); John Cimprich, *Fort Pillow, a Civil War Massacre, and Public Memory* (Baton Rouge: Louisiana State University Press, 2005).

39. *HW,* January 2, 1864, 52–54; August 29, 1863, 553; *FL,* March 7, 1863, 369.

40. *FL,* January 16, 1864, 264–265.

41. Ibid., February 13, 1864, 336.

42. *HW,* February 18, 1865, 97–98; February 11, 1865, 83; *FL,* February 18, 1865, 337, 344–345. Interestingly, the same issue of *Harper's* that merely noted passage of the amendment in the House included a long piece on the repeal of Black Laws in Illinois. "The monstrous subjection of this country to the prejudice against color," stated the article, "is not, as many who are under its influence suppose, 'a natural instinct;' it is only the natural result of a system which arbitrarily and forcibly makes color the sign of hopeless servitude" (p. 82).

43. *HW,* April 22, 1865, 256. On May 19, 1866, *Harper's* published a woodcut of black soldiers mustered out at Little Rock, Arkansas.

44. Valentine C. Randolph, *A Civil War Soldier's Diary: Valentine C. Randolph, 39th Illinois Regiment,* ed. David D. Roe and Stephen R. Wise (DeKalb: Northern Illinois University Press, 2006), 141; William B. Styple, ed., *Writing and Fighting the Civil War: Soldier Correspondence to the New York Sunday Mercury,* 2nd rev. ed. (Kearny, N.J.: Belle Grove, 2004), 301–302; Benjamin West to Dear Brother, December 14, 1864, item DL0999, JLNC. The letter in the *Sunday Mercury* from the 16th New York Heavy Artillery was signed "Jackson" and dated October 16, 1864.

45. Ford, ed., *War Letters 1862–1865 of Gray and Ropes,* 452, 62; Robert F. Engs and Cory M. Brooks, eds., *Their Patriotic Duty: The Civil War Letters of the Evans Family of Brown, Ohio* (New York: Fordham University Press, 2007), 95–96; Thomas L. Waterman, *Upon the Tented Field* (Red Bank, N.J.: Historic Projects, 1993), 80. Evans subsequently became a company commander in the 59th USCT Infantry. His father denounced the decision to join a black regiment, remarking that he "would rather clean out S__thouses at ten cents pr day" than serve in such "a degraded position" (p. xviii). The exchanges between son and father regarding emancipation and race are exceptionally revealing.

46. Andrea R. Foroughi, ed., *Go If You Think It Your Duty: A Minnesota Couple's Civil War Letters* (Saint Paul: Minnesota Historical Society Press, 2008), 126, 190; James Oliver, "Civil War Diary of Dr. James Oliver, 1862–1864," 4–5; Thomas P. Lowry, ed., *Swamp Doctor: The Diary of a Union Surgeon in the Virginia and North Carolina Marshes* (Mechanicsburg, Pa.: Stackpole, 2001), 58–59; George W. Snell to Dear Brother, March 18, 1863, item DL1068, JLNC. I thank Prof. Michael W. Carter for making available a copy of the typescript of Oliver's diary, adapted, in part, from James Oliver, *Ancestry, Early Life and War Record of James Oliver, M.D. Practicing Physician Fifty Years* (Athol, Mass.: Athol Transcript Company, 1916).

47. Jacob Behm, "Emancipation: A Soldier's View," *Civil War Times Illustrated* 21 (February 1983):46–47; James A. Connolly, *Three Years in the Army of the Cumberland: The Letters and Diary of Major James A. Connolly,* ed. Paul M. Angle (Bloomington: Indiana University Press, 1959), 58; George H. Mellish to his parents, May 2, 1865, Papers of George H. Mellish, HEHL; Henry C. Baldwin to My Old Friend Charley, February 1, 1863, item DL1109, JLNC.

48. Styple, ed., *Writing and Fighting the Civil War,* 161–162. On July 31, 1864. The *Sunday Mercury* claimed its circulation "in the Army exceeds that of all other papers published. The soldier would sooner go without his rations than his favorite paper" (p. 274).

49. William Bluffton Miller, *Fighting for Liberty and Right: The Civil War Diary of William Bluffton Miller, First Sergeant, Company K, Seventy-Fifth Indiana Volunteer Infantry,* ed. Jeffrey L. Patrick and Robert J. Willey (Knoxville: University of Tennessee Press, 2005), 69, 112, 162–164, 308.

50. Benjamin F. McIntyre, *Federals on the Frontier: The Diary of Benjamin F. McIntyre, 1862–1864,* ed. Nannie M. Tilley (Austin: University of Texas Press, 1963), 253, 326–327; Daniel W. Sawtelle, *All's for the Best: The Civil War Reminiscences and Letters of Daniel W. Sawtelle, Eighth Maine Volunteer Infantry,* ed. Peter H. Buckingham (Knoxville: University of Tennessee Press, 2001), 221–222.

51. Grant, *Papers,* 9:218; Frederick Law Olmsted, *The Papers of Frederick Law Olmsted.* Volume 4: *Defending the Union: The Civil War and the U.S. Sanitary Commission, 1861–1863,* ed. Jane Turner Censer (Baltimore: Johns Hopkins University Press, 1986), 540–541. In April 1861, Grant prophesied the end of slavery as a vigorous institution: "In all this I can but see the doom of Slavery. The North do not want, nor will they want, to interfere with the institution. But they will refuse for all time to give protection unless the South shall return soon to their allegiance, and then too this disturbance will give such an impetus to the production of their staple, cotton, in other parts of the world that they can never recover the control of the market again for that commodity. This will reduce the value of negroes so much that they will never be worth fighting over again." Grant to Frederick Dent, April 19, 1861, in Grant, *Papers,* 2:3–4.

52. For an emancipation-centered argument, see David E. Long, *The Jewel of Liberty: Abraham Lincoln's Re-Election and the End of Slavery* (Harrisburg, Pa.: Stackpole, 1994). For a discussion of literature on the election, see Adam I. P. Smith, "Review Essay," *Journal of the Abraham Lincoln Association* 20 (Winter 1999):67–84.

53. Waugh, *Reelecting Lincoln,* 340–341; McPherson, *Battle Cry of Freedom,* 804–805.

54. Edward King Wightman, *From Antietam to Fort Fisher: The Civil War Letters of Edward King Wightman, 1862–1865,* ed. Edward G. Longacre (Rutherford, N.J.: Fairleigh Dickinson University Press, 1985), 212; Beverly Hayes Kallgren and James L. Crouthamel, eds., *"Dear Friend Anna": The Civil War Letters of a Common Soldier from Maine* (Orono: University of Maine Press, 1992), 100–101, 107–108; Karen Marihugh-Loeffelman, ed., *Except for Hope, the Heart Would Break: A Family's Story Based on Original Civil War Letters* (n.p.: n.p., n.d. [circa 2003–04]), 344–345.

55. Henry E. Richmond to Harriett Richmond, October 23, November 6, 1864 (from near Petersburg, Virginia), items DL0560, DL0576; Lyman U. Humphrey to Dearest Mother, October 21, 1864, item DL0558; Asa M. Weston to Dear Sister, September 11, 1864, item DL1293, all in JLNC.

56. Thomas M. Stevenson, *History of the 78th Regiment O. V. V. I., from Its "Muster-*

In" to Its *"Muster-Out;"* Comprising Its Organization, Marches, Campaigns, Battles and Skirmishes (Zanesville, Ohio: Hugh Dunne, 1865), 182–183; Pound Sterling [William Maxson], *Camp Fires of the Twenty-Third: Sketches of the Camp Life, Marches, and Battles of the Twenty-Third Regiment, N.Y.V., during the Term of Two Years in the Service of the United States* . . . (New York: Davies and Kent, Printers, 1863), 104.

57. Wales W. Wood, *A History of the Ninety-Fifth Regiment Illinois Infantry Volunteers, from Its Organization in the Fall of 1862, until Its Final Discharge from the United States Service in 1865* (Chicago: Tribune Company, 1865), 62–63, 86–88; David Lathrop, *The History of the Fifty-Ninth Regiment Illinois Volunteers* . . . (Indianapolis, Ind.: Hall and Hutchinson Printers and Binders, 1865), 41.

58. Ovando J. Hollister, *History of the First Regiment of Colorado Volunteers* (Denver, Colo. Territory: Thos. Gibson and Co., 1863), 131–132.

59. Bartholomew B. S. De Forest, *Random Sketches and Wandering Thoughts; or, What I Saw in Camp, on the March, the Bivouac, the Battle Field and Hospital, While with the Army in Virginia, North and South Carolina, during the Late Rebellion. With a Historical Sketch of the Second Oswego Regiment, Eighty-First New York V.I* . . . (Albany, N.Y.: Avery Herrick, 1866), 192–193, 204–205.

60. Mowris, *History of the One Hundred and Seventeenth Regiment,* 113–114; James H. Clark, *The Iron-Hearted Regiment: Being an Account of the Battles, Marches and Gallant Deeds Performed by the 115th Regiment N.Y. Vols.* (Albany, N.Y.: J. Munsell, 1865), 85. Clark offered a mixed review of USCT units at the battle of the Crater, crediting them with gallantry under heavy Confederate musketry in the initial attacks but blaming eventual Union failure on "panic stricken" black soldiers who created "a wild scene of confusion" (p. 151).

61. Powers, *Story of the Thirty Eighth Regiment,* 90–91.

62. Evarts, *History of the Ninth New Jersey,* 127; Charles T. Bowen, *Dear Friends at Home: The Civil War Letters and Diaries of Sergeant Charles T. Bowen, Twelfth United States Infantry, 1861–1864,* ed. Edward K. Cassedy (Baltimore: Butternut and Blue, 2001), 508–509.

63. W. W. H. Davis, *History of the 104th Pennsylvania Regiment, from August 22nd, 1861, to September 30th, 1864* (Philadelphia: Jas. B. Rogers, Printer, 1866), 181–182.

64. Joseph Grecian, *History of the Eighty-Third Regiment, Indiana Volunteer Infantry. For Three Years with Sherman. Compiled from the Regimental and Company Books, and Other Sources, as Well as from the Writer's Own Observations and Experience* (Cincinnati: John F. Uhlhorn, Printer, 1865), 92; De Forest, *Historical Sketch of the . . . Eighty-First New York,* 204–205.

65. Henry T. Johns, *Life with the Forty-Ninth Massachusetts Volunteers* (Pittsfield, Mass.: C. A. Alvord, printer [for the author], 1864), 154, 285, 347.

66. Myers, *A Daily Journal of the 192d Reg't Penn'a Volunteers,* 157.

67. John W. Hanson, *Historical Sketch of the Old Sixth Regiment of Massachusetts Volunteers, during Its Three Campaigns in 1861, 1862, 1863, and 1864. Containing the History of the Several Companies Previous to 1861, and the Name and Military Record of*

Each Man Connected with the Regiment during the War (Boston: Lee and Shepard, 1866), 160–162.

68. Powers, *Story of the Thirty Eighth Regiment,* 126; Lyman B. Pierce, *History of the Second Iowa Cavalry; Containing a Detailed Account of Its Organization, Marches, and the Battles in which It Has Participated; Also, A Complete Roster of Each Company* (Burlington, Iowa: Hawk-Eye Steam Book and Job Printing Establishment, 1865), 52–53; Stevenson, *History of the 78th Regiment,* 313–314, 317.

69. A. F. Sperry, *History of the 33d Iowa Infantry Volunteer Regiment 1863–6* (Des Moines, Iowa: Mills and Company, 1866), 58.

70. Orlando P. Cutter, *Our Battery, or the Journal of Company B, 1st O.V.A.* (Cleveland, Ohio: Nevins' Book and Job Printing, 1864), 39; William Grunert, *History of the One Hundred and Twenty-Ninth Regiment Illinois Volunteer Infantry, Containing the Marches, Events and Battles of the Army Commanded by Gen. Sherman, from the Commencement of the Campaign against Atlanta, Georgia, to the Arrival at Washington, D.C.; Also, the Return of the Regiment from Washington to Chicago, Ills., and Events on the Route and in Chicago* (Winchester, Ill.: R. B. Dedman, 1866), 159.

71. Evan M. Woodward, *Our Campaigns; or, the Marches, Bivouacs, Battles, Incidents of Camp Life and History of Our Regiment during Its Three Years Term of Service* (Philadelphia: John E. Potter, 1865), 94.

72. Solon W. Pierce, *Battle Fields and Camp Fires of the Thirty-Eighth. An Authentic Narrative and Record of the Organization of the Thirty-Eighth Regiment of Wis. Vol. Inf'y, and the Part Taken by It in the Late War . . .* (Milwaukee: Daily Wisconsin Printing House, 1866), 126; W. H. Chamberlin, *History of the Eighty-First Regiment of Ohio Infantry Volunteers, during the War of the Rebellion* (Cincinnati: Gazette Steam Printing House, 1865), 37.

73. [No Author], *Lloyd's Battle History of the Great Rebellion* (New York: H. H. Lloyd and Co., 1866), 5, 12, 686–687, 712; Thomas P. Kettell, *History of the Great Rebellion* (Hartford, Conn.: L. Stebbins, 1865), 756–757.

74. Benson J. Lossing, *Pictorial History of the Civil War in the United States of America,* 3 vols. (Philadelphia: George W. Childs, 1866 [vol. 1]; Hartford, Conn.: T. Belknap, 1868 [vols. 2–3]), 1:4, 2:564. See also J. T. Headley, *The Great Rebellion; A History of the Civil War in the United States,* 2 vols. (Hartford, Conn.: Hurlbut, Williams and Company, 1863, 1866); and Frazar Kirkland, *The Pictorial Book of Anecdotes and Incidents of the War of the Rebellion* (Hartford, Conn.: Hartford Publishing, 1866).

75. On Ball's controversial sculpture, see Kirk Savage, *Standing Soldiers, Kneeling Slaves: Race, War, and Monument in Nineteenth-century America* (Princeton, N.J.: Princeton University Press, 1997), chapter 4. For Douglass's speech at the dedication, which included a revealing assessment of Lincoln and emancipation, see Thomas J. Brown, *The Public Art of Civil War Commemoration: A Brief History with Documents* (Boston and New York: Bedford/St. Martin's, 2004), 149–154. On the trajectory of Lincoln's various images, including that of the Great Emancipator, see Merrill D. Peterson, *Lincoln in American Memory* (New York: Oxford University Press, 1994).

4. The Armies

1. *CW,* 7:22–23, 8:332–333; Grant, *Papers,* 15:120–121.

2. John R. Neff, *Honoring the Civil War Dead: Commemoration and the Problem of Reconciliation* (Lawrence: University Press of Kansas, 1998), [243–247] (list of national cemeteries); Drew Gilpin Faust, *This Republic of Suffering: Death and the American Civil War* (New York: Knopf, 2008), 240–241; David W. Blight, *Race and Reunion: The Civil War in American Memory* (Cambridge, Mass.: Harvard University Press, 2001), 71; Mary R. Dearing, *Veterans in Politics: The Story of the G.A.R.* (Baton Rouge: Louisiana State University Press, 1952), 176–180; Mildred C. Baruch and Ellen J. Beckman, *Civil War Union Monuments: A List of Union Monuments, Markers and Memorials of the American Civil War, 1861–1865* ([Washington, D.C.]: Daughters of Union Veterans of the Civil War 1861–1865 Inc., 1978), 181. Baruch and Beckman list hundreds of monuments and provide photographs of approximately 250, but their roster is far from complete. Blight's book and William Blair, *Cities of the Dead: Contesting the Memory of the Civil War in the South, 1865–1914* (Chapel Hill: University of North Carolina Press, 2004), examine the different approaches to memorial days among white and black people in the North and South.

3. The next four paragraphs draw extensively on my published lecture titled *"The Progress of Our Arms": Whither Civil War Military History?* 44th Annual Fortenbaugh Memorial Lecture (Gettysburg, Pa.: Gettysburg College, 2006), 11–15.

4. For examples of comparing the American Civil War to Homer, see Charles P. Roland, *An American Iliad: The Story of the Civil War,* 2nd ed. (Lexington: University Press of Kentucky, 2004); and Ralph G. Newman and Otto Eisenschiml, eds., *The American Iliad: The Story of the Civil War as Narrated by Eyewitnesses and Contemporaries* (Indianapolis: Bobbs-Merrill, 1947). The battle of Gettysburg has inspired by far the largest number of books and essays. See Richard A. Sauers, *The Gettysburg Campaign, June 3–August 1, 1863: A Comprehensive, Selectively Annotated Bibliography,* 2nd ed. (Baltimore: Butternut and Blue, 2004), which lists 6,193 items.

5. The Sanitary Commission has received extensive scholarly attention. For two very different approaches to the topic, see William Quentin Maxwell, *Lincoln's Fifth Wheel: The Political History of the U.S. Sanitary Commission* (New York: Longman's, 1956); Lori D. Ginzberg, *Women and the Work of Benevolence: Morality, Politics, and Class in the 19th-Century United States* (New Haven, Conn.: Yale University Press, 1990).

6. There have been encouraging examples of political, social, and cultural historians who explore the reciprocal relationship between military and nonmilitary factors—among them James M. McPherson, George C. Rable, Kenneth W. Noe, Mark E. Neely, Jr., Drew Gilpin Faust, and Daniel E. Sutherland.

7. *Testimony of James B. Gardner, Deputy Executive Director American Historical Association, Before the Subcommittee on National Parks and Public Lands, Committee on Interior and Insular Affairs of the U.S. House of Representatives, H.R. 3513 and S. 1770, September 4, 1990* (Washington: American Historical Association, 1990), 2–3; Eric

Foner, ed., *The New American History* (Philadelphia: Temple University Press, 1990), 79–81.

8. Ken Gewertz, "War and Remembrance," *Harvard Gazette,* July 13, 1995; McPherson, *Battle Cry of Freedom,* xviii–xix. A clipping of Gewertz's article, without page numbers, was provided to me by T. Michael Parrish of Baylor University. The professor in question was William E. Gienapp, an eminent historian of mid-nineteenth-century American political history.

9. On American attitudes toward professional versus volunteer soldiers before the Civil War, see Russell F. Weigley, *History of the United States Army,* rev. ed. (Bloomington: Indiana University Press, 1984), chs. 1–9; Marcus Cunliffe, *Soldiers and Civilians: The Martial Spirit in America, 1775–1865* (Boston: Little, Brown, 1968). On the tension between professional officers and volunteer soldiers, see Steven J. Ramold, *Baring the Iron Hand: Discipline in the Union Army* (DeKalb: Northern Illinois University Press, 2010), especially chapter 2; Wayne Wei-siang Hsieh, *West Pointers and the Civil War: The Old Army in War and Peace* (Chapel Hill: University of North Carolina Press, 2009).

10. Marvin A. Kreidberg and Merton G. Henry, *History of Mobilization in the United States Army, 1775–1945* (1955; reprint, Washington, D.C.: Center of Military History, 1984), 141; Holberton, *Homeward Bound,* 8–9; Alan R. Millet and Peter Maslowski, *For the Common Defense: A Military History of the United States of America* (New York: Free Press, 1984), 233; "German History in Documents and Images," http://germanhistorydocs.ghidc.org/pdf/eng/617_Strength%20German%20Army_121.pdf (accessed June, 2010); "Effective Strength of the French Army," *New York Times,* November 12, 1892, http://query.nytimes.com/mem/archive-free/pdf?res=9506E4DF1638E233A25751C1A9679D94639ED7CF (accessed December, 2010).

11. Jacob Gantz, *Such Are the Trials: The Civil War Letters of Jacob Gantz,* ed. Kathleen Davis (Ames: Iowa State University Press, 1991), 95. Winslow also returned to civilian life to pursue a successful career as a railroad executive. Roger D. Hunt, *Brevet Brigadier Generals in Blue* (Gaithersburg, Md.: Olde Soldier Books, 1990), 683.

12. John W. Haley, *The Rebel Yell and the Yankee Hurrah: The Civil War Journal of a Maine Volunteer,* ed. Ruth L. Silliker (Camden, Me.: Down East Books, 1985), 280–283, 13.

13. William Wiley, *The Civil War Diary of a Common Soldier: William Wiley of the 77th Illinois Infantry,* ed. Terrence J. Winschel (Baton Rouge: Louisiana State University Press, 2001), 174–175, 182–184.

14. Arnold H. Sturtevant, ed., *Josiah Volunteered: A Collection of Diaries, Letters and Photographs of Josiah H. Sturtevant and His Wife, Helen, and His Four Children* (Farmington, Me.: Knowlton and McLeary, 1977), 128–130. Sturtevant began the war with the 17th Maine Infantry.

15. Charles O. Musser, *Soldier Boy: The Civil War Letters of Charles O. Musser, 29th Iowa,* ed. Barry Popchock (Iowa City: University of Iowa Press, 1995), 214–217.

16. William Garrigues Bentley, *"Burning Rails as We Pleased": The Civil War Letters*

of William Garrigues Bentley, 104th Ohio Volunteer Infantry, ed. Barbara Bentley Smith and Nina Bentley Baker (Jefferson, N.C.: McFarland, 2004), 153–155, 158.

17. John Bennitt, *"I Hope to Do My Country Service": The Civil War Letters of John Bennitt, M.D., Surgeon, 19th Michigan Infantry,* ed. Robert Beasecker (Detroit: Wayne State University Press, 2005), 374–377. Some soldiers dealt with the end of their service more tersely. Corporal George W. Belles of the 139th Pennsylvania Infantry wrote in his diary on June 26, 1865: "This morning is wet. We got our discharge and pay at noon and left for home gay and happy. I arrived at home in the evening. *This ends my soldiering mission in the great Rebellion!*" George W. Belles, *Preserve It Reader in Remembrance of Me: The Writings and Saga of American Civil War Soldier George W. Belles,* ed. Ron Bardnell (Bennington, Vt.: Merriam Press, 2009), 239.

18. Jake Hart to Dear Companion, October 3, 1864, item DL1136, JLNC; Harrison Washburn to Mr. Neff, February 13, 1863, item DL1395, JLNC. For discussions of soldiers' disenchantment with the home front, see Wiley, *Life of Bill Yank,* 286–288; Reid Mitchell, *The Vacant Chair: The Northern Soldier Leaves Home* (New York: Oxford University Press, 1993), 32–34; McPherson, *For Cause and Comrades,* 142–144; Timothy J. Orr, "'A Viler Enemy in Our Rear': Pennsylvania Soldiers Confront the North's Antiwar Movement," in Aaron Sheehan-Dean, ed., *The View from the Ground: Experiences of Civil War Soldiers* (Lexington: University Press of Kentucky, 2007), 171–198.

19. Arnold Yeckley to My Dear Friend, March 4, 1863, item DL1121, JLNC.

20. Twenty-seven covers between the bombardment of Fort Sumter and the end of 1861 dealt with military topics, forty-seven in 1862, forty in 1863, forty-three in 1864, and fifteen in the first half of 1865 (several others depicted people and events associated with Lincoln's assassination).

21. *New York Times,* April 21, June 2, 1864; *New York Herald,* May 6, 14, 1864.

22. *Chicago Tribune,* May 18, 1864, 1–2; May 16, 1864, 2. The allusion to dying with one's face to the enemy stemmed from reports about the final words of Brig. Gen. James Clay Rice, who was mortally wounded in fighting at Spotsylvania Court House on May 10, 1864.

23. *New York Herald,* April 20, 1864, 4; *New York Times,* May 14, 1864, 6; *Philadelphia Daily Evening Bulletin,* May 13, 1864, 4.

24. *FL,* November 9, 1861, 386; *HW,* April 19, 1862, 248–249; Robert Gould Shaw, *Blue-Eyed Child of Fortune: The Civil War Letters of Robert Gould Shaw,* ed. Russell Duncan (Athens: University of Georgia Press, 1992), 73.

25. Joan Waugh, *U.S. Grant: American Hero, American Myth* (Chapel Hill: University of North Carolina Press, 2009), 1. Winfield Scott had been a lieutenant general by brevet (an honorary rank that carried some privileges) since 1855, but his formal rank always remained major general. See Timothy D. Johnson, *Winfield Scott: The Quest for Military Glory* (Lawrence: University Press of Kansas, 1998), 218–219.

26. Brooks D. Simpson, *Ulysses S. Grant: Triumph Over Adversity, 1822–1865* (Boston: Houghton, Mifflin, 2000), 256–258; Grant, *Papers,* 10:195.

27. McIntyre, *Federals on the Frontier,* 172–173; *Chicago Tribune,* May 14, 1864, 2; *New York Herald,* May 10, 1864, 4.

28. *Philadelphia Daily Evening Bulletin,* June 7, 1864, 4.

29. *New York Tribune,* June 11, 1864, 9. The paper quoted French historian and political figure François Pierre Guillaume Guizot regarding common sense and determination. The piece on Grant was reprinted from *U.S. Service Magazine.*

30. Grant, *Papers,* 9:219n1 (Wilson quoting Dana to Elihu B. Washburne, July 25, 1863); *New York Herald,* March 12, 1864, 4. Stanton appointed Dana assistant secretary of war in the summer of 1863. For a specific allusion to Grant as a possible presidential candidate, see the *New York Herald,* June 1, 1864, 4: "This is a man of whom it may be truly said that the Presidency seeks him, instead of his seeking the Presidency."

31. *FL,* March 19, 1864, 407; *New York Herald,* March 11, 1864, 4; May 16, 1864, 4.

32. For examples of newspapers that consistently supported Grant, though noting, and often trying to place in context, the enormous Union casualties during the Overland campaign, see: *Chicago Tribune,* May 14, 16, June 6, 15, 29, 1864; *New York Herald,* June 4, 6, 17, 28, 1864; *New York Times,* May 19, 30, June 6, 7, 18, 1864; *New York Tribune,* May 14, June 7, 28, 1864; *Philadelphia Daily Evening Bulletin,* May 31, June 6, 1864. For an article that discussed Sheridan's Valley campaign as part of Grant's overall strategic plan, see *FL,* October 8, 1864, 33–34.

33. For an example of harsh comments about Grant in the northern press, see *New York Mercury,* June 5, 1864, in Styple, ed., *Writing and Fighting the Civil War,* 264–265. Such comments were far more common in the Confederate press. See examples in *Richmond Daily Dispatch,* June 7, 9, 24, 1864; *Richmond Enquirer,* June 16, 1864; *The Confederate Union (Milledgeville, Ga.),* May 31, 1864. For war weariness among Democrats, see Frank L. Klement, *The Copperheads of the Middle West* (Chicago: University of Chicago Press, 1960), 232–233; Weber, *Copperheads,* 135–156. For examples of books that claim a broad criticism in the North of Grant as a butcher, see Fellman, Gordon, and Sutherland, *This Terrible War,* 269; Randall and Donald, *Civil War and Reconstruction,* 420, 424.

34. McAllister, *Civil War Letters,* 434; Maria Lydig Daly, *Diary of a Union Lady, 1861–1865* (1962; reprint, Lincoln: University of Nebraska Press, 2000), 299. See also Joseph Hopkins Twichell, *The Civil War Letters of Joseph Hopkins Twichell: A Chaplain's Story,* ed. Peter Messent and Steve Courtney (Athens: University of Georgia Press, 2006). A three-year volunteer in the 71st New York Infantry and a Republican, Twichell wrote his mother on June 1, 1864, from near Richmond: "The Great Campaign is proceeding amid blood and hardship. The army was never in better spirits, or more confident of success than now . . . Gen. Grant has gained a strong point in winning the confidence of his army, and is playing the grand game as if he understood his business. God bless him. The more the war costs, the more imperatively is the nation called upon to support it" (pp. 304–305).

35. Frank Wilkeson, *Recollections of a Private Soldier in the Army of the Potomac* (New York: G. P. Putnam's, 1887), 192, 196.

36. *The Old Guard, A Monthly Journal Devoted to the Principles of 1776 and 1787,* vol. 2, no. 7 (July 1864):165; vol. 2, no. 8 (August 1864):189.

37. *HW,* April 22, 1865, 242.

38. Waugh, *U.S. Grant,* 120, 243, 249, 297–99; Grant, *Papers,* 18:264; Mark E. Neely, Jr., and Harold Holzer, *The Union Image: Popular Prints of the Civil War North* (Chapel Hill: University of North Carolina Press, 2000), 177, 183.

39. Waugh, *U.S. Grant,* 250–251, 247; Walt Whitman, "As One by One Withdraw the Lofty Actors," *HW,* May 16, 1885, 310. The poem was reprinted as "Grant" in *Critic* 7 (August 15, 1885):80, and revised as "Death of General Grant" in the "Sands at Seventy" annex to the 1888 edition of *Leaves of Grass.*

40. Peter Parish, *The American Civil War* (New York: Holmes and Meier, 1975), 637; Susan-Mary Grant, *North Over South: Northern Nationalism and American Identity in the Antebellum Era* (Lawrence: University Press of Kansas, 2000), 161; Waugh, *U.S. Grant,* especially the discussion of Grant's *Personal Memoirs* in chapter 4. See also Parish's essay titled "Abraham Lincoln and American Nationhood" in Smith and Grant, eds., *The North and the Nation,* 200–226. Although focused on Lincoln, Parish obliquely credits the armies with a major role: "The successful fight to save the Union was the essential prerequisite for all of Lincoln's other contributions to the making of American nationhood" (p. 206).

41. Lawson, *Patriot Fires,* 12–23. On the U.S. Sanitary Commission as a force to overcome "local prejudices" and promote "National ideas . . . the great Federal idea for which we are contending at such cost of blood and treasure," see George Templeton Strong, *Origin, Struggles and Principles of the U.S. Sanitary Commission* (Boston: n.p., 1864), 27–31.

42. *HW,* May 4, 1861, 274.

43. Nina Silber and Mary Beth Sievens, eds., *Yankee Correspondence: Civil War Letters between New England Soldiers and the Home Front* (Charlottesville: University Press of Virginia, 1996), 90–91. See also pp. 84–85 for this from an artillerist in Company A of the 3rd Rhode Island Artillery on December 15, 1861: "The curley headed contraband is here, in great quantities, male and female, old and young; I can tell you honestly that if our army stays he[re] much longer there will be more niggers than soldiers for they are coming into our camps every day."

44. Shaw, *Blue-Eyed Child of Fortune,* 252.

45. Josiah Bradford to Dear Wife, December 11, 1863, item DL0901, JLNC.

46. Charles Mosher, *Charlie Mosher's Civil War: From Fair Oaks to Andersonville with the Plymouth Pilgrims (85th N.Y. Infantry),* ed. Wayne Mahood (Hightstown, N.J.: Longstreet House, 1994), 166. Innumerable officers and men in the ranks commented about black expectations regarding the Union army. Brigadier General Alpheus S. Williams, a division and corps commander under Sherman in Georgia and the Carolinas, wrote from Savannah in January 1865: "I have been astonished to find how widespread amongst field hands, as well as house servants, the idea is that the

Yankees are coming to set the captive free, and how long this feeling has existed." Alpheus S. Williams, *From the Cannon's Mouth: The Civil War Letters of General Alpheus Williams,* ed. Milo M. Quaife (Detroit: Wayne State University Press, 1959), 370–371.

47. Styple, ed., *Writing and Fighting the Civil War,* 199–200.

48. Grunert, *History of the One Hundred and Twenty-Ninth Regiment,* 125–126; S. F. Fleharty, *Our Regiment. A History of the 102d Illinois Infantry Volunteers, with Sketches of the Atlanta Campaign, the Georgia Raid, and the Campaign in the Carolinas* (Chicago: Brewster and Hanscom Printers, 1865), 120; Marion Morrison, *A History of the Ninth Regiment Illinois Volunteer Infantry* (Monmouth, Ill.: John S. Clark, Printer, 1864), 80.

49. James Marten, "A Feeling of Restless Anxiety: Loyalty and Race in the Peninsula Campaign and Beyond," in Gary W. Gallagher, ed., *The Richmond Campaign of 1862* (Chapel Hill: University of North Carolina Press, 2000), 121–152 (*Richmond Enquirer* quotation p. 136); Edmund Ruffin, *The Diary of Edmund Ruffin,* ed. William Kauffman Scarborough, 3 vols. (Baton Rouge: Louisiana State University Press, 1972–1989), 2:346–347.

50. Philip D. Dillard, "'What Price Must We Pay for Victory?': Views on Arming Slaves from Lynchburg, Virginia, to Galveston, Texas," in Lesley J. Gordon and John C. Inscoe, eds., *Inside the Confederate Nation: Essays in Honor of Emory M. Thomas* (Baton Rouge: Louisiana State University Press, 2005), 316–334.

51. Amanda Virginia Edmonds, *Journals of Amanda Virginia Edmonds: Lass of the Mosby Confederacy, 1859–1867,* ed. Nancy Chappelear Baird (Stephens City, Va.: by the editor, 1984), 116; Anne S. Frobel, *The Civil War Diary of Anne S. Frobel of Winton Hill in Virginia,* ed. Mary H. and Dallas M. Lancaster (Birmingham, Ala.: by the editors, 1986), 70.

52. *OR,* ser. 3, vol. 5:138–139; Ira Berlin, Joseph P. Reidy, and Leslie S. Rowland, eds., *Freedom: A Documentary History of Emancipation, 1861–1867,* ser. 2, *The Black Military Experience* (New York: Cambridge University Press, 1982), 10–15.

53. Sperry, *History of the 33rd Iowa,* 129–130.

54. James M. McPherson, "Who Freed the Slaves?" in McPherson, *Drawn with the Sword: Reflections on the American Civil War* (New York: Oxford University Press, 1996), 192–207 (quotation p. 206). See also Mark E. Neely, Jr., "Lincoln and the Theory of Self-Emancipation," in John Y. Simon and Barbara Hughett, eds., *The Continuing Civil War: Essays in Honor of the Civil War Round Table of Chicago* (Dayton, Ohio: Morningside, 1992), 45–60. Neely directs readers toward "occupied Union territory" for the answer to who freed the slaves but says very little about United States military forces (p. 51).

55. Berlin, Reidy, and Rowland, eds., *The Black Military Experience,* 1; Berlin, Fields, Miller, Reidy, and Rowland, *Slaves No More,* 5–6; Leon F. Litwack, *Been in the Storm So Long: The Aftermath of Slavery* (New York: Random House, 1979), xi.

56. Fields, "Who Freed the Slaves?" 179–181. For a detailed estimate that approximately 500,000 slaves in the Confederacy had been freed by war's end, see Ira

Berlin, Thavolia Glymph, Steven F. Miller, Joseph P. Reidy, Leslie S. Rowland, and Julie Saville, eds., *Freedom: A Documentary History of Emancipation, 1861–1867*, ser. 1, vol. 3, *The Wartime Genesis of Free Labor: The Lower South* (New York: Cambridge University Press, 1990), 77–80.

57. W. E. B. Du Bois, *Black Reconstruction: An Essay Toward a History of the Part Which Black Folk Played in the Attempt to Reconstruct Democracy in America, 1860–1880* (1935; reprint, Milwood, N.Y.: Kraus-Thomson, 1963), 55; Steven Hahn, *The Political Worlds of Slavery and Freedom* (Cambridge, Mass.: Harvard University Press, 2009), 58. See also Hahn's *A Nation Under Our Feet: Black Political Struggles in the Rural South from Slavery to the Great Depression* (Cambridge, Mass.: Harvard University Press, 2003), which posits "what became the largest slave rebellion in modern history . . . a rebellion that culminated in tens of thousands of former slaves taking up arms to help the Union army crush the Confederacy and complete the destruction of slavery" (p. 7). Yet Hahn also notes that "the decided majority of blacks most everywhere in the Confederacy—and especially in much of the Deep South—remained on plantations and farms in presumptive slavery" (pp. 82–83, 87; quotation on p. 83).

58. The 1994 stamp showed Lincoln as president, but the text on the back was silent about emancipation. The bicentennial stamps depicted Lincoln as a "Rail Splitter," "Lawyer," "Politician" (debating Stephen A. Douglas in the 1858 Illinois senatorial context), and "President" (conferring with U.S. Grant, W. T. Sherman, and Admiral David Dixon Porter in 1865). The pennies featured his birthplace in Kentucky, his formative years in Indiana (a rail splitter reading a book on a large log), his professional life as a lawyer in Illinois, and his presidency in Washington, D.C. (the unfinished Capitol Dome of 1861).

59. For a fascinating discussion of how the loyal citizenry dealt with "the somewhat uncomfortable implications" of deciding the "highly contentious legal question [of secession] through violence," see Cynthia Nicoletti, "The Great Question of the War: The Legal Status of Secession in the Aftermath of the American Civil War, 1861–1865" (Ph.D. diss., University of Virginia, 2010), chapter 7 (quotation p. 405); Nicoletti, "The American Civil War as a Trial by Battle," *Law and History Review* 28 (February 2010):71–110.

5. Affirmation

1. On reaction to Lincoln's assassination, see Thomas Reed Turner, *Beware the People Weeping: Public Opinion and the Assassination of Abraham Lincoln* (Baton Rouge: Louisiana State University Press, 1982); Elizabeth D. Leonard, *Lincoln's Avengers: Justice, Revenge, and Reunion after the Civil War* (New York: W. W. Norton, 2004). Eight conspirators were tried by a military commission, and four, including Mary Surratt, were hanged in Washington on July 7, 1865. On attitudes toward Wirz and his trial, see William Marvel, *Andersonville: The Last Depot* (Chapel Hill: University of North Carolina Press, 1994), 243–247; Leonard, *Lincoln's Avengers*, 152–163.

2. For a succinct treatment of the factors that distressed loyal citizens in the aftermath of the war, see Eric Foner, *Reconstruction: America's Unfinished Revolution, 1863–1877* (New York: Harper and Row, 1988), 176–227.

3. For examples of the idea of a lost moment, see Kenneth M. Stampp, *The Era of Reconstruction, 1865–1877* (New York: Knopf, 1965), 214–215 (Stampp fully appreciates the long-term significance of the amendments); Blum, *Reforging the White Republic*, 2–3; Michael FitzGerald, *Splendid Failure: Postwar Reconstruction in the American South* (Chicago: Ivan R. Dee, 2007). The subtitle of Foner's detailed narrative—"America's Unfinished Revolution"—also suggests that the nation lost an opportunity to complete work begun during Reconstruction.

4. Blight, *Race and Reunion*, 2. The invitation from the Philadelphia Brigade caused controversy north and south of the Potomac River. See Carol Reardon, *Pickett's Charge in History and Memory* (Chapel Hill: University of North Carolina Press, 1997), 93–103.

5. Grant, *Memoirs and Selected Letters*, 735.

6. Grant, *Papers*, 14:433.

7. W. H. Redman to Catherine Redman [mother], May 2, December 21, 1865, W. H. Redman to Nelson Redman [brother], May 31, 1865, Papers of William Henry Redman, Albert and Shirley Small Special Collections Library, University of Virginia, Charlottesville.

8. Mathew Woodruff, *A Union Soldier in the Land of the Vanquished: The Diary of Sergeant Mathew Woodruff, June–December, 1865*, ed. F. N. Boney (University: University of Alabama Press, 1969), 48–50.

9. Grant, *Memoirs and Selected Letters*, 752–753, 761.

10. Baruch and Beckman, *Civil War Union Monuments*, 113, 156, 55. This volume includes photographs of all but the monument in Santa Fe. The overwhelming dominance of Union stands out in the inscriptions quoted in this book.

11. Ibid., 40, 112, 9.

12. Brown, *Public Art of Civil War Commemoration*, 38 (quotation). Far more people probably visited Grant's Tomb, which officially was designated a "monument," than any of the public artworks Brown discusses except the Lincoln Memorial in Washington.

13. Executive Committee of the Maine Commissioners, *Maine at Gettysburg* (1898; reprint, Gettysburg, Pa.: Stan Clarke Military Books, 1994), 546–547, 551, 555.

14. New York Monuments Commission for the Battlefields of Gettysburg and Chattanooga, *Final Report for the Battlefield of Gettysburg*, 3 vols. (Albany: J. B. Lyon, 1902), 2:671–672.

15. [L. S. Trowbridge and Fred. E. Farnsworth, eds.], *Michigan at Gettysburg, July 1st, 2nd, 3rd, 1863: Proceedings Incident to the Dedication of the Michigan Monuments upon the Battlefield at Gettysburg, June 12th, 1889* . . . (Detroit: Winn and Hammond, 1889), 53–54; New York Monuments Commission, *Final Report* 2:807–808.

16. [Ohio Gettysburg Memorial Commission], *Report of the Gettysburg Memorial*

Commission (1889; reprint, Baltimore: Butternut and Blue, 1998), 79, 88; John Page Nicholson, comp., *Pennsylvania at Gettysburg: Ceremonies at the Dedication of the Monuments Erected by the Commonwealth of Pennsylvania to Mark the Positions of the Pennsylvania Commands Engaged in the Battle,* 2 vols. (Harrisburg: E. K. Meyers, 1893), 1:225.

17. [Gettysburg Battle-field Commission of New Jersey], *Final Report of the Gettysburg Battle-field Commission of New Jersey* (Trenton: John L. Murphy, 1891), 84; [Trowbridge and Farnsworth, eds.], *Michigan at Gettysburg,* 54, 66; Nicholson, comp., *Pennsylvania at Gettysburg* 1:167 (the captain was H. B. Piper, who spoke in September 1889).

18. [Gettysburg Battle-field Commission of New Jersey], *Final Report,* 48; Executive Committee, *Maine at Gettysburg,* 220–221. For casualties of all units at Gettysburg, see John W. Busey and David G. Martin, *Regimental Strengths and Losses at Gettysburg,* 4th ed. (Hightstown, N.J.: Longstreet House, 2005), 132 (for the 17th Maine Infantry).

19. Ward, *The Civil War,* 273. Foote's contribution to this book, titled "Men at War: An Interview with Shelby Foote" (pp. 264–273), repeats some of his most memorable lines from the documentary.

20. Grant, *Papers,* 28:412–413. See Grant, *Memoirs and Personal Letters,* for examples of his using "National armies" (pp. 452, 515) and "army of the United States" (p. 739). For another tribute to American citizen-soldiers, see ibid., 766: "Our armies were composed of men who were able to read, men who knew what they were fighting for, and could not be induced to serve as soldiers, except in an emergency when the safety of the nation was involved."

ACKNOWLEDGMENTS

....

I first discussed this book with Joyce Seltzer more than ten years ago. I initially envisioned writing a military history of the Civil War, but the passage of time, and my own changing interests, brought a shift in focus to how the loyal population of the United States framed their understanding of the conflict. The result is a book that serves as a companion to *The Confederate War,* for which Joyce also served as my editor. Throughout these many years, and in response to my repeated requests for more time, Joyce has exhibited understanding and patience beyond reckoning. She also improved the manuscript in many ways, as I knew she would. I am much in her debt and count myself fortunate indeed to have been able to work with her on two books. My thanks go as well to Kate Brick at Harvard University Press, who pointed out infelicities of phrasing and otherwise strengthened my prose, and to Jeannette Estruth, who looked after many of the details requisite to moving a manuscript along toward publication.

I also owe a great deal to a number of friends and colleagues—none of whom, I hasten to add, should be held accountable for the interpretations in this book. At the University of Virginia, Peter Onuf listened without complaint inside and outside the classroom as I worked through various elements of my argument. He also read the entire manuscript and helped me sharpen my thinking regarding many key points. Steve Cushman and Bill Bergen similarly critiqued the whole text, and I am especially grateful for Steve's suggestions regarding some crucial material from Walt Whitman. Peter Luebke first directed me to the regimental histories published between 1863 and 1866—a body of evidence on which I drew extensively. I have come to expect excellent suggestions from him, many of which come in the course of long discussions about antiquarian books.

A number of colleagues outside Virginia graciously took the time to read all my chapters and respond to myriad questions about sources and analysis. Bill Blair, Carrie Janney, Mike Parrish, Aaron Sheehan-Dean, and Joan Waugh compose this hearty band, and their contributions are evident throughout the text. Carrie also shared a substantial body of her research on the early postwar years, and Joan helped immeasurably as I sought to situate U. S. Grant within my larger framework. Mike always has forwarded pertinent materials that turn up in his own research and reading, a habit that has been of immense value to me over the years and was especially useful with this project.

Matt Gallman, Joe Glatthaar, and George Rable read the manuscript for Harvard University Press. As a trio of the most senior and influential scholars in the field, they brought a range of perspectives and special expertise to the task and collectively provided a substantial body of invaluable suggestions and criticisms. I appreciate their willingness to add the burden of reading my manuscript to their very busy schedules.

Much of the work on this book took place at the Huntington Library in San Marino, California. I am indebted to Robert C. Ritchie, the W. M. Keck Director of Research at the Huntington, for the opportunity to spend all of 2008 at what I consider the best place in the world to research and write about the mid-nineteenth-century United States. The Huntington's combination of spectacular holdings, professional staff, and beautiful setting is simply unmatched—and powerfully conducive to getting things done.

John Nau and I have spent a great deal of very pleasant time over the past decade discussing things related to the Civil War—much of it while walking various battlefields. Despite our many conversations, I had formed only a vague idea about the scope of his collection of soldier manuscripts. At breakfast one morning, our talk came to focus on some letters he had recently acquired. I asked if I could examine them, and he said I could see the entire collection if I liked and put me in touch with Sally Anne Schmidt, who oversees the John L. Nau, III Civil War Collection in Houston. Sally Anne proved unbelievably helpful in supplying hundreds of items, none of which had been used by other scholars. The material yielded immensely valuable evidence for *The Union War,* and I am very much in John's, and Sally Anne's, debt.

The book's dedication reflects my appreciation for the accomplishments of the company of scholars who completed their doctoral studies under my supervision over the past seventeen years. At Penn State University, Joe Fischer, Bill Blair, Peter Carmichael, and Clarissa Confer worked with me. Without any intent of claiming more than I should, I also will mention Jonathan Berkey, Keith Bohannon, Barb Gannon, Christian Keller, Bob Sandow, Andrew Slap, and Jim Weeks—all of whom began their careers under me but finished with others at Penn State after I moved to the University of Virginia in 1998. At UVA, the list includes Aaron Sheehan-Dean, Wayne Hsieh, Carrie Janney, Andre Fleche, Jaime Martinez, Matt Speiser, Katy Shively Meir, Adam Dean, Kid Wongsrichanalai, Cynthia Nicoletti, Keith Harris, and David Zimring. I have watched with admiration as they published their books and articles, took on important editorships, assumed posts of leadership in departments, and otherwise shaped the field of Civil War studies. That they are a genuinely thoughtful and generous group who consistently exhibit an ability to think beyond themselves makes their accomplishments all the more impressive.

INDEX

....

Abolitionists, 20–21, 34, 39, 90, 101, 103, 112, 135, 141, 142–143

Adams, John Quincy, 46

Adams, Lois Bryan, 20, 25, 28

African Americans: as contrabands, 5, 19, 57, 94, 95, 96, 104, 105, 109, 114–116, 141–147, 148–149, 169n22, 196n43; as pioneers in Union army, 19, 20, 21, 75, 95; suffrage for, 42, 152, 155–156; population in free states and territories, 42–43; stereotypes of, 94, 96; role in Emancipation, 147–150; during Reconstruction, 152–153. *See also* Race; United States Colored Troops (USCT)

Alabama, 150; USCT from, 146

Albany Evening Journal, 130

American exceptionalism, 3, 4, 6, 52; and Union, 36–37, 45, 62, 70, 73, 172n37

American Historical Association, 123

American militarism, 39, 41

American nationalism, 6, 29, 37, 39, 47, 140–141, 166n7

American Revolution, 82, 117, 166n6; Washington, 3, 26, 27, 59, 133, 136, 139, 178n44; founding generation and Union, 6, 7, 16, 26, 27, 34, 35, 47–48, 48, 49, 58, 59, 62–63, 83, 85, 119, 150, 161

Andersonville prison, 151

Antietam, battle of, 90, 121, 124, 142, 145, 185n27

Appomattox Court House, 11, 22, 64, 79, 153–154

Aristocracy: in Europe, 5, 6, 17, 49, 70, 72–73, 117; slaveholders as, 34, 46, 62, 63, 68–69, 72–73, 77, 98, 106, 120, 151, 159

Arkansas, USCT from, 146

Armies of the Tennessee and Georgia, 22, 66, 82, 173n1; at Grand Review, 8, 10–11, 13, 14–15, 18, 19–20, 23, 24, 25, 26–27, 29, 30, 31–32, 92–93,